CONCISE REVISION COURSE
CSEC®
Physics

Peter DeFreitas

T0340425

Collins

HarperCollins Publishers Ltd
The News Building
1 London Bridge Street
London SE1 9GF

HarperCollins *Publishers*
Macken House, 39/40 Mayor Street Upper,
Dublin 1, D01 C9W8, Ireland

First edition 2016

10

© HarperCollins *Publishers* Limited 2016

ISBN 978-0-00-815789-0

www.collins.co.uk/caribbeanschools

A catalogue record for this book is available from the British Library.

Typeset by QBS
Printed in India

Author: Peter DeFreitas
Publisher: Elaine Higgleton
Commissioning Editor: Peter Dennis and Tom Hardy
Managing Editor: Sarah Thomas
Copy Editor: Jane Roth
Editor: Aidan Gill
Proofreader: Tim Jackson
Artwork: QBS
Cover: Kevin Robbins and Gordon MacGilp

Acknowledgements

I am grateful to my employers and to all the parents who have shown appreciation for my work and dedication to education. I am also thankful to my students who have encouraged me in writing this text, and above all, to my wife Christere and children, Zoe, Zachary and Jenna for supporting me in my efforts.

Peter DeFreitas

Contents

iv   Contents

Failure is not an option

Why this book is so very important to you

The author has taught Physics for over 35 years. He is well aware of the issues which pose problems to students and of how to present the material in a manner so as to avoid such problems. This book is specifically designed to meet the needs of students preparing for the CSEC® Physics examination.

- **The CSEC® Physics syllabus has been closely followed** in the layout of the book with respect to its **5 Sections (A to E)** as well as to the **order of the topics** within each section.

  - ◆ Section A   Chapters 1 – 9   Mechanics
  - ◆ Section B   Chapters 10 – 18   Thermal Physics and Kinetic Theory
  - ◆ Section C   Chapters 19 – 25   Waves and Optics
  - ◆ Section D   Chapters 26 – 32   Electricity and Magnetism
  - ◆ Section E   Chapters 33 – 34   The Physics of the Atom

- **Every specific objective** has been carefully addressed in a **complete and concise** manner.

- **Clear, annotated diagrams** make it **easier to fully understand the content of the text.**

- **Laws and definitions** are printed in **colored, italic font** so that they are **emphasized for improved learning** and are **easily located.**

- A **complete summary of necessary formulae** is provided at the end of this introduction.

- **Worked examples** are included to **reinforce the theory** of each topic. These demonstrate the application of **the laws and equations** to various situations as well as show the **format to be used** in calculations.

- **Revision questions**, included at the end of each chapter, are designed to test your **knowledge and comprehension** of the content of the chapter.

- **Exam-style questions,** included at the end of each section, are specifically prepared to assess your **knowledge and comprehension** in the relevant areas as well as to test your **use of knowledge** in application to various situations. These questions are **accompanied by the marks** allotted to them, allowing you to obtain an **accurate measure of your performance** in relation to the CSEC® method of assessment.

- **Answers** to the **revision questions of each chapter** and to the **exam-style questions of each section** are available online at www.collins.co.uk/caribbeanschools.

The CSEC® Physics examination

A starting point for all students in preparing for the CSEC® examination is to obtain a copy of the relevant syllabus. This is available online at http://cxc-store.com and provides an in-depth overview of the specific objectives together with important information regarding the School-Based Assessment (SBA) and the examination itself. A brief outline of the assessment profiles, the examination format and the SBA is provided below.

Assessment profiles

Your final grade will be determined by assessing your performance using the following profiles:

- Knowledge and comprehension
- Use of knowledge
- Experimental skills

Examination format

Paper 01 (1¼ hours):

Worth 60 marks (30% of the total exam mark) and comprised of 60 multiple choice questions.

Paper 02 (2½ hours):

Worth 100 marks (50% of the total exam mark) and is comprised of Section A (questions 1 to 3) and Section B (questions 4 to 6). All questions are compulsory.

- **Section A** consists of **three structured questions.**
  - **Question 1** tests **data analysis** and is worth **25 marks**. It usually involves completing a table of readings, plotting a graph and determining its slope, finding an intercept and making predictions from the plot. This is generally followed by questions testing your knowledge of the particular topic. **Dedicate 35 minutes** to this question.
  - **Questions 2 and 3** are each worth **15 marks**. Usually you will be required to complete a table or diagram and then to answer questions on the same topic. **Dedicate 20 minutes** to each question.
- **Section B** consists of **three extended response questions**, each worth **15 marks**. Usually you will be asked to describe an experiment or discuss certain issues related to Physics. Your **essay writing skills** and your **ability to 'think outside the box'** is more dominant in this section. Calculations are also generally included. **Dedicate 20 minutes** to each question.

Paper 03/1 (School-Based Assessment) Developed throughout the course (20% of total exam mark)

Paper 03/2 (For private candidates not doing SBA) 2 hours 10 minutes (20% of total exam mark)

School-Based Assessment (SBA)

School-Based Assessment provides a significant and unique influence on the development of necessary skills applicable to the subject together with a means of assessing and rewarding students for their accomplishments. For the diligent student, these laboratory exercises provide a golden opportunity to achieve a good grade since they are not performed under the usual stresses of examination conditions.

- Your achievements under the profiles of **Experimental Skills** and **Use of Knowledge** (Analysis and Interpretation) will be assessed during Terms 1 to 5 of the two-year period leading up to your CSEC® examinations.
- Competence in the following **skills** will be assessed:
  - Manipulation/Measurement
  - Observation/Recording/Reporting
  - Planning and Designing
  - Analysis and Interpretation
- Assessments will be made during the usual practical sessions. You are required to keep a separate practical workbook for all your practical work. This must be **maintained in good condition** and must be **available on demand for moderation** by CXC. Your workbook should be collected at the end of each practical session.

- An **Investigative Project**, to be carried out in Year 2, is assessed in two parts; *Planning and Designing*, and *Analysis and Interpretation*. Students pursuing two or more of the subjects, Biology, Chemistry and Physics, **may opt to carry out ONE investigation only** from any of these subjects.

Keywords used in Paper 02

In order to accurately interpret what is being asked, you must be familiar with the following keywords.

Annotate	provide a short note to a label
Apply	solve problems using knowledge and principles
Assess	give reasons for the importance of particular structures, relationships or processes
Calculate	provide a numerical solution to a problem
Cite	quote or make reference to
Classify	partition into groups according to observed characteristics
Comment	state an opinion or point of view **validated by reasons**
Compare	state similarities and differences
Construct	Represent data using a specific format to draw a graph, scale drawing or other device.
Deduce	logically connect two or more pieces of information; arrive at a conclusion by using data
Define	concisely state the meaning of a word or term
Demonstrate	show
Derive	determine a relationship, formula or result from data by the use of a logical procedure
Describe	give detailed factual information on the form of a structure or the sequence of a process
Determine	find the value of a physical quality
Design	plan and present , with relevant practical detail
Develop	expand on an idea or argument with the use of supportive reasoning
Distinguish	briefly identify differences between items which can place them in separate categories
Discuss	present the relative merits of a situation with reasons **for and against**
Draw	produce a line illustration depicting an accurate relationship between components
Estimate	arrive at an approximate quantitative result
Evaluate	make judgements based on given criteria by consideration of supporting evidence
Explain	make an account giving reasons based on recall
Find	locate or extract information of a feature
Formulate	develop a hypothesis
Identify	point out specific constituents or characteristics
Illustrate	clearly present by the use of examples, diagrams or sketches
Investigate	observe, log data and arrive at logical conclusions by using basic systematic procedures
Label	Identify parts of a diagram by means of names and pointers

Failure is not an option

List	produce a series of related items without detail
Measure	make accurate quantitative observations with the use of suitable measuring instruments
Name	state the name only
Note	record observations
Observe	examine and record changes which occur during a particular situation
Plan	make preparation for the operation of a particular exercise
Predict	suggest a possible conclusion based on given information
Record	give an accurate account of all observations made during a procedure
Relate	show connections between sets of facts or data
Sketch	a freehand diagram illustrating relevant approximate proportions and characteristics
State	give facts in concise form without explanations
Suggest	explain based on given information or on recall
Test	discover by the use of a set of procedures

Revising efficiently and effectively

Throughout the course

From the onset of the two year CSEC® programme you should be in a mode of regular revision. This will keep you on top of things and boost your confidence in the subject.

- New material should be reviewed as early as the day of receiving it and then periodically browsed as the school year progresses. This reinforces the concepts and reveals weaker areas; it alerts the brain of the importance of the topic, allowing it to be readily available in our memory.
- Notes should be kept up-to-date.
- All assignments and tests should be filed in an organized manner.
- Weak areas should be overcome immediately and not left to later in the term.

The term before the examination

About twelve weeks before the CSEC® examination, a concentrated revision technique should be employed. Due to the increased work-load, this period should be accompanied by maintaining a healthy balanced diet and leaving adequate time for rest and exercise.

- Obtain the dates of your CSEC® examinations from www.cxc.org and prepare a revision timetable. This may be a bit difficult to stick to during the week due to homework assignments, but the times allotted for weekend study should be fairly stable. The Easter holidays provide a great opportunity to increase the number of hours dedicated to revision.
- Select a suitable location for your revision, **free from noise and other distractions**.
- A **large desk** which can hold all your texts, notebooks, a copy of the syllabus, past tests and examination papers, calculator and other items you may need for revision, is preferred. This avoids you having to break your concentration to locate materials during the sessions. The desk should be **kept free of clutter** to maintain an organized mood.
- Six to eight hours of revision is recommended on days when you are not at school. This may be divided into **TWO sessions** positioned at times when your concentration is best. Relax and do unrelated things during the remainder of the day.

- Your posture should be comfortable since you will be seated for long periods, but not such that you feel drowsy; no lying or sitting in bed!
- Take **short breaks** after each hour of study to walk around and have a **brief stretch**. This allows you to better focus and consolidate the information.
- The following outlines some techniques which may be used to enhance your learning skills. The more you apply these techniques the greater will be your recall.
  - Carefully read through the topic, identifying key points with reference to definitions, laws, concepts, etc. Having a good understanding of the subject matter makes it much easier to reserve a high priority space in your memory.
  - Group discussions are very important since they help to
    - increase your confidence
    - alert you of things you were not aware of
    - improve understanding of your weaker areas
  - Create flow charts or other forms of **linking diagrams** to act as **mind maps**. By placing large amounts of information on one page you make it easier to review; the individual parts are then more meaningful and therefore readily remembered.
  - Prepare **flash cards** with important queues to information on a topic
  - Practice **drawing, labeling and annotating diagrams**
  - Use a **key word, a short phrase, a mnemonic or an acronym**, as a queue to trigger the recall of important information.
    - '**R**ichard **O**f **Y**ork **G**ave **B**attle **I**n **V**ain' is a mnemonic to remember the colours of the visible spectrum; '**R**ed, **O**range, **Y**ellow, **G**reen, **B**lue, **I**ndigo and **V**iolet'
    - '**LED**' is an acronym for '**L**ight **E**mitting **D**iode'
- Topics are of varying length and complexity and therefore some sessions will cover more items than others. **Set time periods** for each session and **goal/goals** for what you want to accomplish within them. Finish each session with a **brief overview** of the items covered.
- **Read through the relevant section** in the syllabus before you revise each topic and **mark it off as you complete the revision**.
- Answer the end of **Chapter revision questions** at the end of each chapter and the **Exam-style questions** at the end of each section to obtain a measure of your competence. The answers can be checked online at www.collins.co.uk/caribbeanschools.
- **Past CSEC® examination papers** are available online through the CXC Store. Work through as many of these as possible.
- Read through all your **past tests and assignments** and ensure that you understand the areas where you lost marks.

Optimum examination technique

- Preliminaries – just before the examination
  - Ensure that you are certain of the start time for the examination
  - Have 8 hours sleep
  - Have a healthy breakfast
  - Arrive early to the venue
  - Stay away from those who panic; think positive

Failure is not an option

- **Carefully** read and **follow** the instructions on the opening page, doing **exactly** as you are asked.
- **Plan the period of time to be applied to answer each question.** This should be known before hand since you would have practiced on past CSEC® papers with the same format.
- Although all questions must be answered, you should still read through the paper before attempting them. You would then be able to select the ones you can do well and **start on the simplest first.** This will enhance your confidence.
- Before attempting a question, read it **at least twice, circling important keywords and phrases.**
- Dedicate time to each part of a question in **proportion to the marks allotted to it**
- As you do a question, recheck to ensure that you have **attempted all the parts** and have **accurately answered** what was asked. The **typical CSEC® keywords** listed earlier would be very important here in order for you to acquire the marks assigned to the question.
- Appropriate **scientific jargon** makes your answers more meaningful and impressive.
- **Check the time periodically** (could be at the beginning of each question) to ensure that you are in good standing to finish the paper.
- **For calculations:**
    - Start by **listing the equation** in general form
    - Substitute the known values
    - **Show each step** in the solution, preferably on a new line
    - Represent your final answer with the **correct SI unit**
    - Show **all working** as well as any **assisting statements**
- If several points are required in an answer, **use bullets** to clearly indicate their individuality.
- If you are asked to list the pros and cons or benefits and costs, etc. of an issue, make sure to place **sub headings** over each list to distinguish between them.
- Any time left over at the end of the exam should be spent on **reading through your answers** to ensure that they are free of errors. Pay special attention to calculations and to the use of units.

Important Formulae

One of the most important things to learn for a Physics examination is the formulae necessary for your calculations. The symbols used below have already been defined in the text.

SECTION A   MECHANICS

density
$$\rho = \frac{m}{V}$$

acceleration
$$a = \frac{v - u}{t}$$

force
$$F = ma \qquad F = \frac{m(v - u)}{t}$$

weight
$$W = mg$$

pressure	$P = \dfrac{F}{A}$	$P = h\rho g$

momentum $\quad p = mv$

moment $\quad T = Fd_\perp$

work or energy $\quad W = Fd_\parallel$

power $\qquad P = \dfrac{E}{t} \qquad\qquad P = \dfrac{W}{t} \qquad\qquad P = Fv$

efficiency $= \dfrac{\text{useful work or energy output}}{\text{work or energy input}} \times 100 = \dfrac{\text{useful power output}}{\text{power input}} \times 100$

kinetic energy $\qquad\qquad\qquad\qquad E_K = \dfrac{1}{2}mv^2$

change in gravitational potential energy $\qquad \Delta E_p = mg\Delta h$

displacement – time graphs $\quad$ **velocity** $\quad v = \dfrac{\Delta d}{\Delta t}$ (i.e. gradient)

velocity – time graphs $\qquad$ **acceleration** $\;a = \dfrac{\Delta v}{\Delta t}$ (i.e. gradient)

distance = area between graph line and t – axis $\qquad$ (all areas positive)

displacement = area between graph line and t – axis $\quad \begin{pmatrix}\text{areas above axis are positive} \\ \text{areas below axis are negative}\end{pmatrix}$

SECTION B THERMAL PHYSICS AND KINETIC THEORY

heat energy $\qquad\qquad E_H = mc\Delta T \qquad E_H = ml$

heat power $\qquad\qquad P_H = \dfrac{mc\Delta T}{t} \qquad P_H = \dfrac{ml}{t}$

equation of Ideal Gas $\dfrac{P_1 V_1}{T_1} = \dfrac{P_2 V_2}{T_2} \qquad$ (note: T must be in kelvin)

SECTION C WAVES AND OPTICS

within a medium $v = \lambda f \quad$ **changing mediums** $\dfrac{v_1}{v_2} = \dfrac{\lambda_1}{\lambda_2} = \dfrac{\sin\theta_1}{\sin\theta_2} = \dfrac{\eta_2}{\eta_1} \qquad$ **frequency** $f = \dfrac{1}{T}$

lens equation $\dfrac{1}{u} + \dfrac{1}{v} = \dfrac{1}{f} \quad$ **magnification** $m = \dfrac{v}{u} \qquad m = \dfrac{h_i}{h_o}$

SECTION D ELECTRICITY AND MAGNETISM

charge $\qquad\qquad Q = It \qquad Q = Nq$

energy and work $\quad E = VQ \qquad E = VIt \qquad E = I^2Rt \qquad E = \dfrac{V^2 t}{R}$

power $\qquad\qquad P = VI \qquad P = I^2R \qquad P = \dfrac{V^2}{R}$

emf = sum of pd's in circuit $\quad V = IR$

transformers $\dfrac{N_p}{N_s} = \dfrac{V_p}{V_s} \qquad$ **efficiency** $= \dfrac{P_s}{P_p} \times 100 \qquad$ **efficiency** $= \dfrac{V_s I_s}{V_p I_p} \times 100$

ideal transformers (100% efficient) $\quad \dfrac{N_p}{N_s} = \dfrac{V_p}{V_s} = \dfrac{I_s}{I_p}$

SECTION E THE PHYSICS OF THE ATOM

Einstein's equation of mass – energy equivalence $\quad \Delta E = \Delta mc^2$

1 Scientific method

Galileo's contribution to scientific methodology

Galileo Galilei was an Italian mathematics professor of the 16th century. He was the first to implement a scientific approach in order to investigate a problem, and is often referred to as the 'father of modern scientific methodology'. Today's scientists have the advantage of added tools for investigation, such as calculus mathematics invented by Newton, the processing speed of the computer and the web of pooled information available on the internet. However, the basis of Galileo's method is still adopted by scientists for their current investigations:

1. **Observation**: Observe an event in nature which needs to be investigated.

2. **Hypothesis**: Suggest a possible explanation based on the observation.

3. **Experiment**: Use **quantitative data** to obtain objective generalisations and perform several experiments to test the generalisations. The experiments should investigate only one variable at a time.

4. **Conclusion**: Make a solid conclusion on the truth of the hypothesis based on calculations from the experiments. The conclusion itself should be expressed in terms of an equation. For example, Galileo showed that an object fell through a distance (s) in a time (t) according to the equation $s = \frac{1}{2} kt^2$ where k is a constant.

Experimental data and its analysis

- A procedure to be undertaken is designed using the following types of variable.

  Independent variable: The variable that is being altered or investigated

  Dependent variable: The variable that may be affected by a change in the independent variable

  Control variable: A variable that is kept constant

- The procedure is implemented.

  In an investigation of how the factors mass (m) and length (l) affect the period (T) of a simple pendulum, the variables could be as shown in Table 1.1.

  Table 1.1 *Types of variables*

	Independent	Dependent	Control
Expt 1	length of string	period	mass of bob
Expt 2	mass of bob	period	length of string

  If a third variable is to be investigated, such as the angular displacement of the string, the length of the string as well as the mass of the bob will have to be controlled as the angle is varied.

- The experimental data in tables, charts and graphs is **analysed**.

Drawing graphs

Figure 1.1 illustrates the format used in presenting the plot of a graph.

- The graph should have a title stating the variables being plotted and the purpose of the plot.
- The first variable mentioned is placed on the y-axis; the other, on the x-axis.
- Each axis is labelled with quantity and unit (if any).
- Scales are selected which are easy to use; simple ratios such as 1:1, 1:2, 1:5.
- Suitable scales should utilise at least two-thirds of the graph sheet.

- Points are plotted either as × or ⊙ using a sharp pencil.
- Sometimes, if both axes start at zero, the experimental points are all cluttered together in one small section of the graph paper. In such cases the scale should be broken.
- A long transparent ruler should be used to draw a line of best fit for straight-line graphs.
- If the graph is not a straight line, the best smooth curve through the points is sketched.
- Whether the graph is a straight line or a curve, the following should be noted:

  a) The line will not necessarily pass through all the points.

  b) The mean deviation of the points from either side of the line should balance in order to reduce random error (discussed later) which may have occurred during the experiment.

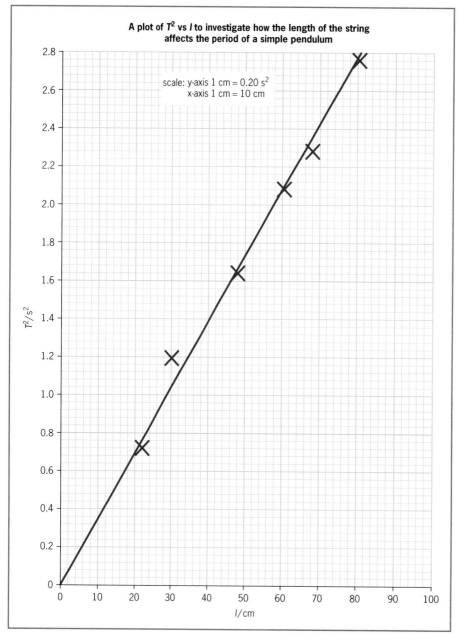

Figure 1.1 *Drawing graphs*

Finding the gradient (slope) of a straight-line graph

- Select two points on the line, (x_1, y_1) and (x_2, y_2), which are *far apart*. Each point should be exactly on a corner of one of the small squares of the graph sheet. Mark these points and use them to construct a *large* right-angled triangle as shown in Figure 1.2.

- Determine the gradient, m (slope) from the equation

$$m = \frac{y_2 - y_1}{x_2 - x_1}$$

- The point (x_2, y_2) is always to the right of (x_1, y_1), which sometimes makes the slope *negative*.

- The **unit** of the slope is the ratio:

$$\frac{\text{unit of } y\text{-axis}}{\text{unit of } x\text{-axis}}$$

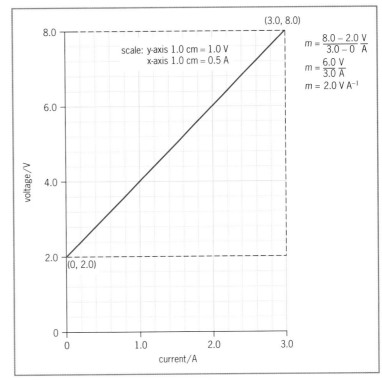

Figure 1.2 *Gradient of a straight-line graph*

In the figure:

scale: y-axis 1.0 cm = 1.0 V
x-axis 1.0 cm = 0.5 A

$$m = \frac{8.0 - 2.0}{3.0 - 0} \frac{\text{V}}{\text{A}}$$

$$m = \frac{6.0}{3.0} \frac{\text{V}}{\text{A}}$$

$$m = 2.0 \text{ V A}^{-1}$$

(3.0, 8.0)

(0, 2.0)

voltage/V

current/A

Significant figures in measurements and calculations

Measurements

Generally, a reading can be read to the nearest half of an interval of the scale. For example, a reading on a metre rule, calibrated in mm, could be 23.5 mm.

Calculations involving products and/or quotients

Express to the *least number of significant figures of the items in the calculation.*

$$P = \frac{4.2 \times 375 \times 41.3}{27} = 2409.166667 \text{ from calculator}$$

$$P = 2400 \text{ to 2 sig. fig.}$$

Calculations involving addition and/or subtraction

We examine *precision* here, rather than significant figures.

$$X = 21.3 + 325 + 2132.1 = 2478.4 \text{ from calculator}$$

$$X = 2478 \text{ to the correct level of precision}$$

The least precise of the three numbers is 325. Its *least significant figure* is in the units place value position and therefore the result must also have its least significant figure in the units place value position.

Random errors

Random errors are those which have equal chance of causing the result to be greater or lesser than the true value.

They may be caused by poor judgement or by slightly fluctuating conditions during the experiment which cannot be controlled. A typical example is **parallax error**. This occurs when the marking viewed on a scale is not coincident in position with the point to which the measurement should be made (Figure 1.3).

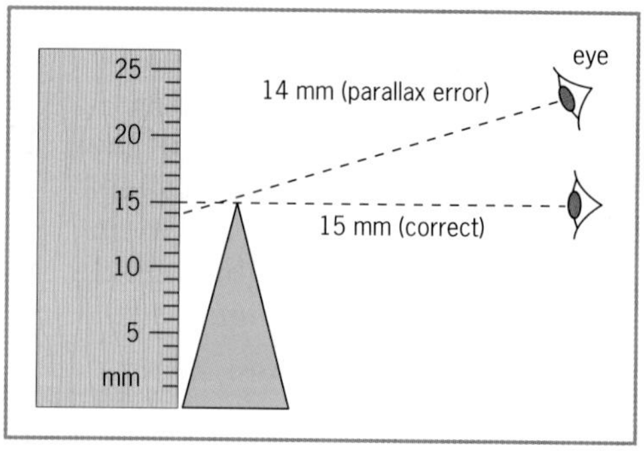

Figure 1.3 *Parallax error*

Reducing parallax error

- Ammeters and voltmeters with moving pointers usually have a mirror placed behind their scales. Readings should be taken from a position where the pointer is directly in front of the image it produces.
- Observations should be made with the line of sight perpendicular to the scale.
- The pointer should be as close as possible to the scale when taking readings.
- If the scale is vertical, such as with a measuring cylinder, eye level readings should be taken.

Reducing the effects of random errors

- The mean of several readings should be taken.
- The line of the graph should have minimum deviation from its points.

Systematic errors

Systematic errors are those which make the result always too small or always too large by the same amount.

They are due to some inaccuracy in the system. They usually arise because of some problem with the measuring instrument, but can also be due to the experimenter. Examples are:

- **zero error** of ammeters or voltmeters with moving pointers (when no current flows, the pointer may not be at the zero mark)
- poorly **calibrated** scale.

Reading systematic errors

Systematic errors are not reduced by the methods that reduce random errors. They may be reduced by one of the following methods:

- The value of the error must be discovered and then added or subtracted from each reading.
- The instrument must be adjusted.

Reading measuring instruments

Measuring instruments can usually be read to the nearest half of an interval on a scale. However, the **vernier calliper** and the **micrometer screw gauge** require the examination of *two* scales before the actual reading is determined.

Vernier calliper

The vernier calliper (Figure 1.4) has an extra scale known as a **vernier scale** which is capable of measuring to one extra decimal place over that measured by the main scale. This calliper is suitable for measuring lengths between 1 cm and 10 cm. The following should be noted when using the instrument:

- The jaws are adjusted by sliding the vernier scale over the main scale.
- The main scale is read to the mark just before the zero marking on the vernier scale.
- The marking on the vernier scale that best aligns with a mark on the main scale gives the added significant figure.

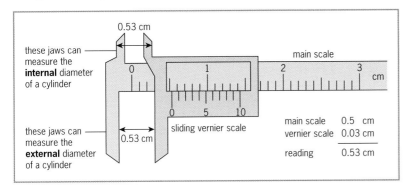

Figure 1.4 *Vernier calliper*

Micrometer screw gauge

Figure 1.5 shows a micrometer screw gauge. It is used mainly for measurements which are less than 1 cm. Like the vernier calliper, it produces a reading with greater precision than that of just the main scale. One revolution of the thimble moves the jaws by 0.5 mm. It is useful for measuring small lengths such as the diameter of a wire. The following should be noted when reading the instrument:

- The main scale of the sleeve is read to the marking just before the thimble.
- The thimble scale is read at the marking that coincides with the horizontal line on the sleeve.
- The two readings are summed.

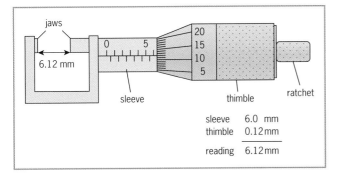

Figure 1.5 *Micrometer screw gauge*

Suitability of instruments

The sensitivity, accuracy and range of an instrument determine its suitability for making particular measurements.

- A metre rule is used to measure the height of a table because it has the necessary range required. In most cases, accuracy to the nearest mm is sufficient for such a measurement.
- A vernier calliper is used for measuring the internal diameter of a water pipe. Its sensitivity, accuracy and range are suitable, as well as its physical design of expanding jaws.

- A micrometer is suitable for measuring the diameter of an electrical wire because it has the required range, sensitivity and accuracy required by an engineer, as well as jaws for holding the wire firmly.
- A mercury-in-glass laboratory thermometer is suitable for measuring temperatures in the school laboratory because the experiments generally performed are within its range. It does not have to be as accurate as a clinical thermometer.
- A clinical thermometer needs to be very sensitive and accurate for the doctor or nurse to make adequate decisions regarding the patient. It requires only a small range because the temperatures for which it is used are only between 35 °C and 42 °C.

Quantities and units

Table 1.2 shows the fundamental quantities with their **SI base units**. 'SI' denotes the International System of units.

Table 1.2 *Fundamental quantities and their SI base units*

SI fundamental quantity	SI base unit	Symbol of SI unit
mass	kilogram	kg
length	metre	m
time	second	s
current	ampere	A
temperature	kelvin	K
amount of substance	mole	mol
luminous intensity	candela	cd

Other quantities are derived from these fundamental ones, and **SI derived units** are combinations of the base units.

For example, acceleration has the unit m s^{-2}. Force (F) can be calculated from the product of mass (m) and acceleration (a), so its unit can be determined:

Quantities $F = ma$

SI units $N = kg\ m\ s^{-2}$

The newton (N) is assigned as the SI unit of force. Instead of speaking of a force of 25 kg m s^{-2}, we say 25 N. Table 1.3 lists several derived quantities and their SI units.

Table 1.3 *Derived quantities and their SI units*

Derived quantity	Common symbol	Formula	SI unit symbol	SI unit combinations using the formula column	Constituent SI base units
force	F	$F = ma$	N	kg m s^{-2}	kg m s^{-2}
work or energy	W or E	$E = Fd$	J	N m	kg m^2 s^{-2}
power	P	$P = \dfrac{W}{t}$	W	J s^{-1}	kg m^2 s^{-3}
pressure	P	$P = \dfrac{F}{A}$	Pa	N m^{-2}	kg m^{-1} s^{-2}

Table 1.3 *Derived quantities and their SI units continued*

Derived quantity	Common symbol	Formula	SI unit symbol	SI unit combinations using the formula column	Constituent SI base units
charge	Q	$Q = It$	C	A s	A s
voltage (pd or emf)	V	$V = \dfrac{E}{Q}$	V	J C^{-1}	kg m^2 A^{-1} s^{-3}
resistance	R	$R = \dfrac{V}{I}$	Ω	V A^{-1}	kg m^2 A^{-2} s^{-3}
frequency	f	$f = \dfrac{1}{T}$	Hz	s^{-1}	s^{-1}

Index notation

A number expressed in **standard form** or **index notation** is represented as a power of 10: $M \times 10^p$.

M (the 'mantissa') is a number in decimal form with *only one non-zero digit before the decimal point* and p is an integer. The value of p is obtained from the number of decimal places moved in representing the mantissa. A negative value of p indicates that the number being expressed is less than 1.

$$37\ 000 = 3.7 \times 10^4$$

$$0.000\ 000\ 55 = 5.5 \times 10^{-7}$$

Prefixes

As an alternative to index notation, prefixes may also be used to express a quantity in a shorter way, as Table 1.4 shows.

Table 1.4 *Prefixes*

Prefix	pico	nano	micro	milli	*no prefix*	kilo	mega	giga	tera
Abbreviation	p	n	μ	m	*no prefix*	k	M	G	T
Power of 10	$\times 10^{-12}$	$\times 10^{-9}$	$\times 10^{-6}$	$\times 10^{-3}$	$\times 10^{0}$	$\times 10^{3}$	$\times 10^{6}$	$\times 10^{9}$	$\times 10^{12}$

- For each jump to an adjacent column in the table of prefixes, there is a shift of 3 decimal places.
- Using a larger unit produces a smaller number; using a smaller unit produces a larger number.

$$0.004\ 56\ \text{km} = 4.56\ \text{m}$$

This is a jump of 1 column (3 decimal places) from kilo to *no prefix*; a larger to a smaller unit and therefore a smaller to a larger number.

$$5\ 200\ 000\ 000\ \text{W} = 5.2\ \text{GW}$$

This is a jump of 3 columns (9 decimal places) from *no prefix* to giga; a smaller to a larger unit and therefore a larger to a smaller number.

Density

*The **density** of a substance is its mass per unit volume.*

$$\text{density} = \frac{\text{mass}}{\text{volume}} \qquad \rho = \frac{m}{V}$$

The mass of the body can be obtained by the use of an electronic balance.

The volume of the body can be obtained by one of the following methods:

- If it is a liquid, it can simply be poured into a measuring cylinder and the reading taken.
- If it is a regularly shaped solid, its dimensions are measured and the necessary calculation performed.
- If it is an irregularly shaped solid, it is immersed into a measuring cylinder of liquid in which it is insoluble; the increase in the reading gives its volume.

Unit of density

Density is usually expressed in kg m^{-3} or g cm^{-3}. This can be deduced from the relation $\rho = \dfrac{m}{V}$ where kg and g are units of mass, and m^3 and cm^3 are units of volume.

Revision questions

1 Express the following to the correct number of significant figures.

   a $27.2 \times 14 \times 12.22$ **b** $17.62 + 11.2 - 7.5$

2 State what is meant by each of the following terms, giving an example of each.

   a random error   **b** systematic error

3 Calculate the gradient of the graph in Figure 1.6.

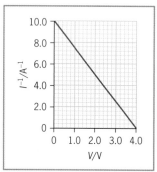

Figure 1.6

4 State the instrument which is most suitable for measuring each of the following lengths.

   a The thickness of a piece of window glass

   b The width of a microwave oven

   c The width of a box of playing cards

5 What are the readings on the micrometer screw gauge and the vernier calliper shown in Figure 1.7?

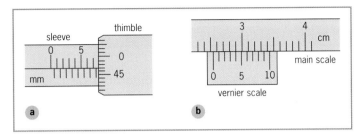

Figure 1.7

6 List FIVE fundamental quantities with their SI base units.

7 What are the derived SI units for each of the following?

   a pressure   **b** work   **c** force   **d** power

8 Express the following in standard form.

   a 555.22   **b** 0.000 123

9 Express:

   a 55 000 000 J in MJ   **b** 0.0333 mA in µA   **c** 400 mW in kW

10 Calculate the mass of a stone of volume 4.0 cm³ if its density is 2.0 g cm⁻³.

2 Scalars and vectors

Table 2.1 *Scalars and vectors*

	Scalar	Vector
Definition	*a quantity that has only magnitude*	*a quantity that has magnitude and direction*
Common examples	mass, length, time, temperature, area, volume, speed, pressure, distance, work, energy, power, resistance, current	force, momentum, displacement, velocity, acceleration
How added	algebraic summation	vector summation

Finding the resultant of two vectors

Oblique vectors by scale diagram

Figure 2.1 shows four cases of forces *A* and *B* either pushing or pulling on a particle. In each case, *B* is horizontal and *A* is at an angle, θ, above the horizontal. The resultant force can be found by using either of the following methods, which are illustrated in Figure 2.2.

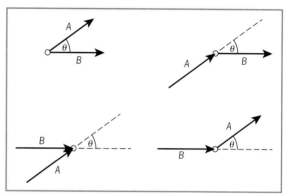

Figure 2.1 *Oblique vectors*

- **Parallelogram method**: The vectors are represented to scale in magnitude and direction by arrows, *starting at the same point* and forming the adjacent sides of a parallelogram. The resultant vector is then represented in magnitude and direction by the arrow forming the diagonal of the parallelogram *originating at the same point as the vectors being added.*

- **Polygon method**: The vectors are represented in magnitude and direction by arrows *joined head to tail* forming a chain. The resultant vector is then represented to scale by the arrow closing the polygon and *originating from the beginning of the chain.*

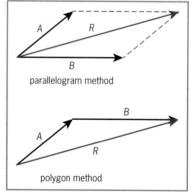

Figure 2.2 *Parallelogram and polygon methods of adding vectors*

A and B pull on an object with forces of *A* = 40 N and *B* = 30 N. By means of a scale diagram, determine their resultant force if the angle between the forces is 30°.

A scale of 1 cm = 10 N is appropriate.

The resultant force has magnitude 68 N and direction 17° anticlockwise from the direction of force *B*. See Figure 2.3.

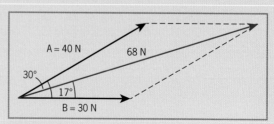

Figure 2.3

Parallel and anti-parallel vectors

In cases like those in Figure 2.4, forces to the right are assigned positive values and those to the left are assigned negative values.

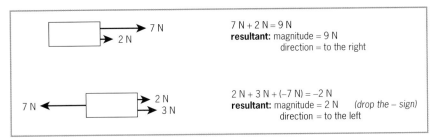

Figure 2.4 *Parallel and anti-parallel vectors*

Perpendicular vectors

In cases like that in Figure 2.5(a), upward forces and forces to the right are assigned positive values; downward forces and forces to the left are assigned negative values.

- The resultant horizontal and vertical vectors are first found as in Figure 2.5(a).
- These resultants can then be combined using Pythagoras' theorem as shown in Figure 2.5(b).

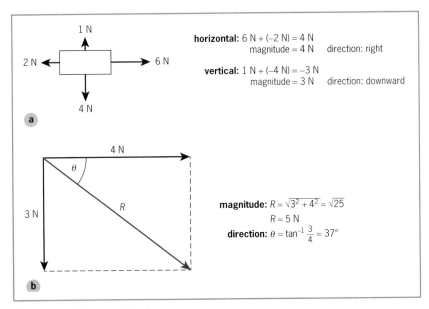

Figure 2.5 *Perpendicular vectors*

Resolving vectors into two perpendicular components

A single vector, F, can be analysed as two perpendicular vectors as shown in Figure 2.6.

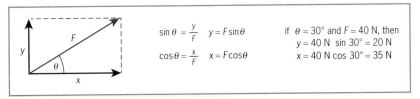

Figure 2.6 *Resolving vectors into perpendicular components*

Examples of vector components

- The velocity vector of a football kicked through the air has a vertical component causing it to rise and fall, and a horizontal component causing it to move across the field.
- The force vector due to a groundsman pushing a heavy roller across a cricket pitch has a vertical component pushing it onto the ground and a horizontal component pushing it across the surface.

Revision questions

1 List FIVE vectors and FIVE scalars.

2 A force of 50 N acts in an easterly direction on an object at the same time as a force of 80 N pushes on it in a direction N 45° E. Determine the magnitude and direction of the resultant force.

3 A man runs at 7.5 m s⁻¹ due east across the deck of a ship which moves at 10.0 m s⁻¹ due north. Determine the resultant velocity of the man (his velocity relative to the water).

4 At a particular instant, a football has a velocity of 25 m s⁻¹ and its direction makes an angle of 30° above the horizontal. Determine the vertical and horizontal components of its velocity.

5 Find the resultant of the following four forces.

A = 25 N due north
B = 50 N due east
C = 30 N due west
D = 40 N due south

3 Forces, mass and weight

Forces

*A **force** is an action that changes the size, shape or motion of a body.*

There are several types of force.

- **Gravitational forces** are attractive forces that exist between bodies due to their masses. The gravitational force of a planet on an object is the object's **weight**. The Moon is kept in orbit around the Earth by gravitational force.

- **Magnetic forces** are attractive or repulsive forces that exist between bodies due to their magnetic polarities (see Chapter 31).

- **Electrostatic forces** are attractive or repulsive forces that exist between bodies due to their electric charge (see Chapter 26). Electrons are kept in orbit around the atomic nucleus by such forces.

- **Nuclear forces** are extremely strong attractive forces which bind together the subatomic particles of an atomic nucleus.

- **Elastic forces** are restoring forces produced when a body is stretched or compressed.

- **Mechanical forces** are those that exist between bodies in contact. These can be pushes, pulls, normal reactions, friction, etc. **Friction** is a mechanical force that opposes the relative motion of the surfaces of bodies in contact with each other.

Mass and weight

*The **mass** of a body is the quantity of matter making up the body.*

*The **weight** of a body is the force of gravity on the body.*

The weight of a body depends on the gravitational field strength that acts on it. On Earth, the generally accepted value of the **gravitational field strength** is 10 N kg^{-1}. This is equal in value to the **acceleration due to gravity** = 10 m s^{-2}. Both are given the symbol g. The units are equivalent.

$$\text{weight} = \text{mass} \times \text{gravitational field strength}$$
$$W = mg$$

An object of mass 1 kg therefore has a weight $W = 1 \text{ kg} \times 10 \text{ N kg}^{-1} = 10 \text{ N}$.

A breadfruit of mass 2.0 kg has a weight of 20 N on Earth but only just over 3.2 N on the Moon where the gravitational field strength is much lower; it is completely weightless in outer space where there is no gravity. The *mass* of the breadfruit is the same at each location since it is comprised of the *same quantity of matter*.

Revision questions

1 List FOUR types of forces other than friction.

2 What is a frictional force?

3 Define:

   a mass   **b** weight

4 **a** Determine the mass of a football which has a weight of 0.80 N on a planet where the acceleration due to gravity is 2.0 m s^{-2}.

   b What would be the football's weight on Earth?

4 Moments

When we open a door, sit on a seesaw, use a spanner, raise the handles of a wheelbarrow or use a bottle opener, we are using forces that have a turning effect or **moment** about some pivot point.

*The **moment** of a force about a point is the product of the force and the perpendicular distance of its line of action from the point.*

$$moment = force \times perpendicular\ distance$$

$$T = Fd$$

The SI unit of moment is N m. Other units may be used, such as N cm or kN m, depending on the size of the moment.

Note that work (see Chapter 8) is the product of a force and the *distance moved in the direction* of the force. Its unit is therefore also the product N m. To indicate the difference between the two, the unit joule (J) is assigned to work.

The direction of a moment must be stated as *clockwise* or *anticlockwise*.

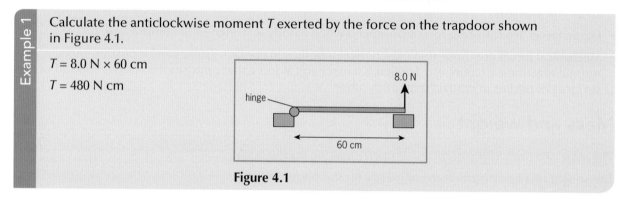

Example 1

Calculate the anticlockwise moment T exerted by the force on the trapdoor shown in Figure 4.1.

$T = 8.0\ N \times 60\ cm$

$T = 480\ N\ cm$

Figure 4.1

Calculations on the equilibrium of bodies

The following conditions hold for a system of coplanar forces in equilibrium:

1. *The sum of the forces in any direction is equal to the sum of the forces in the opposite direction (translational equilibrium).*
2. *The sum of the clockwise moments about any point is equal to the sum of the anticlockwise moments about that same point (rotational equilibrium). This is the **principle of moments**.*

Tackling problems involving moments

- *Sketch a diagram* showing all the forces acting on the body in equilibrium. These are:

   i) the weight, which acts through the centre of gravity

   ii) all other forces of the environment, which act on the body at points of contact.
- Select a suitable point about which to take moments.

   If more than one force is unknown, choose a point through which one of them acts. That force then has no moment about the point and is excluded from the calculation.
- Use the rules of translational and rotational equilibrium to formulate equations and solve for unknown forces and distances.
- Whenever there is only *one unknown force*, it can easily be found from the rule of translational equilibrium.

Example 2

Figure 4.2 shows a uniform metre rule of weight 2.0 N resting on a fulcrum and supported by a spring balance registering 5.0 N. Calculate:

a the weight X   **b** the reaction R

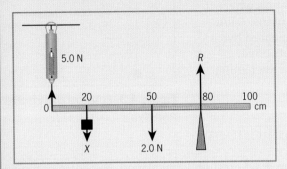

Figure 4.2

Note the following:

- Since the metre rule is *uniform*, its centre of gravity is at the 50 cm mark.
- The downward force of the rule on the fulcrum and the downward force of the rule on the spring balance are not considered, because these forces are *not on the rule.*
- A suitable point must be selected from which to take moments in order to eliminate one of the two unknown forces from the equation. Taking moments about the fulcrum eliminates R.

a $\sum$ anticlockwise moments = $\sum$ clockwise moments

$$(2.0 \times 30) + (60X) = (5.0 \times 80)$$

$$60 + 60X = 400$$

$$60X = 340$$

$$X = \frac{340}{60}$$

$$X = 5.67 \text{ N} = 5.7 \text{ N to 2 sig. fig.}$$

b $\sum$ upward forces = $\sum$ downward forces

$$5.0 + R = 5.67 + 2.0$$

$$R = 5.67 + 2.0 - 5.0$$

$$R = 2.67 \text{ N} = 2.7 \text{ N to 2 sig. fig.}$$

Determining the centre of gravity of an object

*The **centre of gravity** of a body is the point through which the resultant gravitational force on the body acts.*

A straight rod

The rod is balanced on the edge of a fulcrum or is suspended horizontally from a string until it balances. The point of support is then the centre of gravity.

An irregularly shaped lamina

The lamina is hung so that it swings freely from a pin placed through a small hole near its edge as shown in Figure 4.3. A plumb line is suspended from the pin and the position where it passes in front of the lamina is marked by small crosses. A line is drawn through the crosses. The procedure is repeated twice by suspending the lamina from other points near its edge. Where the lines intersect is the centre of gravity of the lamina.

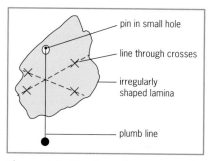

Figure 4.3 *Finding the centre of gravity of a lamina*

Stable, unstable and neutral equilibrium

- **Stable equilibrium**: A body is in stable equilibrium if, when slightly displaced, its centre of gravity rises and a restoring moment is created that returns the body to its base.

- **Unstable equilibrium**: A body is in unstable equilibrium if, when slightly displaced, its centre of gravity falls and a toppling moment is created which removes the body from its base.

- **Neutral equilibrium**: A body is in neutral equilibrium if, when slightly displaced, the height of its centre of gravity is unchanged and the body remains at rest in its new position.

See Figure 4.4.

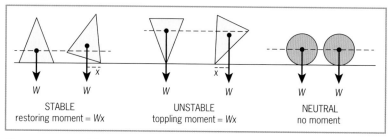

Figure 4.4 *Stable, unstable and neutral equilibrium*

Factors affecting the stability of an object

1. Height of its centre of gravity (see Figure 4.5(a))

2. Width of its base (see Figure 4.5(b))

3. Its weight. A larger weight increases the restoring moment of a stable body thereby increasing its stability. It also increases the toppling moment of an unstable body, thereby decreasing its stability.

- Go-karts have wide wheel bases and low centres of gravity in order to be more stable.

- Large cargo buses have their baggage compartments under the floor in order to lower the centre of gravity of the vehicle and to enhance stability.

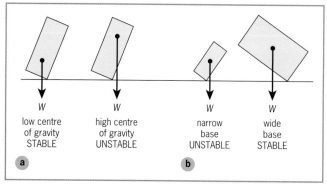

Figure 4.5 *Factors affecting the stability of an object*

Common devices utilising the principle of moments

For a given moment, the greater the *perpendicular distance from the pivot to the force*, the smaller is the force. In each device of Figure 4.6, since d_E is greater than d_L, the force of the effort (E) is less than the force of the load (L). For this reason, these devices are known as *force multipliers*.

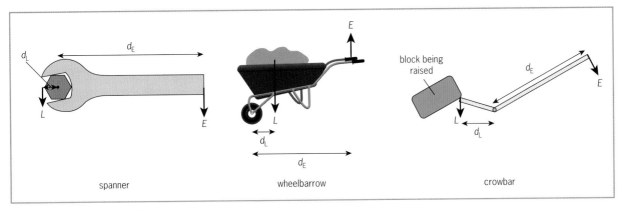

Figure 4.6 *Devices utilising the principle of moments*

Revision questions

1 **a** Define the term *moment about a point*.

   b State the TWO conditions necessary for a system of coplanar forces to be in equilibrium.

   c Which of the two conditions is known as the principle of moments?

2 What is meant by each of the following?

   a The centre of gravity of a body

   b Stable equilibrium

   c Unstable equilibrium

3 Describe with the aid of a diagram how you can determine the position of the centre of gravity of an irregularly shaped lamina.

4 State THREE factors which affect the stability of an object.

5 Figure 4.7 shows a *non-uniform* rod of length 3.0 m balancing on a fulcrum. The centre of gravity of the rod is 1.2 m to the right of the fulcrum. Calculate the weight of the rod and the reaction from its support.

Figure 4.7

5 Deformation

Hooke's law states that the force applied to a spring is proportional to its extension.

Verifying Hooke's law

- The apparatus is set up as shown in Figure 5.1.
- The position of the pointer is recorded using the metre rule.
- A mass of 20 g is placed on the mass holder and the new position of the pointer is recorded.
- The process is repeated by adding masses, one at a time, until six readings are taken.
- The masses are removed, individually, and the position of the pointer on the scale is measured and recorded each time.
- The average scale reading and the extension for each load is calculated and tabulated.
- A graph of load against extension is plotted.

Provided the spring is not stretched to the extent that it is damaged, a *straight-line graph through the origin* should be obtained, thus verifying Hooke's law. The slope of the graph is the **force constant** (k) of the spring.

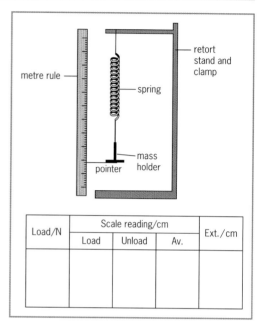

Load/N	Scale reading/cm			Ext./cm
	Load	Unload	Av.	

Figure 5.1 *Verifying Hooke's law*

Precautions to minimise errors

- It is ensured that the pointer is fixed firmly to the mass holder during the experiment.
- Eye level readings are taken to avoid parallax error.
- Readings are taken when the spring is at rest.
- To reduce random error, the spring is loaded and unloaded and the average scale reading is calculated.
- It is ensured that the spring's support is firm so that it does not shift during the experiment.

Analysing force–extension graphs

Springs

Figure 5.2 shows the relation between force and extension for a spring which has been stretched to the extent that it is damaged.

- The **proportional limit** (P) is the point beyond which any further increase in the load applied to a spring will produce an extension that is no longer proportional to the force.
- The **elastic limit** (E) is the point beyond which any further increase in the load applied to a spring will produce a permanent stretch.

For loads (forces) within the elastic limit, there is **elastic deformation**; if the load is removed the spring returns to its original size and shape.

Beyond the elastic limit, there is **plastic deformation**; the material is permanently stretched.

The area between the graph line and the extension axis represents the **work done** on stretching the spring. If this is within the proportional limit, it is represented by the area of the enclosed triangle.

Elastic bands

Unlike springs, elastic rubber bands *never obey Hooke's law*; Figure 5.3 shows that the graph is nowhere a straight line. As the elastic band is unloaded, the extension for a particular load is greater than when it was being loaded. Heat energy is dissipated in the process.

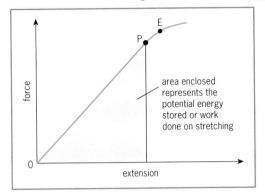

Figure 5.2 *Force–extension graph for a spring*

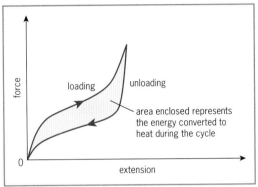

Figure 5.3 *Force–extension graph for an elastic band*

Example

A load of 5.0 N stretches a spring by 10 cm. The relaxed length of the spring is 40 cm. Assuming that the proportional limit is not exceeded, determine the following:

a the force constant of the spring

b the load which will stretch it to 60 cm.

Sketch:

c a graph of force against extension of the spring

d a graph of force against length of the spring.

Calculate:

e the work done in stretching the spring to 60 cm

f the potential energy stored in the spring when it is stretched to 60 cm.

a Hooke's law can be stated as $F = ke$ where k is the force constant of the spring and e is the extension.

$$5.0 = k(0.10)$$

$$k = \frac{5.0}{0.10}$$

$$k = 50 \text{ N m}^{-1}$$

b $F = ke$

$$F = 50(0.60 - 0.40)$$

$$F = 10 \text{ N}$$

c, d See Figure 5.4.

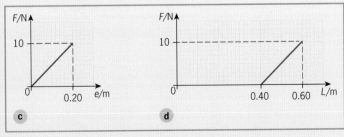

Figure 5.4 *Force–extension and force–length graphs*

e Work done = area under force–extension graph

$$W = \frac{10 \times 0.20}{2}$$

$$W = 1.0\ \text{J}$$

f Potential energy stored = work done = 1.0 J

Revision questions

1 State what you understand by each of the following terms associated with stretched springs.

    a Hooke's law   **b** the elastic limit   **c** elastic deformation

2 Sketch graphs of force against extension for each of the following:

    a a spring being stretched without exceeding the proportional limit

    b an elastic band being loaded and then unloaded.

3 A load of 80 N applied to a spring of length 40 cm extends it by 20 mm. Assuming that the proportional limit is not exceeded, calculate the following:

    a the force constant of the spring

    b the length of the spring when a load of 40 N is applied

    c the potential energy stored in the spring when the extension is 20 mm. (A simple sketch graph of force against extension can help you here.)

6 Kinematics

Table 6.1 *Variables in kinematics*

Quantity	Definition	Scalar/vector	SI base unit
distance d	*length between two points*	scalar	m
displacement s	*distance in a specified direction*	vector	m
speed v	*rate of change of distance*	scalar	m s^{-1}
velocity v	*rate of change of distance in a specified direction (rate of change of displacement)*	vector	m s^{-1}
acceleration a	*rate of change of velocity*	vector	m s^{-2}

Displacement–time and velocity–time graphs

Displacement–time (s–t) graph

Examples of obtaining velocity from displacement–time graphs are shown in Figure 6.1.

- **velocity** $= \dfrac{\Delta s}{\Delta t}$ which is the gradient

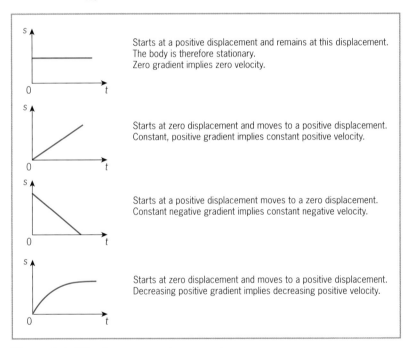

Starts at a positive displacement and remains at this displacement. The body is therefore stationary. Zero gradient implies zero velocity.

Starts at zero displacement and moves to a positive displacement. Constant, positive gradient implies constant positive velocity.

Starts at a positive displacement moves to a zero displacement. Constant negative gradient implies constant negative velocity.

Starts at zero displacement and moves to a positive displacement. Decreasing positive gradient implies decreasing positive velocity.

Figure 6.1 *Displacement–time graphs*

Velocity–time (v–t) graph

Examples of obtaining acceleration from velocity–time graphs are shown in Figure 6.2.

- **acceleration** $= \dfrac{\Delta v}{\Delta t}$ which is the gradient
- distance = area between graph line and time axis (all areas are positive)
- displacement = area between graph line and time axis (areas above time axis are positive; areas below time axis are negative)

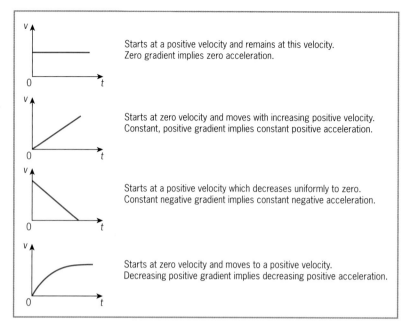

Figure 6.2 *Velocity–time graphs*

$$\text{average speed} = \frac{\text{total distance}}{\text{time}} \qquad \text{average velocity} = \frac{\text{total displacement}}{\text{time}}$$

Distance–time and speed–time graphs

- The gradient of a distance–time graph is the speed.
- The gradient of a speed–time graph is the magnitude of the acceleration *if the motion is in a straight line*.

Determine the velocity during each stage, A, B and C, shown in the displacement–time graph of Figure 6.3.

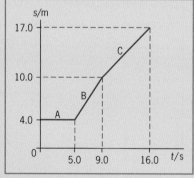

Figure 6.3

$$v = \frac{\Delta s}{\Delta t} = \text{gradient}$$

$$v_A = \frac{4.0 - 4.0}{5.0 - 0} = \frac{0}{5.0} = 0 \text{ m s}^{-1}$$

$$v_B = \frac{10.0 - 4.0}{9.0 - 5.0} = \frac{6.0}{4.0} = 1.5 \text{ m s}^{-1}$$

$$v_C = \frac{17.0 - 10.0}{16.0 - 9.0} = \frac{7.0}{7.0} = 1.0 \text{ m s}^{-1}$$

Example 2

Figure 6.4 shows a velocity–time graph of an object *moving to the left and then to the right*. Determine:

a the acceleration during the first 6.0 s

b the acceleration during the last 2.0 s

c the distance travelled in the first 6.0 s

d the displacement during the first 6.0 s

e the average speed during the first 6.0 s

f the average velocity during the first 6.0 s

g the time at which the object changed direction.

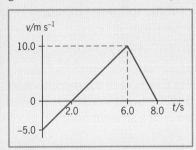

Figure 6.4

By inspection of the graph it can be seen that the initial velocity to the left has been assigned a negative value. Motion to the right is therefore positive.

a $a = \dfrac{\Delta v}{\Delta t} = \dfrac{10.0 - -5.0}{6.0 - 0} = \dfrac{15.0}{6.0} = 2.5$

$a = 2.5 \text{ m s}^{-2}$

The positive value indicates that the acceleration is directed to the right. During the first 2.0 s this is in the opposite direction to the velocity, so the object is slowing down. This is known as a *deceleration*. For the next 4.0 s it is speeding up as it moves to the right.

b $a = \dfrac{\Delta v}{\Delta t} = \dfrac{0 - 10}{8 - 6} = \dfrac{-10}{2} = -5.0$

$a = 5 \text{ m s}^{-2}$ in magnitude

The negative value indicates that the acceleration is directed to the left and the object is slowing down while still moving to the right. It is therefore *decelerating* at 5.0 m s^{-2}.

c distance = area of triangles

$d = \dfrac{5.0 \times 2.0}{2} + \dfrac{4.0 \times 10.0}{2} = 25$

$d = 25 \text{ m}$

d displacement $s = - \dfrac{5.0 \times 2.0}{2} + \dfrac{4.0 \times 10.0}{2} = 15$

$s = 15 \text{ m}$

The positive value indicates that the displacement is to the right.

e average speed $= \dfrac{\text{distance}}{\text{time}}$

average speed $= \dfrac{25}{6.0} = 4.2 \text{ m s}^{-1}$

f average velocity $= \dfrac{\text{displacement}}{\text{time}}$

average velocity $= \dfrac{15}{6.0} = 2.5 \text{ m s}^{-1}$

The positive value indicates that the average velocity is directed to the right.

g The object changed direction at $t = 2.0$ s. This occurs when the velocity changes from negative to positive.

Revision questions

1 Define each of the following terms:

    a distance   **b** displacement   **c** speed   **d** velocity   **e** acceleration

2 **a** Without using values, sketch displacement–time graphs for the following motions:

    i a stationary object

    ii an object moving at constant velocity

    iii an object accelerating.

    b Without using values, sketch velocity–time graphs for the following motions:

    i an object moving at constant velocity

    ii an object accelerating uniformly.

3 A car accelerates uniformly from rest to 20 m s^{-1} during a period of 5.0 seconds and then remains at this constant velocity for the next 4.0 s. The brakes are then applied, bringing it uniformly to rest in a final 3.0 s. *The motion is in a straight line.*

    a Sketch a velocity–time graph of the motion.

    b Calculate:

    i the acceleration during each stage of the motion

    ii the distance travelled during the first 9.0 seconds

    iii the average velocity for the first 9.0 seconds.

7 Newton's laws and momentum

Aristotle's theory

Aristotle, a renowned Ancient Greek philosopher, believed that the force applied to a body determined its velocity, that is, $F \propto v$. His arguments were based on *observations*, rather than on *experiment*. They were:

1. To pull a chariot at a greater speed required more horses which provided a greater force.

2. A moving body comes to rest when the force on it is removed.

But Aristotle's observations were of real-life situations, with friction. If friction is negligible, an object will *accelerate* when pushed along a level surface by a *constant force*. There is no force that results in a unique velocity for the object and therefore Aristotle's 'law of motion', $F \propto v$, cannot be correct. His theory was eventually discredited and replaced by that of Newton.

Newton's laws of motion

1st law: A body continues in its state of rest or uniform motion in a straight line unless acted on by a resultant force.

2nd law: The rate of change of momentum of a body is proportional to the applied force and takes place in the direction of the force.

$$F_R = \frac{mv - mu}{t}$$

F_R = resultant force, m = mass, u = initial velocity, v = final velocity, t = time of action of force, a = acceleration

$$F_R = \frac{mv - mu}{t} = \frac{m(v - u)}{t} = ma$$

Momentum is discussed later in the chapter.

3rd law: If body A exerts a force on body B, then body B exerts an equal but oppositely directed force on body A. In other words, 'every action has an equal, but oppositely directed reaction'.

Only one of the two forces in the pair acts on a particular body.

Applications of Newton's laws

- A rocket, with its engines off, moves through outer space at constant velocity in a straight line. The resultant force on the rocket is zero; there is no forward force since the engines are off and there is no opposing force since there is no atmosphere to create friction with its surface. It will continue in a straight line at the particular velocity it has acquired due to forces which *previously* acted on it. (*1st law: uniform velocity if $F_R = 0$*)

    If an astronaut steps out of the rocket as it moves at 200 m s⁻¹ and then gently releases the door handle, he or she will continue to move at 200 m s⁻¹ alongside the vehicle. The velocity of the astronaut was 200 m s⁻¹ and remains at 200 m s⁻¹ until some resultant force acts to change this. (*1st law: uniform velocity if $F_R = 0$*)

- As a car crashes into a wall, a force acts against its motion for a particular time. It quickly decelerates to rest (experiences an acceleration with a direction in opposition to its motion). (*2nd law: $F_R = ma$*)

  If the occupants are not wearing seatbelts, they will continue their motion (*1st law: uniform velocity if $F_R = 0$*) until they collide with the windscreen, dashboard or some other object. An opposing force from the object then changes their motion, causing them to decelerate to rest. (*2nd law: $F_R = ma$*)

- As an aircraft accelerates along a runway, the backrest of a seat presses forward on its occupant. This, together with the forward forces of friction from the seat, armrest and carpet, on the person's body, produces a resultant force that causes the passenger to accelerate. (*2nd law: $F_R = ma$*)

  Each object producing a force *on* the passenger's body experiences an equal but oppositely directed reaction force *from* his/her body. For example, the forward force of the seat on the passenger's back gives rise to a backward force from his/her back onto the seat. (*3rd law: action = reaction*)

- If the aircraft moves at *constant velocity*, the resultant force on the passenger along the line of motion must be zero. The passenger will no longer feel the seat pushing on his/her back or friction at the arms. (*1st law: uniform velocity if $F_R = 0$*)

  As the aircraft decelerates to rest due to the opposing force of the brakes on its wheels, the occupant also decelerates to rest due to the opposing resultant force experienced from the seatbelt, armrests and seat. (*2nd law: $F_R = ma$*)

  The forward force of the passenger's body on the seatbelt is equal in magnitude to the backward force of the seatbelt on his/her body. (*3rd law: action = reaction*)

- A car uses a *greater driving force* from its engine to travel at a *higher constant velocity*. This is because the frictional force from the air is greater at higher velocity. The *resultant force* in each case is zero and hence the acceleration in each case is zero. (*1st law: uniform velocity if $F_R = 0$*)

- As a raindrop falls through the air, it quickly attains a constant velocity. Initially, the only force on the drop is its weight (the force of gravity) which causes it to accelerate at approximately 10 m s^{-2}. (*2nd law: $F_R = ma$*)

  As the velocity of the drop increases, the upward force of the air friction on it increases and hence the resultant downward force on the drop decreases. At some point the weight of the drop becomes equal in magnitude but opposite in direction to the opposing frictional force; the resultant force and acceleration are then zero and the velocity no longer increases. This maximum velocity reached is known as the **terminal velocity**. (*1st law: uniform velocity if $F_R = 0$*)

- As a child springs upward from a trampoline, an upward force acts on his/her feet resulting in an acceleration (*2nd law: $F_R = ma$*). The force exerted by the child on the trampoline is equal but opposite in direction to the force exerted by the trampoline on the child. (*3rd law: action = reaction*)

- As water spouts from a rotating garden sprinkler, the force of the device pushing on the water results in an equal but oppositely directed force from the water on the device. This causes the sprinkler arm to rotate. (*3rd law: action = reaction*)

- An object being whirled in a circle at the end of a string is constantly changing direction and therefore its velocity is constantly changing, even if its speed is constant. It is accelerating under the influence of an external force from the tension in the string. (*2nd law: $F_R = ma$*)

Constant velocity implies zero resultant force

From Newton's 1st law, if the resultant force on a body is zero, then one of the following is true:

a) the body is at rest, or

b) the body is moving at constant velocity.

The net force is therefore zero in each of the following cases:

- a humming bird hovering above a flower
- a raindrop falling at constant terminal velocity
- a car moving at constant velocity (constant speed in a straight line).

Abdul pulls a block of mass 8.0 kg by means of a horizontal string across a horizontal surface. The tension in the string is 29 N and the frictional force opposing the motion is 17 N. Determine the acceleration.

$$F_R = ma$$

$$(29 - 17) = 8.0 \times a$$

$$\frac{12}{8.0} = a$$

$$a = 1.5 \text{ m s}^{-2}$$

Simran leapt into the air and spiked the ball horizontally. It rocketed away at 25 m s^{-1} but found the palms of Zakira who struck it back along its path with the same speed. If the force exerted by Zakira was 1250 N and the mass of the ball was 500 g, determine the period of impact.

Take the original direction of the ball's motion as positive.

$$F_R = \frac{m(v - u)}{t}$$

$u = 25 \text{ m s}^{-1} \longrightarrow$ $v = -25 \text{ m s}^{-1} \longleftarrow$

$$-1250 = \frac{0.500(-25 - 25)}{t}$$

$F_R = -1250 \text{ N} \longleftarrow$

$$t = \frac{0.500(-50)}{-1250}$$

$$t = 0.020 \text{ s}$$

Momentum

*The **linear momentum** of a body is the product of its mass and its velocity.*

$$\text{momentum} = \text{mass} \times \text{velocity}$$

The unit of momentum is kg m s^{-1}. It may also be expressed as N s:

From Newton's 2nd law,

$$F = \frac{mv - mu}{t}$$

and therefore

$$Ft = mv - mu \text{ (the change in momentum)}$$

The units on both sides of the equation must be equal and therefore, using the left side, the unit of momentum can be N s.

Momentum is a VECTOR quantity and therefore its direction is significant. For motion along a straight line, positive values are assigned to one direction and negative values to the opposite direction.

Conservation of linear momentum

*The **law of conservation of linear momentum** states that, in the absence of external forces, the total momentum of a system of bodies is constant.*

- The greater the mass of the head of a golf club, the more momentum it has when swung at a given speed, and the greater is the momentum it will impart to the ball which it strikes.

- When a bullet is fired, the forward momentum of the bullet is equal but oppositely directed to the backward (recoil) momentum of the gun. The total momentum after the explosion is therefore zero, as it was before the shot was released.

Tackling problems involving the conservation of linear momentum

- Select one direction as positive and the opposite direction as negative.

- Sketch a block diagram in equation form (see examples which follow), including all objects immediately before and after the collision or explosion, indicating the mass and velocity of each.

  Be very careful with the signs (+/–) and arrows for each velocity. Do not place an arrow or – sign on any unknown velocity.

- Use the conservation law and the diagram to formulate a numerical equation.

- If the solution to the equation is a velocity or momentum, you should state its magnitude and its direction (obtained from its sign, +/–).

- Since 'mass × velocity' is the only quantity on each side of the conservation equation, any unit of mass or of velocity can be used, so long as it is applied consistently within the calculation.

Example 3

A car of mass 1000 kg travels north at 20 m s^{-1} and collides head-on with another car of mass 1500 kg, which is moving south at 18 m s^{-1}. Determine the common velocity of the vehicles after the collision if they stick together.

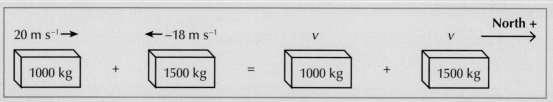

Figure 7.1

Total momentum before collision = total momentum after collision

$$(1000 \times 20) + (1500 \times -18) = 1000v + 1500v$$

$$20000 - 27000 = 2500v$$

$$-7000 = 2500v$$

$$\frac{-7000}{2500} = v$$

$$-2.8 = v$$

The negative sign indicates the direction is south.

Common velocity after collision $v = 2.8$ m s^{-1} towards south

Example 4

A body of mass 800 g moves to the right at 4.0 m s⁻¹ and collides head-on with a lighter body of mass 200 g which is moving to the left at 20 m s⁻¹. After the collision, the heavier body rebounds at 5.6 m s⁻¹. Determine the velocity of the lighter body immediately after the collision.

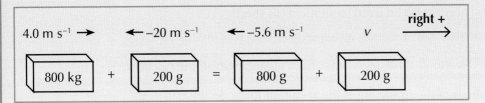

Figure 7.2

Total momentum before collision = total momentum after collision

$$(800 \times 4.0) + (200 \times -20) = (800 \times -5.6) + 200v$$
$$3200 - 4000 = -4480 + 200v$$
$$-800 = -4480 + 200v$$
$$-800 + 4480 = 200v$$
$$3680 = 200v$$
$$\frac{3680}{200} = v$$
$$18.4 = v$$

Velocity of lighter object after collision $v = 18$ m s⁻¹ (to 2 sig. fig.) towards the right

Example 5

A stationary gun of mass 1.2 kg is loaded with a bullet of mass 20 g. Determine the recoil velocity of the gun as the bullet leaves its nozzle at 200 m s⁻¹.

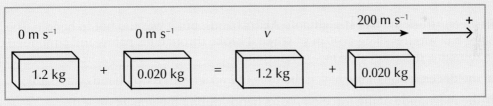

Figure 7.3

Total momentum before collision = total momentum after collision

$$(1.2 + 0.020)\, 0 = 1.2v + 0.020 \times 200$$
$$0 = 1.2v + 4.0$$
$$-4.0 = 1.2v$$
$$\frac{-4.0}{1.2} = v$$
$$-3.3 = v$$

Recoil velocity of gun = 3.3 m s⁻¹ (in the opposite direction to the bullet)

Revision questions

1. State:
   a. Aristotle's 'law of motion'
   b. the arguments he used to support his theory
   c. one example that indicates that his belief was incorrect.

2. State Newton's three laws of motion, giving an example of each.

3. In which of the following is the resultant force on the ball zero?
   a. A ball at rest on the ground
   b. A ball moving to the right with uniform velocity of 4.0 m s^{-1}
   c. A ball rising vertically through the air after being shot from a spring gun
   d. A ball, fastened to a string, and whirled in a circle at constant speed

4. a. Define *momentum*.
   b. Give TWO units that can be used to express the momentum of a body.
   c. State the law of conservation of linear momentum.
   d. Is momentum a scalar or vector quantity?
   e. How is it possible for two moving bodies to have a total momentum of zero?

5. Rikita of mass 40 kg steps from an initially stationary raft onto a nearby pier. Calculate the magnitude of her velocity if the raft is of mass 20 kg and moves away at 5.0 m s^{-1}.

6. Omorade of mass 50 kg runs and jumps with a velocity of 4.0 m s^{-1} onto a stationary trolley of mass 30 kg. Determine their common velocity immediately after they make contact.

7. Rasheed struck the ball straight into Akib's hands, but it was too hot to handle. The 500 g ball was travelling at 40 m s^{-1} when it broke through his palms and continued on in the same direction at 10 m s^{-1}. Determine:
   a. the deceleration of the ball, if the time of impact with Akib's hands was 0.020 s
   b. the magnitude of the force on Akib's hands during the impact period.

8 Energy

Work is the product of a force and the distance moved by its point of application in the direction of the force.

Energy is the ability to do work.

Power is the rate of doing work or of using energy.

$$\text{work} = \text{force} \times \text{displacement} \qquad W = F \times s$$

$$\text{energy} = \text{force} \times \text{displacement} \qquad E = F \times s$$

$$\text{power} = \frac{\text{work}}{\text{time}} \qquad P = \frac{W}{t}$$

1 **joule** (1 J) of work is done when the point of application of a force of 1 N moves through a distance of 1 m in the direction of the force.

1 **watt** (1 W) is the power used in doing 1 J of work per 1 s.

Some types of energy

- mechanical energy:

  a) potential (gravitational or elastic)

  b) kinetic

- electromagnetic energy (the energy of radio waves, microwaves, infrared waves, light waves, ultraviolet waves, X-waves and gamma waves; see Chapter 21)
- chemical energy (the energy stored in the bonds of chemical compounds)
- sound energy (the energy transferred by vibrating particles of a sound wave)
- thermal energy (the energy due to the motion of the particles of a body)
- heat energy (thermal energy *in the process of being transferred* from one point to a next, due to a temperature difference between them)
- electrical energy (the energy resulting from charged particles being in electric fields)
- nuclear potential energy (the energy binding the particles of the nucleus of an atom)

Kinetic and potential energy

Kinetic energy is the energy a body has due to its motion.

The kinetic energy, E_K, of a body of mass m and speed v is given by:

$$E_K = \tfrac{1}{2}mv^2$$

Potential energy is the energy a body has due to:
a) its position in a force field, or
b) its state (for example stretched/compressed/chemical).

The change in **gravitational potential energy**, ΔE_p, of a body of mass m, as it moves through a height change Δh in a gravitational field of strength g is given by:

$$\Delta E_p = mg\,\Delta h$$

Examples of kinetic and potential energy

- A fast-moving cricket ball has *kinetic* energy, mainly due to its high velocity.
- A football kicked into the air has *gravitational potential* energy due to its position (height) in the gravitational force field.
- A stretched elastic band has *elastic potential* energy due to its stretched state.
- A compressed spring has *elastic potential* energy due to its compressed state.
- Gasoline, food and batteries have *chemical potential* energy due to their chemical state.

The principle of conservation of energy

The **principle of conservation of energy** *states that energy cannot be created or destroyed but can be transformed from one type to another.*

Note that whenever energy is transformed, an equal amount of work is done.

Examples of energy transformations

The transformations listed below show the MAIN energy changes in each situation.

Note that kinetic energy is constant when velocity is constant. If it is not increasing or decreasing, it does not take part in the transformation.

- A coconut falling from a tree and striking the ground below (not rebounding):

  gravitational potential energy ⟶ kinetic energy ⟶ thermal energy + sound energy
- A gasoline-fuelled car accelerating on a level road:

  chemical potential energy ⟶ kinetic energy + thermal energy + sound energy
- A gasoline-fuelled car moving at constant velocity on a level road:

  chemical potential energy ⟶ thermal energy + sound energy
- A boy running up stairs at constant velocity:

  chemical potential energy (from food) ⟶
  gravitational potential energy + thermal energy + sound energy
- An aircraft taking off:

  chemical potential energy (from fuel) ⟶
  gravitational potential energy + kinetic energy + thermal energy + sound energy
- A swinging pendulum, neglecting friction:

  gravitational potential energy ⟶ kinetic energy ⟶ gravitational potential energy ⟶
  kinetic energy *and so on*
- A battery charging:

  electrical energy ⟶ chemical potential energy
- An electric fan:

  electrical energy ⟶ kinetic energy
- An electric oven:

  electrical energy ⟶ thermal energy + electromagnetic (infrared and light) energy
- An electric lamp:

  electrical energy ⟶ thermal energy + electromagnetic (infrared and light) energy

- A loudspeaker:

  electrical energy in speaker coil ⟶ kinetic energy of speaker coil and cone ⟶
  kinetic energy of vibrating air layers (sound energy)

- A microphone:

  kinetic energy of vibrating air of the sound wave ⟶
  kinetic energy of microphone coil and diaphragm ⟶ electrical energy in coil

- Hydroelectric power:

  gravitational potential energy of water at top of falls ⟶ kinetic energy of falling water ⟶
  kinetic energy of spinning generator turbine ⟶ electrical energy in generator coil

- A diesel-fuelled electrical power station:

  chemical potential energy of diesel ⟶ thermal energy (to boil water to produce steam) ⟶
  kinetic energy of spinning generator turbine (turned by steam pressure) ⟶
  electrical energy in generator coil

- A battery used by a crane to lift an object at constant velocity:
  chemical potential energy ⟶ electrical energy ⟶ gravitational potential energy

---

Example 1

Asabi pushes a block 25 m across a floor with a horizontal force of 20 N in a time of 4.0 s.

Determine:

a the work done   b the energy used   c the power used.

a $W = Fs$

   $W = 20 \times 25$

   $W = 500 \text{ J}$

b $E = 500 \text{ J}$

c $P = \dfrac{W}{t}$

   $P = \dfrac{500}{4.0}$

   $P = 125 \text{ W}$

Example 2

A bullet of mass 20 g is shot vertically into the air with a velocity of 200 m s⁻¹. Determine:

a the kinetic energy of the bullet on leaving the gun

b the maximum potential energy gained by the bullet.

a $E_K = \dfrac{1}{2} mv^2$

   $E_K = \dfrac{1}{2} \times 0.020 \times 200^2$

   $E_K = 400 \text{ J}$

b The maximum E_K of the bullet transforms completely to E_P at the maximum height.
   Therefore max. $E_P = 400$ J.

Example 3

Raveena grabs on to one of the vines in the tree and starts to swing. She has a velocity of 6.0 m s⁻¹ at the lowest point of her motion. Determine the maximum change of height, Δh, she swings through. (Gravitational field strength = 10 N kg⁻¹)

The required height, Δh, is shown in Figure 8.1.

ΔE_p at the highest point transforms completely to E_K at the lowest point.

$$\frac{1}{2}mv^2 = mg\,\Delta h$$

$$\frac{1}{2}v^2 = g\,\Delta h \ (m \text{ cancels})$$

$$\frac{1}{2}6.0^2 = 10\,\Delta h$$

$$\frac{1}{2}\frac{6.0^2}{10} = \Delta h$$

$$\Delta h = 1.8 \text{ m}$$

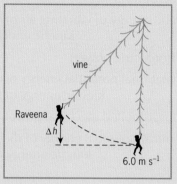

Figure 8.1

Example 4

If the block in Example 1 is being pushed at constant velocity across a horizontal floor, determine the thermal energy generated.

500 J of chemical potential energy stored in Asabi's muscles transforms into 500 J of thermal energy produced by friction between the block and floor.

(Note that the kinetic energy and gravitational potential energy are unchanged since the velocity is constant and the floor is level.)

Energy sources

Renewable energy sources are those which are readily replaced.

Examples are: solar, hydroelectric, geothermal, tidal, and wind energy. Wood and biomass (organic material) may be considered renewable if the trees and crops are replanted.

Non-renewable energy sources are those which are not readily replaced and become scarce with time.

Examples are **fossil fuels** (coal, oil and natural gas) and nuclear fuel.

Problems associated with obtaining electricity from fossil fuels

- Limited reserves: Supplies are rapidly diminishing.
- Pollution: Burning fossil fuels contaminates the environment with several pollutants including **greenhouse gas** emissions.
- Fluctuating oil prices: The price has been low recently and this has highlighted the high risk of investing in crude oil companies.
- Health care costs: Government funding is needed for health care facilities to deal with illnesses associated with pollutants from the burning of fossil fuels.

Alternative sources of energy

The Caribbean depends heavily on fossil fuels for the generation of electricity and there is an urgent need for utilising alternative sources of energy. Some possible sources are listed below.

Solar energy: Solar water heaters heat water directly and are relatively cheap to install. **Photovoltaic panels** convert solar radiation into electrical energy. These have a relatively high installation cost but provide a clean source of electricity. The energy can be returned to the electricity grid or stored in batteries to be used at night.

Hydroelectricity: Water is collected behind a dam in a river and then released. The kinetic energy of the water then turns the turbine of an electrical generator. Guyana has great potential for providing this form of energy, but the landscape of most Caribbean territories is unsuitable.

Tidal energy: Water from the ocean can be collected at high tide and then released at low tide to produce powerful water pressure which can turn electrical generators. Alternatively, energy of wave motion and ocean currents can be harnessed to turn the generators.

Geothermal energy: Thermal energy from the hot interior of the Earth can be brought to the surface as steam under pressure and released in hot water springs or geysers. Volcanic islands are capable of providing large amounts of this type of energy.

Wind energy: Kinetic energy from the wind can be used to turn wind turbines. This form of energy generation, however, has the drawbacks of noise pollution, spoiling the scenery and being vulnerable to unpredictable stormy weather.

Biomass energy: This is the energy obtained from plant or animal matter.

- Biogas is obtained from the decay of animal wastes. It is comprised mainly of methane and is being used to drive electrical generators on farms that deal with livestock.
- Wood can be used as a fuel for cooking.
- Alcohol, produced from sugar cane, can be used to make **gasohol**, a useful fuel.

Efficiency

*The **efficiency** of a system is the ratio of the useful energy output to the energy input.*

It is commonly represented as a percentage.

$$\text{efficiency} = \frac{\text{useful work or energy output}}{\text{work or energy input}} \times 100\%$$

It can also be calculated as the ratio of useful *power output* to *power input*.

$$\text{efficiency} = \frac{\text{useful power output}}{\text{power input}} \times 100\%$$

Thermal energy produced due to friction is the main reason for systems having low efficiency.

Example 5

The fuel tank of a toy car contains gasoline capable of releasing 3.0 kJ of energy. Calculate the efficiency of the conversion if the car moves 50 m, exerting a driving force of 20 N before it is out of fuel.

$$\text{efficiency} = \frac{\text{useful energy output}}{\text{energy input}} \times 100\%$$

$$\text{efficiency} = \frac{F \times d}{E_{in}} \times 100\% = \frac{20 \times 50}{3000} \times 100 = 33\%$$

Example 6

A mass of 200 kg is raised by an electric motor through a height of 25 m. Calculate the electrical energy used if the efficiency of the system is 80%. (Gravitational field strength = 10 N kg^{-1})

$$\text{efficiency} = \frac{\text{useful energy output}}{\text{energy input}} \times 100\%$$

$$\text{efficiency} = \frac{mg \, \Delta h}{E_{in}} \times 100$$

$$80 = \frac{200 \times 10 \times 25}{E_{in}} \times 100$$

$$E_{in} = \frac{5\,000\,000}{80} = 62\,500 \text{ J}$$

Revision questions

1 Define:

    a work   **b** energy   **c** power   **d** potential energy   **e** kinetic energy

2 **a** State the principle of conservation of energy.

    b Describe the MAIN energy transformations occurring for each of the following situations.

       i A gasoline-fuelled car accelerating along a level road

      ii A gasoline-fuelled bus driving along a level road at constant velocity

     iii The bob of a swinging pendulum

     iv The generation of hydroelectricity

      v The generation of electricity from diesel

     vii A battery-powered motor of a crane lifting an object at constant velocity

3 Mukesh, of weight 400 N, runs up a staircase of height 4.0 m at constant speed in a time of 2.5 s. Determine:

    a the energy transformation occurring (neglect thermal and sound energy)

    b the energy used

    c the power used.

4 A bullet of mass 20 g and speed 400 m s^{-1} embeds itself 12 cm into a block. Determine:

    a the kinetic energy of the bullet before entering the block

    b the energy transformed in boring the hole

    c the work done in boring the hole

    d the average force of the bullet on the block as it bores the hole.

5 List:

    a THREE problems associated with the use of fossil fuels

    b FOUR alternative sources of energy.

6 Radiation from the Sun reaches the panel of a solar water heater at a rate of 500 W. If the efficiency of the conversion is 20%, calculate the rate of energy supplied to the water.

9 Pressure and buoyancy

Pressure is the force acting normally per unit area.

$$\text{pressure} = \frac{\text{force}}{\text{area}} \qquad P = \frac{F}{A}$$

The SI unit of pressure is N m^{-2} which has been assigned the name **pascal** (Pa).

Example 1

Gravitational field strength = 10 N kg^{-1}

Determine the maximum pressure that can be exerted on a horizontal surface by a rectangular block of mass 50 kg and dimensions 20 cm × 50 cm × 1.2 m when resting on one of its faces.

The maximum pressure is obtained when the block rests on its smallest face as shown in Figure 9.1.

$$P = \frac{F}{A}$$

$$P = \frac{mg}{A} \text{ (the force is the weight)}$$

$$P_{max} = \frac{50 \times 10}{0.20 \times 0.50}$$

$$P_{max} = 5000 \text{ Pa}$$

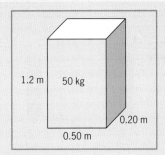

Figure 9.1

Pressure in fluids

The pressure at a point in a fluid increases with increased depth and with increased density of the fluid.

increase in pressure =
depth × density × gravitational field strength

$$\Delta P = \Delta h \rho g$$

Figure 9.2 shows a tall can of water with small holes in its sides at different depths. Water spouts with equal strength from holes on the same level, indicating that the pressure is the same in all directions at a particular depth. Water spouts with greater force from holes at greater depth, indicating that the pressure increases with depth.

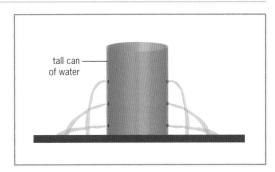

Figure 9.2 *Pressure in a fluid increases with depth*

Example 2

Gravitational field strength = 10 N kg^{-1}

Figure 9.3 shows a fish at a depth of $h = 40$ m in a lake where the density of the water is 1000 kg m^{-3}. Determine:

a   the pressure due to the water on the fish

b   the total pressure on the fish if the atmospheric pressure is 1.0×10^5 Pa.

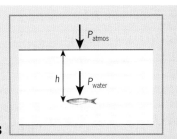

Figure 9.3

a $P_{water} = h\rho g$

$P_{water} = 40 \times 1000 \times 10 = 400\,000$ Pa

b $P_{tot} = P_{atmos} + P_{water}$

$P_{tot} = 1.0 \times 10^5 + 4.0 \times 10^5 = 5.0 \times 10^5$ Pa

Archimedes' principle

*Archimedes' principle states that when a body is completely or partially immersed in a fluid, it experiences an **upthrust** equal to the weight of the fluid displaced.*

Figure 9.4 shows how the principle can be verified.

- An object is first weighed in air and then again when immersed in a displacement can filled to the spout with water. The difference between these weights is the upthrust of the water on the immersed object.

- The displaced water is collected in a beaker and weighed. The weight of the empty beaker is subtracted from the weight of the beaker of water to find the weight of water displaced.

The readings verify that the upthrust is equal to the weight of the fluid displaced.

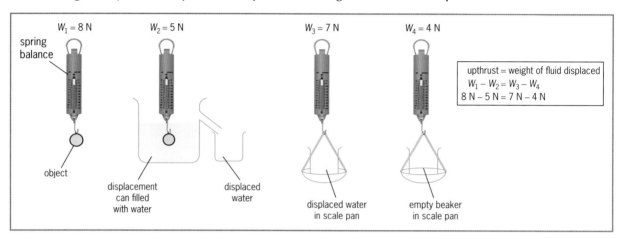

Figure 9.4 *Verifying Archimedes' principle*

Floating

A body floats if its own weight is equal to the upthrust on it (the weight of fluid displaced by it).

Example 3

A rectangular block of base dimensions 20 cm × 20 cm and weight 50 N floats as shown in Figure 9.5. Calculate the depth, h, to which it is submerged, given that the density of water is 1000 kg m^{-3}. (Gravitational field strength = 10 N kg^{-1})

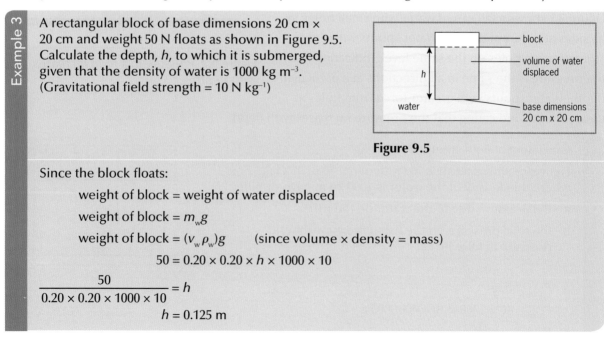

Figure 9.5

Since the block floats:

weight of block = weight of water displaced

weight of block = $m_w g$

weight of block = $(v_w \rho_w)g$ (since volume × density = mass)

$$50 = 0.20 \times 0.20 \times h \times 1000 \times 10$$

$$\frac{50}{0.20 \times 0.20 \times 1000 \times 10} = h$$

$$h = 0.125 \text{ m}$$

Submarines

Figure 9.6 shows a toy submarine that has a ballast tank which can hold water. If water is taken into the tank until the submarine's weight exceeds the weight of water displaced (upthrust), the submarine will accelerate downwards. The resultant force on it is downwards, and it will descend without the use of its engines.

To accelerate upwards, air under pressure expels water from the ballast tank, decreasing the weight of the submarine. When decreased to a value less than the weight of water displaced (upthrust), the submarine will accelerate upwards. Floating occurs if the weight is equal to the weight of water displaced (upthrust).

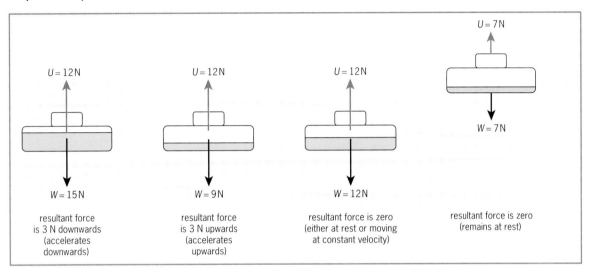

Figure 9.6 *Upthrust and submarines*

Balloons

Figure 9.7(a) shows a balloon containing air. If the air in the balloon is heated, it will become less dense and will expand. The upthrust on the balloon will increase since it will now displace more of the cooler surrounding air. It will accelerate upwards if its weight plus the weight of its contents is less than the weight of the air it displaces (upthrust).

If the balloon contains a gas of low density such as helium, as in Figure 9.7(b), it will accelerate upwards even without its contents being heated.

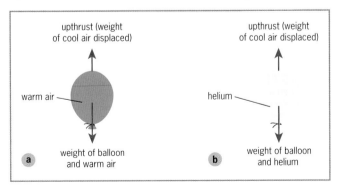

Figure 9.7 *Upthrust and balloons*

Note that air becomes less dense at higher altitudes and therefore the weight of the air displaced (upthrust) becomes less. When the upthrust has decreased to the weight of the balloon and its contents, the resultant force is zero and acceleration ceases. The balloon continues upwards but there is then a net downward force since the upthrust is further reduced. The balloon thus begins to bob up and down until it settles at a height where the net force on it is zero.

Measuring Pressure

Example 4

Figure 9.8 shows a simple **mercury barometer**, an instrument used to measure the pressure of the atmosphere. The height, h, of the mercury column is proportional to the atmospheric pressure. Since there is a *vacuum* at the top of the tube, the pressure at Y is due only to the mercury above it. Given the following data, calculate the atmospheric pressure, P_A, indicated by the barometer.

density of mercury = 13 600 kg m^{-3},
gravitational field strength = 10 N kg^{-1}

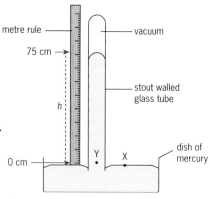

Figure 9.8

P_A = *pressure at X*
P_A = *pressure at Y (since X and Y are at the same level in the mercury)*
$P_A = h\rho g$　　　(*pressure at Y due to the column of mercury above it*)
$\quad = 0.75 \times 13600 \times 10$
$\quad = 1.0 \times 10^5 \ P_a$

Example 5

Figure 9.9 shows a **manometer**, an instrument used to measure the pressure of a gas. One arm of the U-tube is exposed to the atmosphere and the other is connected to the gas supply. The difference in the levels of the liquid in the arms of the tube indicates the difference in pressure between the gas and the atmosphere.

Given the following data, calculate the pressure of the gas supply assuming the liquid in the manometer is mercury.

atmospheric pressure = 1.0×10^5 Pa, h = 20 cm,
density of mercury = 13 600 kg m^{-3}, *gravitational field strength* = 10 N kg^{-1}

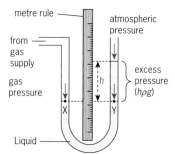

Figure 9.9

gas pressure = pressure at X
$\qquad\qquad$ *= pressure at Y (since X and Y are at the same level in the fluid)*
gas pressure = atmospheric pressure + excess pressure
$\quad P_G = P_A + h\rho g$
$\qquad = 1.0 \times 10^5 + (0.20 \times 13\ 600 \times 10)$
$\qquad = 1.3 \times 10^5 \ P_a$

Revision questions

Acceleration due to gravity = 10 m s^{-2}

1 Shakira, of mass 40 kg, stands in soft mud in her garden. The sole of each of her shoes has an area of 140 cm^2. Determine the pressure she creates on the ground when standing on both feet. (1 m^2 = 100 cm × 100 cm = 10 000 cm^2, therefore 140 cm^2 = 0.0140 m^2, i.e. divide by 10 000)

2 Determine the pressure at the bottom of a swimming pool of depth 2.0 m, on a day when the atmospheric pressure is 1.1×10^5 Pa. The density of water is 1000 kg m^{-3}.

3 a State the principle of Archimedes.

　b Write an equation showing the condition necessary for an object to float.

4 A raft of weight 500 N floats in water of density 1000 kg m^{-3}.

　a What is the upthrust on the raft?

　b Calculate the volume of water displaced by the raft.

5 Explain, in terms of Archimedes' principle, why a hot air balloon rises.

Exam-style questions – Chapters 1 to 9

Structured questions

1 **a)** Define EACH of the following terms.

    i)   Scalar quantity   **(2 marks)**

    ii) Vector quantity   **(2 marks)**

  b) Complete Table 1 by placing EACH of the quantities listed below in the appropriate column.

    energy, force, displacement, pressure, momentum, power

    Table 1

Scalar	Vector

    (3 marks)

  c) Komo's boat can travel across still water at 8.0 m s^{-1}. He tries to cross a river which flows at 6.0 m s^{-1} by directing the front of the boat perpendicular to the banks of the channel. Of course he ends up far downstream!

    i)   By means of a scale drawing, or otherwise, determine the magnitude of the resultant velocity of the boat and its direction in degrees measured from the bank of the river.   **(6 marks)**

    ii) Determine the actual distance travelled if the journey takes 5.0 minutes.   **(2 marks)**

                                                    Total 15 marks

2 **a)** Define EACH of the following terms.

    i)   Displacement   **(2 marks)**

    ii) Velocity   **(2 marks)**

    iii) Acceleration   **(2 marks)**

  b) A car starts from rest and accelerates uniformly for 4.0 s, reaching a maximum velocity of 20 m s^{-1}. It remains at this velocity for the next 6.0 s and then uniformly comes to rest in a period of 8.0 s.

    i)   Sketch a velocity–time graph of the motion.   **(3 marks)**

    ii) Calculate the acceleration during the initial 4.0 s.   **(2 marks)**

    iii) Determine, from your graph, the distance travelled in the first 10 s.   **(3 marks)**

  c) Cite an example where an object accelerates although its speed is constant.   **(1 mark)**

                                                    Total 15 marks

3 **a)** Define EACH of the following terms.

    i)   Moment of a force   **(2 marks)**

    ii) Centre of gravity of a body   **(2 marks)**

  b) i)   State what is meant by the term 'the principle of moments'.   **(2 marks)**

    ii) Write an SI unit to express the moment of a force.   **(1 mark)**

c) Figure 1 shows a uniform cone of mass 2.0 kg and of height 40 cm, resting on its base, of width 30 cm.

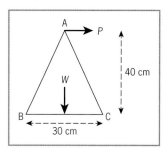

Figure 1

Calculate:

i) the weight, W, of the cone (2 marks)

ii) the minimum horizontal pull, P, which can be applied at A to raise the edge, B, from the floor. (4 marks)

d) Comment on the new value of P required if the height of the cone is doubled. (2 marks)

(Gravitational field strength = 10 N kg^{-1})

Total 15 marks

Extended response questions

4 a) State Newton's three laws of motion. (6 marks)

b) A jet of mass 4.0×10^4 kg accelerates at 3.6 m s^{-2} along a runway.

i) Determine the resultant force producing the acceleration. (2 marks)

ii) Comment on the actual magnitude of the thrust (force) of the engines relative to the value calculated in (b)(i). (2 marks)

iii) Determine the work done along the runway by the resultant force if the length of the runway is 500 m. (3 marks)

c) When the jet is in the air it moves at constant velocity for most of its journey but the engines must still provide a forward thrust. Deduce the resultant force on the jet at this time. (2 marks)

Total 15 marks

5 a) Explain why it is necessary to use alternative sources of energy in the Caribbean, and describe how TWO such sources are being put to use today. (6 marks)

b) Akuna drops a sharp stone of mass 500 g from a height of 30 m and it bores a hole of depth 20 cm into soft soil. Determine:

i) the change in gravitational potential energy of the stone (2 marks)

ii) the kinetic energy just before striking the ground (2 marks)

iii) the work done in boring into the soil (1 mark)

iv) the energy transformed as it bores the hole (1 mark)

v) the average force on the stone as it decelerates and comes to rest. (3 marks)

(Acceleration due to gravity = 10 m s^{-2})

Total 15 marks

10 Nature of heat

Caloric theory

The **caloric theory of heat** is an obsolete theory from the 18th century. Heat was believed to be an invisible fluid called 'caloric', which could combine with matter and raise its temperature.

Arguments for the caloric theory

1. Objects expand when heated because the increased 'caloric' they contain causes them to occupy more space.

2. Heat flows from hotter to cooler bodies because 'caloric' particles *repel* each other.

Arguments against the caloric theory

1. When bodies are heated so that they change state (solid to liquid or liquid to gas), an increase in 'caloric' cannot be detected.

2. When different materials are given the same amount of heat ('caloric'), their temperatures increase by different amounts, indicating that they receive different quantities of 'caloric'.

3. The weight of a body should increase as it is heated, because it should then contain more 'caloric'. However, the weight remains the same.

Rumford's cannon-boring experiment as evidence against caloric theory

Count Rumford was an army officer responsible for the boring of cannons during the late 18th century.

He realised that the heat energy transferred when a cannon was being bored was inexhaustible and depended only on the work done in boring the hole. The 'caloric' theory was therefore not possible; if 'caloric' was a material substance, there would be a time when all of it had left the cannon.

Kinetic theory

The **kinetic theory** of matter states the following.

- The particles of matter (atoms, molecules) are in constant motion of vibration, translation or rotation. The *kinetic energy* they possess is responsible for their temperature, or hotness (see Chapter 11).

- There is space between the particles. Forces (bonds) pull them together when they are near to each other, and so the particles have *potential energy*.

- When a substance is heated, the heat energy supplied could result in an *increase in the kinetic energy* of the particles of the substance, and hence in its thermal energy, causing the temperature to rise.

- When a substance is heated so that it changes state, the heat energy supplied results in an increase in the spacing of the particles and hence an *increase in their potential energy*, allowing them to break bonds with their neighbours and to expand against any surrounding pressure.

Joule's role in establishing the principle of conservation of energy

James Joule proved experimentally that energy can be transformed from one type to another, but is always conserved (see Chapter 8). His experiment is outlined below.

Two bodies, each of mass m, and attached to the ends of a string, were allowed to fall through a height h, as shown in Figure 10.1. As they descended, a pulley mechanism caused the strings to turn paddles in the water, of mass m_w.

On reaching the lowest point, the masses were quickly wound up to the starting position and then were allowed to fall again. This was repeated several times (n times). On analysing the results, Joule concluded that the potential energy of the masses was transformed to kinetic energy of the paddles which then transformed to thermal energy of the water, causing the temperature to rise by an amount ΔT.

The work done by the paddles in churning the water was equal to the gravitational potential energy of the falling masses which transformed to a rise in thermal energy of the water.

$$n(2mgh) = m_w c\, \Delta\theta$$

(See Chapter 15 for calculations of thermal energy changes.)

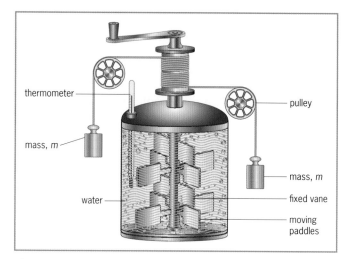

Figure 10.1 *Joule's experiment, establishing the principle of conservation of energy*

Revision questions

1. **a** What was the 'caloric theory' of heat?
   b State TWO arguments for and TWO arguments against the caloric theory.
   c What evidence did Count Rumford use to indicate that the caloric theory was incorrect?

2. **a** What theory replaced the caloric theory?
   b Briefly describe this theory.

3. Describe the experiment of Joule in establishing the principle of conservation of energy.

11 Temperature and thermometers

Temperature is the degree of hotness of a body.

*A **thermometer** is an instrument used to measure temperature.*

Units of temperature

The **kelvin** (K) is the SI unit of temperature, but it is also common in science to express temperature in degrees **Celsius** (°C).

$$\text{temperature } T_K \text{ in K} = \text{temperature } T_C \text{ in °C} + 273$$

This conversion will be further discussed in Chapter 14.

Designing a thermometer

- Select a suitable **thermometric property** – a property of a material which varies with temperature (see Table 11.1).

Table 11.1 *Examples of thermometers and their thermometric properties*

Thermometer	Thermometric property as temperature increases
liquid-in-glass	volume of liquid increases
constant-pressure gas thermometer	volume of gas increases at constant pressure
constant-volume gas thermometer	pressure of gas increases at constant volume
thermoelectric thermometer (thermocouple)	emf produced varies *non-linearly*
resistance thermometer	resistance increases
thermistor	resistance usually decreases but increases for some types

- Select a suitable range.

  A mercury-in-glass laboratory thermometer typically has a range from −10 °C to 110 °C or 0 °C to 100 °C.

  A clinical thermometer typically has a range from about 34 °C to 43 °C.

  A thermoelectric thermometer typically has a range from about −250 °C to about 1500 °C.

- Select a suitable scale. The values of the thermometric property at upper and lower **fixed points** are found and marked on the thermometer (see Figure 11.1), and the interval between the fixed points is then **calibrated**.

Fixed points on the Celsius scale

- *The **upper fixed point** (100 °C) is the temperature of steam from pure boiling water at standard atmospheric pressure* (Figure 11.1(a)).
- *The **lower fixed point** (0 °C) is the temperature of pure melting ice at standard atmospheric pressure* (Figure 11.1(b)).

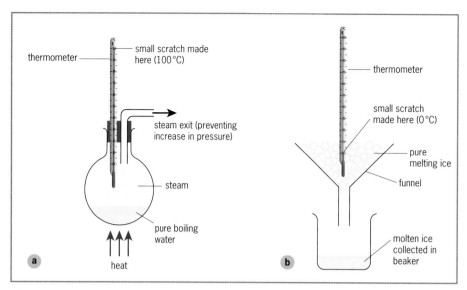

Figure 11.1 *Determining* **(a)** *the upper and* **(b)** *the lower fixed points*

Laboratory mercury thermometer

The laboratory thermometer is a 'liquid-in-glass' thermometer which utilises mercury as the liquid (Figure 11.2).

- The bulb that holds the mercury has a thin wall so that heat can easily transfer through it.

- The bore is very narrow so that any change in volume of the mercury will result in a noticeable change in the length of the mercury thread.

- The bulb is relatively large so that the corresponding expansion or contraction of the mercury it contains is noticeable for small changes in temperature. The larger the bulb, the longer must be the stem and bore; the separation of the intervals on the scale is then greater and it is easier to read.

- The scale is positioned very close to the bore to reduce parallax error (see Chapter 1).

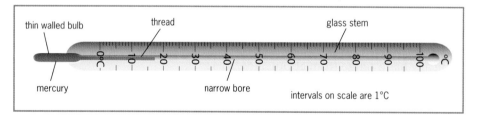

Figure 11.2 *Liquid-in-glass laboratory thermometer*

Advantages of a mercury thermometer

- Mercury is a metal so it has a high conductivity and a low specific heat capacity (see Chapter 15). This means its temperature quickly adjusts to the temperature it is measuring.

- The boiling point of mercury is 357 °C and therefore the thermometer is suitable for most laboratory experiments done at school. If alcohol was used as the liquid, it would evaporate and distil on the upper part of the bore.

- Mercury is bright silver and can easily be seen.

- The thermometer has a linear scale which is easy to read.

Disadvantages of a mercury thermometer

- It cannot be used to measure very cold temperatures because mercury freezes at −39 °C.
- It is expensive.
- Mercury is poisonous.

Clinical mercury thermometer

A clinical thermometer (Figure 11.3) can also be of the liquid-in-glass type. It therefore has many of the features and properties of the laboratory thermometer. However, the following should be noted.

- The scale ranges only from 34 °C or 35 °C to 43 °C because the normal body temperature of a human is 37 °C.
- The interval between markings on the scale is 0.1 °C so that a very precise reading is obtained.
- There is a narrow constriction in the bore. When the thermometer is removed from the patient, the sudden change in temperature causes a rapid contraction of the mercury. As the mercury rushes toward the bulb, the thread breaks at the constriction, leaving the thread above it to be read.
- Mercury is poisonous.
- This type of clinical thermometer is rapidly being replaced by an electronic, digital thermometer.

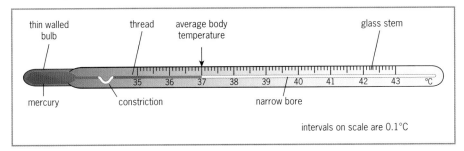

Figure 11.3 *Liquid-in-glass clinical thermometer*

Thermocouple

A **thermocouple** (Figure 11.4) is simply a pair of dissimilar metal wires, A and B, joined at their ends. On heating one of the junctions, an emf is produced which varies with the *temperature difference* between the junctions. By connecting a voltmeter between the junctions, the emf (see Chapter 28) can be detected. The scale of the voltmeter can be calibrated in units of temperature.

Since the thermometer depends on temperature *difference*, the reference junction must always be at the same temperature it had at calibration. The cold junction is generally the reference junction.

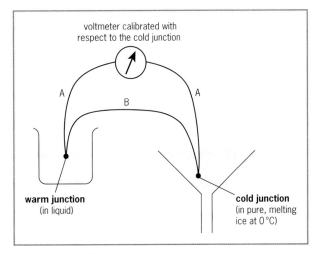

Figure 11.4 *Thermocouple*

Advantages of a thermocouple

- It responds quickly to temperature changes because metals have high conductivities and low specific heat capacities. It is therefore useful for measuring rapidly changing temperatures.
- It takes very little heat from the body it is measuring and is therefore capable of determining the temperature of a small body without noticeably altering its temperature.
- It can withstand very low and very high temperatures and is therefore useful for measuring temperatures in freezers and in furnaces.
- Since it is electrical, it can be connected to digital displays and computer systems.

Disadvantages of a thermocouple

- Large temperature differences produce only small changes in emf. It is therefore not useful for detecting small changes in temperature.
- The measuring instrument used with a thermocouple must be sensitive to small changes in emf and this can be expensive.
- The scale is non-linear and is therefore difficult to read.

Revision questions

1. a Define *temperature*.

   b What is meant by the 'upper fixed point' on the Celsius scale?

2. List TWO types of thermometer together with the thermometric property they each utilise.

3. List TWO advantages and TWO disadvantages of a liquid-in-glass mercury thermometer.

4. State THREE ways that a laboratory mercury thermometer differs from a clinical mercury thermometer.

5. a Describe how a thermocouple can be used as a thermometer.

   b List TWO advantages and TWO disadvantages of this type of thermometer.

12 States of matter

Solids, liquids and gases are all composed of tiny atoms or molecules. Figure 12.1 shows the relative positioning of the particles, and Table 12.1 shows how the forces and distances between these particles can be used to explain their physical properties.

Solids

The attractive forces between the particles of a solid are strong, bringing them *very close* together. However, at even closer distances, these forces are repulsive. The atoms or molecules therefore constantly **vibrate** about some mean position, while being bonded in a fixed lattice.

Liquids

The forces between the particles of a liquid are weaker than in solids. The molecules have more energy and the weaker forces are not enough to make the bonds rigid. They separate slightly more than in solids and are able to **translate** relative to each other.

Gases

Except at times of collision, the particles of a gas are far apart and the forces between the particles are negligible. They therefore **translate** freely, filling the container in which they are enclosed.

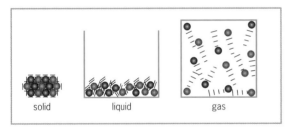

solid   liquid   gas

Figure 12.1 *Particles of a solid, a liquid and a gas*

Table 12.1 *Physical properties of matter explained in terms of forces between particles*

	Solids	Liquids	Gases
Density	High since the particles are *tightly packed*	High since the particles are *tightly packed* – almost as close as in solids	Very low since the particles are *far apart*
Shape	Fixed since there are *rigid bonds* due to strong forces between the particles	The *bonds are not rigid* and therefore liquids take the shape of their container. However, the forces between the particles still cause liquids to have a fixed volume	The forces between the particles only exist at the time of collision and therefore gases spread out to fill the container which encloses them
Ability to flow	The *rigid bonds* between particles prevent solids from flowing	The weaker forces between the particles *cannot form rigid bonds* and therefore liquids can flow	The very weak forces between the particles *cannot form rigid bonds* and therefore gases can flow

Table 12.1 *Physical properties of matter explained in terms of forces between particles continued*

	Solids	Liquids	Gases
Ability to be compressed	Not easily compressed since the particles are *tightly packed*, making it difficult to push them closer	Not easily compressed since the particles are *tightly packed*, making it difficult to push them closer	Easy to compress since there is *much space between the particles*
Main motion of particles	The particles *vibrate* about a mean position, always adjacent to the same set of particles	The particles *vibrate* and *translate*, constantly changing neighbours	The particles *translate freely*, having neighbours only at the time of collision

Revision questions

1. Describe solids, liquids and gases in terms of the separation and motion of their particles, and the forces between those particles.

2. Explain the following properties of a LIQUID in terms of your description in question 1.

   a density

   b shape

   c ability to be compressed

   d ability to flow

13 Expansion

Expansion in terms of the kinetic theory of matter

Solids: When a solid is heated, the heat energy supplied converts into kinetic energy of its particles (which we call thermal energy). The molecules of the solid vibrate faster and with greater amplitude and therefore occupy more space.

Liquids and gases: When a liquid or gas is heated, the heat energy supplied converts to kinetic energy of its particles. The molecules of the liquid or gas translate faster and therefore occupy more space.

Demonstrating expansion

Simple experiments to show expansion in solids, liquids and gases are shown in Figure 13.1.

Solid: At room temperature, the hammer is just able to fit into the space and the ball can just fit through the hole. However, when the hammer or ball is heated, this fit is no longer possible.

Liquid: The flask expands slightly when heated, causing the liquid level to drop initially. With continued heating, however, the liquid expands up the tube. With a narrow tube, the rise is very noticeable.

Gas: The air expands when heated, producing bubbles in the water.

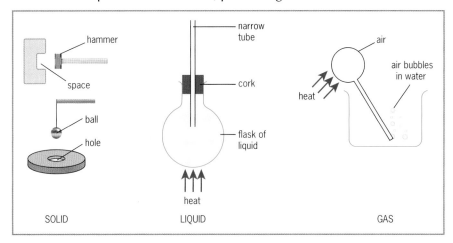

Figure 13.1 *Demonstrating expansion in solids, liquids and gases*

Utilising expansion

- Liquid-in-glass thermometers (see Chapter 11).
- Applications of the **bimetallic strip** (considered later in this chapter).
- Metal plates joined with the use of hot rivets; on cooling, the rivets contract and bind the plates firmly.

Avoiding problems due to expansion

- Concrete surfaces are laid in slabs (Figure 13.2(a)) and the spaces between them are filled with pitch. During expansion of the surface, the soft pitch is compressed, avoiding strong forces in the concrete which would otherwise produce cracks.
- Railway lines are laid in short lengths with their ends bevelled and overlapping (Figure 13.2(b)). This prevents warping because it allows them to freely slide over each other when they expand and contract.

- Pipelines in deserts, or those which carry steam, are laid in a zig-zag formation (Figure 13.2(c)) with flexible joints. On expansion or contraction, these flex without the pipeline being subjected to strong forces.
- Large structures such as bridges can be made with one end on rollers (Figure 13.2(d)). This allows them to expand and contract freely without producing strong forces which could weaken the assembly.
- Baking dishes which undergo large temperature differences are made of materials that expand and contract very little with temperature change. This prevents them from cracking when removed from the oven into the much cooler environment.
- Power lines must be laid slack in summer, so that strong tension forces are not produced when they contract in winter.

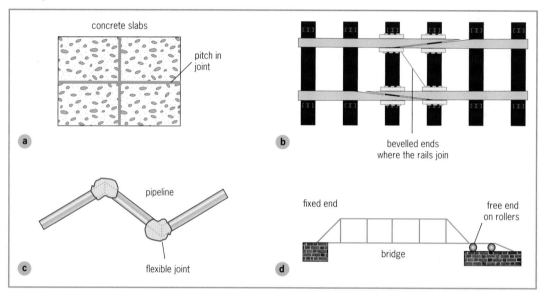

Figure 13.2 *Some ways of dealing with expansion*

Other phenomena involving expansion

- Roofs shrink at night as the temperature falls. Contraction of the wood causes the joints to move relative to each other, producing a creaking sound.
- A tight metal lid on a glass jar is easily removed by running hot water onto it. The lid rapidly expands due to its high thermal conductivity, and becomes loose.

The bimetallic strip

A **bimetallic strip** consists of two metal strips riveted together (Figure 13.3). The strips bend on heating such that the metal that expands more is on the outer side of the curve.

Brass expands much more than invar when heated and so this combination forms a good bimetallic strip. Brass will also contract more on cooling.

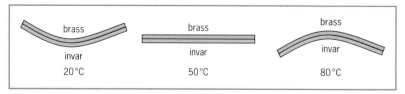

Figure 13.3 *The bimetallic strip*

Simple fire alarm

A simple fire alarm is shown in Figure 13.4. Heat from the fire causes the bimetallic strip to bend upward and closes the contacts. This completes the circuit and sounds the alarm. (See Chapter 29 for interpreting circuit symbols.)

Electric thermostat

An electric **thermostat** is shown in Figure 13.5. This type may control the temperature of an oven. With the switch on, the heater warms the oven. The bimetallic strip then bends causing the sliding contacts to separate and break the circuit. With the heater disconnected, the oven cools, the contacts reconnect, and the process repeats. The temperature control knob is an adjusting screw that can be advanced so that it forces the sliding contacts further over each other. The bimetallic strip must then bend more in order to break the circuit.

By switching the position of the brass and invar, the thermostat can be used to prevent a fridge from becoming too cold.

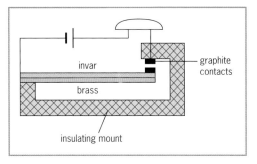

Figure 13.4 *A simple fire alarm using a bimetallic strip*

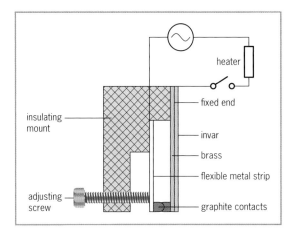

Figure 13.5 *An electric thermostat connected to a heating element*

Revision questions

1. Explain, in terms of the kinetic theory, why matter expands when heated.

2. Describe how you can show that solids expand when heated.

3. State TWO problems associated with expansion and how they may be avoided.

4. Describe and explain the function of a simple fire alarm which utilises a bimetallic strip.

14 The ideal gas laws

Temperature scales

Two important temperature scales are the **Celsius scale** and the **kelvin scale**. The kelvin scale is also known as the **thermodynamic temperature scale** or **absolute temperature scale**.

The relation between the Celsius and the kelvin scales is shown in Figure 14.1. Note that *the intervals of 1 K and 1 °C are equal*. Examples of converting between °C and K are shown in Table 14.1.

Table 14.1 *Converting °C to K*

°C	K
200	273 + 200 = 473
27	273 + 27 = 300
0	273 + 0 = 273
−20	273 − 20 = 253

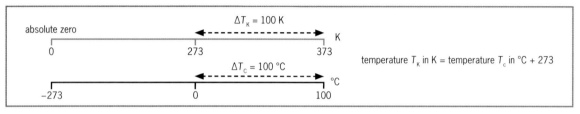

temperature T_K in K = temperature T_c in °C + 273

Figure 14.1 *Temperature scales*

The ideal gas laws

1. **Boyle's law**: *For a fixed mass of gas at constant temperature, the pressure is inversely proportional to its volume.*

$$P \propto \frac{1}{V} \quad \text{or} \quad PV = \text{constant (when } T \text{ constant)}$$

2. **Charles' law**: *For a fixed mass of gas at constant pressure, the volume is directly proportional to its absolute temperature.*

$$V \propto T \quad \text{or} \quad \frac{V}{T} = \text{constant (when } P \text{ constant)}$$

3. **Pressure law**: *For a fixed mass of gas at constant volume, the pressure is directly proportional to its absolute temperature.*

$$P \propto T \quad \text{or} \quad \frac{P}{T} = \text{constant (when } V \text{ constant)}$$

Combining the three laws:

For a fixed mass of an ideal gas changing from state 1 to state 2, the following holds:

$$\frac{P_1 V_1}{T_1} = \frac{P_2 V_2}{T_2}$$

Note the following:

- *P* and *V* may be in any unit of pressure and volume, respectively.
- *T must be measured on the* KELVIN *scale.*
- In problems where one of the variables is constant, it may be omitted from the equation.

There is no such thing as an ideal gas but many gases behave approximately as an ideal gas at easily reached temperatures and pressures. An important assumption of ideal gas theory is that there are no intermolecular forces between its molecules.

Constant temperature

If the vessel is a *very good conductor* (poor insulator), any instantaneous rise or fall in temperature will quickly readjust to that of the environment. It can therefore be assumed that *temperature is constant*.

Constant pressure

If the vessel is *freely expandable*, it can be assumed that the *pressure is constant*. Should the pressure instantaneously rise or fall, the vessel will expand or contract so that its contents have the same pressure as the environment (usually atmospheric pressure). Such is the case with a gas trapped in a syringe with a well oiled piston.

Constant volume

If the container is a *strong, solid vessel,* it can be assumed that the *volume is constant*. An increase in temperature will cause a slight increase in volume of the vessel but this is insignificant when compared to the increase that would have occurred if the gas had freely expanded.

Verifying the gas laws

To verify Boyle's law

Boyle's law can be verified using the apparatus shown in Figure 14.2. The pressure, P, and volume, V, are measured and recorded. The pressure is increased by use of the pump, and the new pressure and volume readings are taken. This is repeated until a total of six pairs of readings are obtained and tabulated.

$\dfrac{1}{V}$ is calculated and recorded for each value of V, and a graph of P against $\dfrac{1}{V}$ is plotted.

* The scale could be of length instead of volume. Since the tube is of uniform cross-sectional area, any change in length will produce a proportional change in volume.

* Increasing the pressure will also increase the temperature. Before taking readings, a short period should be allowed after increasing the pressure for the air to return to room temperature.

* The straight line through the origin of the graph verifies the law.

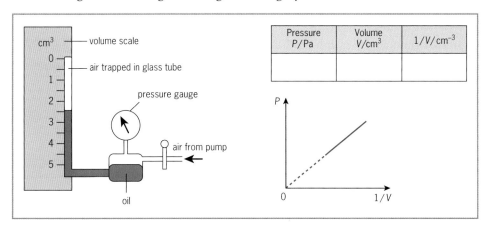

Figure 14.2 *Experimental verification of Boyle's law*

To verify Charles' law

Charles' law can be verified using the apparatus shown in Figure 14.3. The volume, V, of the air trapped by the bead of sulfuric acid is measured and recorded together with the temperature, T_C. The temperature is then increased several times by about 10 degrees Celsius, each time taking a new pair of readings of V and T_C. The temperatures are converted to kelvin temperatures, T_K, and a graph is plotted of V against T_K.

* The scale behind the tube could be of length instead of volume. Since the tube is of uniform cross-sectional area, any change in length will produce a proportional change in volume.

* Readings are only taken when the bead of sulfuric acid is steady, indicating that the pressure of the gas is back to its initial value.

* The straight line through the origin of the graph verifies the law.

Note that zero on the kelvin scale is the temperature at which an ideal gas will occupy no space. This point of **absolute zero** is used in the establishment of the kelvin temperature scale.

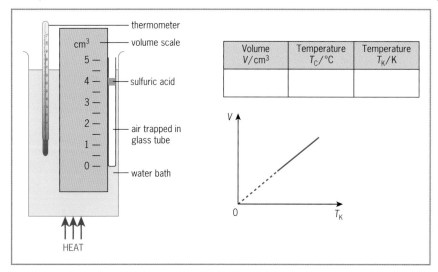

Figure 14.3 *Experimental verification of Charles' law*

To verify the pressure law

The pressure law can be verified using the apparatus shown in Figure 14.4. The pressure, P, and temperature, T_C, of the gas trapped in the spherical flask is measured and recorded. The temperature is increased several times by intervals of about 10 degrees Celsius, each time taking a new pair of readings of P and T_C. The temperatures are converted to kelvin temperatures, T_K, and a graph is plotted of P against T_K.

- It is assumed that the expansion of the vessel is negligible and that the volume of the gas is therefore constant.
- The straight line through the origin of the graph verifies the law.

Zero on the kelvin scale is the temperature at which an ideal gas will exert no pressure. This point of **absolute zero** is used in the establishment of the kelvin temperature scale.

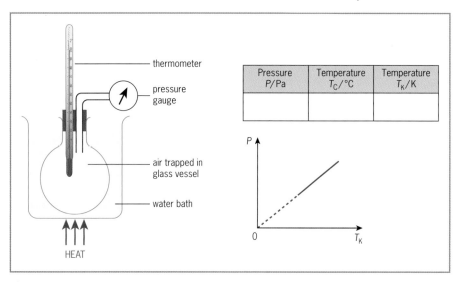

Figure 14.4 *Experimental verification of the pressure law*

Figure 14.5 shows some other important graphs illustrating gas law relationships.

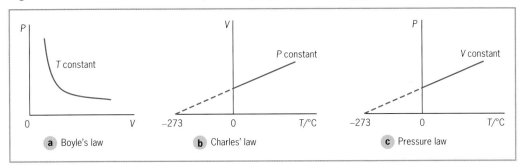

Figure 14.5 *Other important graphs*

Gases and the kinetic theory

The molecules, of mass m, of a gas, bombard each other and the walls of their container. As they rebound, in a short time t, their velocity changes from u to v and they impart forces, F, in accordance with Newton's second law of motion (see Chapter 7).

$$F = \frac{m(v - u)}{t}$$

This force creates a pressure, P, on the area, A, of the walls.

$$P = \frac{F}{A}$$

At higher temperatures, molecules translate at higher velocities and therefore the rate of change in momentum (the force) on collision is greater. The pressure therefore increases.

The three gas laws are individually explained in terms of the kinetic theory, as follows.

Kinetic theory and Boyle's law

As a gas is compressed at constant temperature, the speed of its molecules is unchanged and therefore the *force exerted by its molecules on the walls remains constant*. However, since the volume decreases, the collisions are on a *smaller area*. The force per unit area (pressure) therefore increases. See Figure 14.6(a).

Kinetic theory and Charles' law

As the temperature of a gas rises, the average speed of its molecules increases and therefore the *force exerted by its molecules on the walls is greater*. If the vessel is freely expandable, the volume will increase, and therefore the *area of the walls will also increase*. The force and area increase by the same factor and therefore the pressure remains the same. See Figure 14.6(b).

Kinetic theory and the pressure law

As the temperature of a gas rises, the average speed of its molecules increases and therefore the *force exerted by its molecules on the walls is greater*. If the volume remains constant, the *area of the walls is constant*. Since the force increases as the area remains constant, the pressure on the walls increases. See Figure 14.6(c).

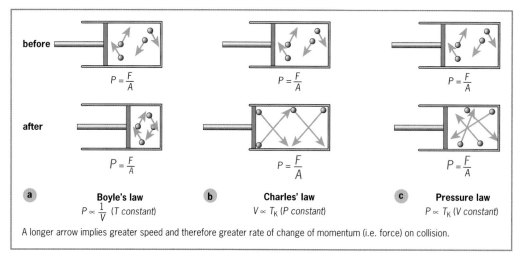

Figure 14.6 *Kinetic theory and the gas laws*

Revision questions

1 Make a sketch comparing the Celsius temperature scale and the kelvin temperature scale. Indicate values on each scale for absolute zero, the melting point of ice and the boiling point of water.

2 Describe an experiment to verify Boyle's law. Your account should include any precautions taken and a statement as to how the law is verified.

3 Explain the following, in terms of the kinetic theory of matter.

a A gas creates a pressure on the walls of its containing vessel.

b The pressure in a car tyre increases as the air in it becomes hotter.

4 40 cm³ of an ideal gas at a temperature of 27 °C is heated to 227 °C in a freely expandable vessel. Determine the new volume of the gas.

15 Heat and temperature change

Heat is thermal energy in the process of transfer from a point of higher temperature to one of lower temperature, due to the temperature difference between them.

Note that a body possesses thermal energy, *but not heat energy*. The thermal energy of a body can rise or fall, for example by the absorption or emission of heat.

*The **specific heat capacity** (c) of a substance is the heat needed to change unit mass of the substance by unit temperature.*

It is the property of a SUBSTANCE.

*The **heat capacity** (C) of a body is the heat needed to change the body by unit temperature.*

It is the property of a BODY.

Calculations

- When heat energy is supplied to a body its temperature may rise. The increase in temperature is the result of an increase in the KINETIC ENERGY of the particles of the substance. The following relation then applies:

$$E = mc\,\Delta T$$

E = heat energy supplied m = mass c = specific heat capacity ΔT = temperature change

- The heat capacity, C, of a body is related to the specific heat capacity, c, of the material from which it is made, by:

$$C = mc$$

- The unit of specific heat capacity is obtained as follows.

Since $mc\,\Delta T = E$

$$c = \frac{E}{m\,\Delta T}$$

so the unit of c is $\dfrac{J}{kg\;°C}$ or $\dfrac{J}{kg\;K}$

- The unit of heat capacity is obtained as follows.

Since $mc\,\Delta T = E$

$$mc = \frac{E}{\Delta T}$$

so the unit of C is $\dfrac{J}{°C}$ or $\dfrac{J}{K}$

- Values of specific heat capacity of some substances are given in Table 15.1. Note that the values for metals are lower than those for non-metals, and that water has the highest value in this list.

Table 15.1 *Specific heat capacity of several substances*

Substance	Specific heat capacity/J kg^{-1} °C^{-1}
ethanol	2400
water	4200
ice	2100
wood	1700
lead	130
copper	390

Tackling problems involving heat and temperature change

- Always draw a temperature diagram before you formulate your equation. This is illustrated in Figures 15.1 to 15.3, in the three Examples below.
- Place hotter bodies on the right and cooler bodies on the left.
- Temperature change, ΔT, is calculated as 'warmer subtract cooler'.
- For situations where *heat gain* and *heat loss* are equated, your diagram should show each chain of arrows having *all bodies meeting at a common temperature*.

Example 1

Determine the heat energy required to change the temperature of a block, of mass 4.0 kg and specific heat capacity 400 J kg^{-1} °C^{-1}, from 20 °C to 60 °C.

$E = mc \, \Delta T$

$E = 4.0 \times 400 \times (60 - 20) = 64\,000$ J

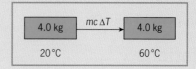

Figure 15.1

Example 2

Determine the thermal energy released when the temperature of water, of mass 2.0 kg and specific heat capacity 4200 J kg^{-1} °C^{-1}, cools from 60 °C to 20 °C.

$E = mc \, \Delta T$

$E = 2.0 \times 4200 \times (60 - 20) = 336\,000$ J

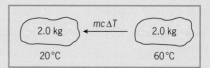

Figure 15.2

Example 3

A copper block of mass 2.0 kg cools from 120 °C to X °C as it is immersed in water of mass 3.0 kg, initially at 25 °C. Determine the final temperature, X °C. (Specific heat capacity of water = 4200 J kg^{-1} °C^{-1}; specific heat capacity of copper = 390 J kg^{-1} °C^{-1})

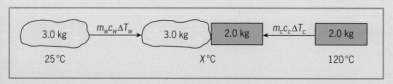

Figure 15.3

heat gain of water = heat loss of copper

$$m_w c_w \, \Delta T_w = m_c c_c \, \Delta T_c$$

$3.0 \times 4200 \times (X - 25) = 2.0 \times 390 \times (120 - X)$

$12\,600\,(X - 25) = 780(120 - X)$

$12\,600X - 315\,000 = 93\,600 - 780X$

$12\,600X + 780X = 93\,600 + 315\,000$

$13\,380X = 408\,600$

$$X = \frac{408\,600}{13\,380} = 30.5$$

Final temperature = 30.5 °C (31 °C to 2 sig. fig.)

Determining specific heat capacity

The specific heat capacity of a metal by the method of mixtures

- The mass, m_c, of a polystyrene cup is measured and recorded. Water is poured into the cup and the new mass, m_{cw}, is measured and recorded.
- The mass of water, m_w, is then calculated from $m_{cw} - m_c$.
- The mass, m_m, of the metal object is measured and recorded.
- The temperature, T_2, of the cool water in the cup is measured and recorded.
- The metal object is heated in boiling water for a few minutes so that it acquires the temperature of the hot water. This temperature, T_1, is measured and recorded.
- The hot metal is removed from the water bath by holding the string; it is quickly shaken and put into the cool water.
- The water is stirred using the thermometer and the highest temperature reached, T_3, is measured and recorded.

Figure 15.4 illustrates the process. Assume that all the thermal energy lost by the metal is gained by the water.

thermal energy gained by water = thermal energy lost by metal

$$m_w c_w (T_3 - T_2) = m_m c_m (T_1 - T_3)$$

$$\frac{m_w c_w (T_3 - T_2)}{m_m (T_1 - T_3)} = c_m$$

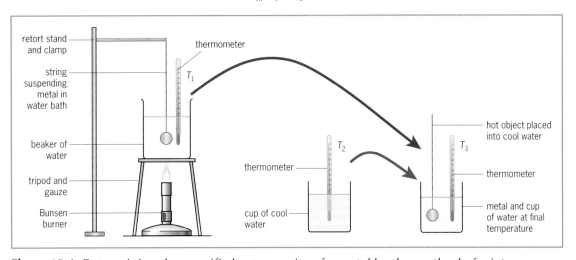

Figure 15.4 *Determining the specific heat capacity of a metal by the method of mixtures*

Precautions to minimise errors

- Some energy from the hot metal is lost to the surrounding air. To keep this to a minimum, the hot metal object is quickly transferred to the cool water.
- The object is briefly shaken to remove water from its surface since this water is not considered in the calculation.
- The water is stirred with the thermometer to ensure that the temperature recorded is the mean temperature reached.

Sources of error

- Thermal energy is transferred by conduction to the cup and to the bench top. Thermal energy is also transferred by radiation to the surrounding air.

- Evaporation of water from the surface of the metal on transferring it to the cool water removes latent heat of vaporisation (see Chapter 16). The temperature of the metal on reaching the cool water is therefore less than T_1.

The specific heat capacity of a liquid by the method of mixtures

- The mass, m_b, of a beaker and the mass, m_c, of a polystyrene cup are measured and recorded.
- The liquid being investigated is poured into the beaker and water is poured into the cup, and the new masses, m_{bL} and m_{cw}, are measured and recorded.
- The mass, m_L, of the liquid, and the mass, m_w, of the water in the cup are calculated from $m_{bL} - m_b = m_L$ and $m_{cw} - m_c = m_w$.
- The temperature, T_2, of the cool water in the cup is measured and recorded.
- The liquid is heated for a few minutes and its temperature, T_1, is then measured and recorded.
- The hot liquid is quickly poured into the cool water.
- The mixture is stirred using the thermometer and the highest temperature reached, T_3, is measured and recorded.

Figure 15.5 illustrates the process. Assuming that all the thermal energy lost by the metal is gained by the water:

thermal energy gained by water = thermal energy lost by liquid

$$m_w c_w (T_3 - T_2) = m_L c_L (T_1 - T_3)$$

$$\frac{m_w c_w (T_3 - T_2)}{m_L (T_1 - T_3)} = c_L$$

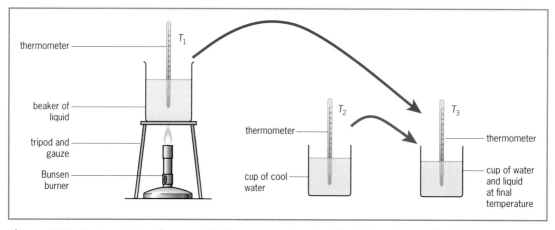

Figure 15.5 *Determining the specific heat capacity of a liquid by the method of mixtures*

Precautions to minimise errors

- Some thermal energy from the hot liquid is lost to the surrounding air. To keep this to a minimum, the hot liquid is quickly poured into the cool water.
- The mixture is stirred with the thermometer to ensure that the temperature recorded is the mean temperature reached.

Sources of error

- Thermal energy is transferred by conduction to the cup and to the bench top. Thermal energy is also transferred by radiation to the surrounding air.
- Evaporation from the warm mixture will absorb latent heat of vaporisation from it (see Chapter 16).

The specific heat capacity of a metal by an electrical method

- A metal block having slots to fit a heater and thermometer is used. The mass, m, of the block is measured and recorded.
- The apparatus is then set up as shown in Figure 15.6 and the heater is switched on.
- After a short while, the initial temperature, T_1, of the block is measured and a stop watch is started simultaneously to measure the time of heating, t.
- The current is kept constant by adjusting the rheostat. Readings of the current, I, and the voltage, V, are measured and recorded.
- When the temperature has risen by about 20 degrees Celsius, the new temperature, T_2, is measured and recorded, and the heater is switched off.

Assuming that all of the electrical energy is responsible for the increase in thermal energy of the block, the specific heat capacity, c, of the metal can be calculated from:

electrical energy = increase in thermal energy of block

$$VIt = mc(T_2 - T_1)$$

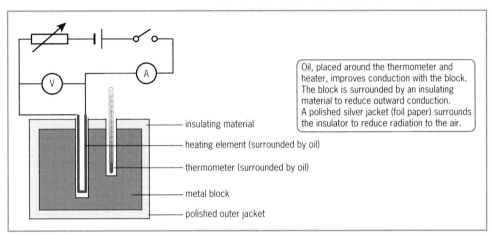

Oil, placed around the thermometer and heater, improves conduction with the block. The block is surrounded by an insulating material to reduce outward conduction. A polished silver jacket (foil paper) surrounds the insulator to reduce radiation to the air.

insulating material

heating element (surrounded by oil)

thermometer (surrounded by oil)

metal block

polished outer jacket

Figure 15.6 *Determining the specific heat capacity of a metal by an electrical method*

Precaution to minimise errors

- It is ensured that the current remains constant during the experiment by adjusting the rheostat.

Source of error

- Thermal energy is transferred to the oil, to the surrounding air and to the bench top.

The specific heat capacity of a liquid by an electrical method

- The mass, m, of the liquid is measured and recorded.
- The apparatus is then set up as shown in Figure 15.7 and the heater is switched on.
- After a short while, the initial temperature, T_1, of the liquid is measured and the stop watch is started simultaneously to measure the time of heating, t.
- The current is kept constant by adjusting the rheostat. Readings of the current, I, and the voltage, V, are measured and recorded.
- When the temperature has risen by about 20 degrees Celsius, the new temperature, T_2, is measured and recorded, and the heater is switched off.

Assuming that all of the electrical energy is responsible for the increase in thermal energy of the liquid, the specific heat capacity, c, can be calculated from:

$$\text{electrical energy} = \text{increase in thermal energy of liquid}$$
$$VIt = mc(T_2 - T_1)$$

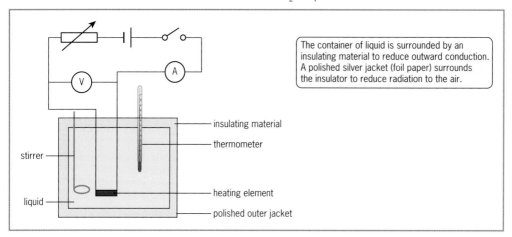

The container of liquid is surrounded by an insulating material to reduce outward conduction. A polished silver jacket (foil paper) surrounds the insulator to reduce radiation to the air.

insulating material

thermometer

stirrer

heating element

liquid

polished outer jacket

Figure 15.7 *Determining the specific heat capacity of a liquid by an electrical method*

Precautions to minimise errors

• The liquid is stirred before measuring the temperature to ensure that the mean temperature is detected.

• It is ensured that the current remains constant during the experiment by adjusting the rheostat.

Source of error

• Thermal energy is transferred to the surrounding air and to the bench top.

Revision questions

1. Define:

   a heat   b specific heat capacity   c heat capacity

2. State SI units for:

   a specific heat capacity   b heat capacity

3. Using data from Table 15.1, determine the heat energy required to change the temperature of 250 g of ethanol from 15 °C to 65 °C.

4. Using the data in Table 15.1, determine the initial temperature of a lump of lead of mass 300 g which when immersed in 400 g of water raises the temperature of the water from 20 °C to 22 °C.

5. Describe how the specific heat capacity of a metal can be found using an electrical method.

16 Heat and state change

The temperature remains constant during a change of state.

Demonstrating a change of state

Liquid to gas

- A beaker of water is heated until about one quarter of it boils away (Figure 16.1). Several readings of temperature and corresponding time are measured and recorded.

- A graph is plotted of temperature against time (a **heating curve**). This reveals that the temperature increases steadily until the water begins to boil, but then remains constant as it changes state.

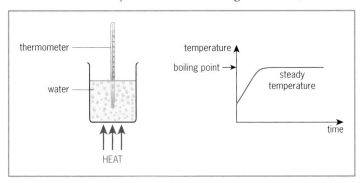

Figure 16.1 *The temperature is constant during boiling*

Liquid to solid

- Figure 16.2 shows wax being heated in a boiling tube by means of a water bath. The water is allowed to boil for a few minutes.

- The wax melts and a thermometer is placed at its centre.

- The tube and the thermometer are removed from the water bath and the wax is allowed to cool.

- Readings of temperature and corresponding time are taken every minute as the wax cools, solidifies, and then cools further.

- A graph is plotted of temperature against time (a **cooling curve**). This reveals that the temperature remains constant as the liquid solidifies.

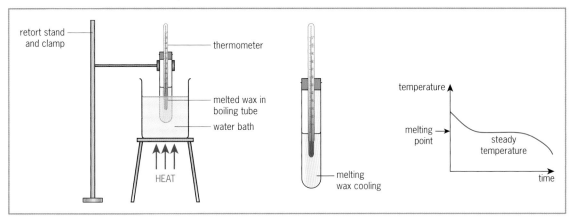

Figure 16.2 *The temperature is constant during solidification*

Latent heat

Latent heat is the heat energy necessary to change the state of a body without a change of temperature.

The **specific latent heat of fusion** (l_f) of a SUBSTANCE is the heat energy needed to change unit mass of the substance from solid to liquid without a change of temperature.

The **specific latent heat of vaporisation** (l_v) of a SUBSTANCE is the heat energy needed to change unit mass of the substance from liquid to gas without a change of temperature.

Table 16.1 *Specific latent heat of ice and water*

Specific latent heat of fusion of ice	3.4×10^5 J kg^{-1} = 3.4×10^2 J g^{-1}
Specific latent heat of vaporisation of water	2.3×10^6 J kg^{-1} = 2.3×10^3 J g^{-1}

Calculations

- When a substance changes from solid to liquid or from liquid to gas, latent heat provides the necessary increase in POTENTIAL ENERGY of the particles of the substance. The following relation then applies:

$$E = ml$$

E = heat energy supplied m = mass l = specific heat of fusion or vaporisation

- The latent heat of fusion is necessary to provide potential energy in order to:

  a) do internal work in *breaking the bonds* between the particles of a solid

  b) do external work as the particles' spacing *expands slightly* against the atmospheric pressure.

- The latent heat of vaporisation is necessary to provide potential energy in order to:

  a) do internal work in *overcoming the attractive forces* between the particles of a liquid

  b) do external work as the particles' spacing *expands significantly* against the atmospheric pressure

- As substances change to a higher energy state, they absorb latent heat, and as they change to a lower energy state, they release latent heat (Figure 16.3).

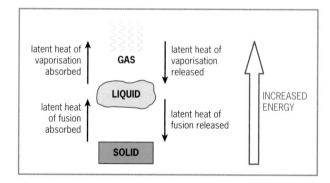

Figure 16.3 *Latent heat and state changes*

Heating curves

Heating curves indicate when the substance changes state (Figure 16.4).

- The *kinetic energy* of the particles increases as the *temperature increases*.

- The *potential energy* of the particles increases as the *state changes* from solid to liquid or from liquid to gas.

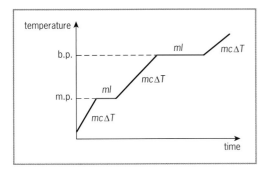

Figure 16.4 *Heating curve showing the changes in internal energy of a substance as it changes* state

Tackling problems involving heat and state change

- Always draw a temperature diagram (like that in Figure 16.5) before you formulate your equation.

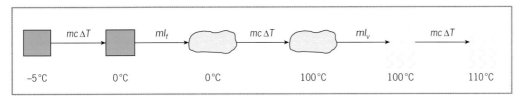

Figure 16.5 *Temperature diagram showing conversion of ice at –5 °C to steam at 110 °C*

- Place hotter bodies on the right and cooler bodies on the left. Temperature change, ΔT, is calculated as 'warmer subtract cooler'.
- A change of state and a change in temperature *cannot occur at the same time*. They must be represented as *separate changes* in the diagram.
- For situations where *heat gain* and *heat loss* are equated, your diagram should show each chain of arrows having *all bodies meeting at a common temperature*.

Example 1

Refer to data in Table 16.1.

Determine the power of a heater which takes 15 minutes to convert 2.0 kg of water at 100 °C to steam at 100 °C.

$$P = \frac{E}{t} = \frac{ml_v}{t}$$

$$P = \frac{2.0 \times 2.3 \times 10^6}{15 \times 60}$$

$$P = 5.1 \times 10^3 \text{ W}$$

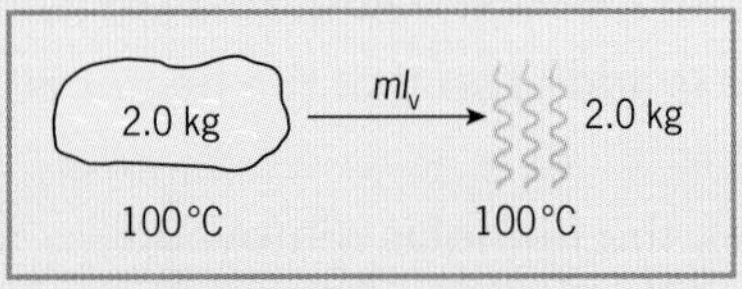

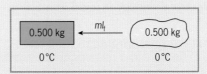

Figure 16.6

Example 2

Refer to data in Table 16.1.

Determine the heat released when 500 g of water at 0 °C converts to ice at 0 °C.

$$E = ml_f$$

$$E = 0.500 \times 3.4 \times 10^5 = 1.7 \times 10^5 \text{ J}$$

Figure 16.7

Example 3

Refer to data in Table 16.1. The specific heat capacity of water = 4200 J kg⁻¹ °C⁻¹.

A mass of 400 g of ice at –10 °C is placed into 5.0 kg of water at 60 °C. Determine the final temperature of the mixture, given that all the ice melts.

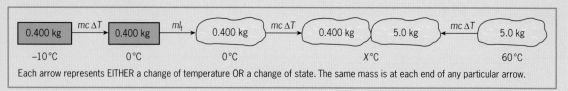

Each arrow represents EITHER a change of temperature OR a change of state. The same mass is at each end of any particular arrow.

Figure 16.8

Heat gained by ice and molten ice = heat lost by warm water

$(0.400 \times 2100 \times 10) + (0.400 \times 3.4 \times 10^5) + (0.400 \times 4200 \times X) = 5.0 \times 4200 \times (60 - X)$

$8400 + 136\,000 + 1680X = 21\,000(60 - X)$

$\qquad 144\,400 + 1680X = 1\,260\,000 - 21\,000X$

$\qquad\qquad 22\,680\,X = 1\,115\,600$

$\qquad\qquad\qquad X = 49$

Final temperature = 49 °C

Determining specific latent heat

The specific latent heat of fusion of ice by an electrical method

- The mass, m_b, of an empty beaker is measured and recorded.
- The apparatus is set up as shown in Figure 16.9 and the heater is switched on.
- Ice chips are packed around the heater element in a funnel so that the heater element is completely immersed, and a stop watch is simultaneously started. The melted ice is collected in the beaker.
- The readings of voltage, V, across the heater, and current, I, through it, are measured and recorded.
- As the ice melts, more is added so that the heater is always submerged.
- After about 10 minutes, the funnel is removed, the watch stopped, and the time, t, measured and recorded.
- The mass, m_{bw}, of the beaker and water is measured and the mass of water, m_w, calculated from $m_w = m_{bw} - m_b$.

Assume that all the electrical energy is used in melting the ice.

electrical energy = heat energy supplied to melt ice

$$VIt = m_w l_f$$
$$\frac{VIt}{m_w} = l_f$$

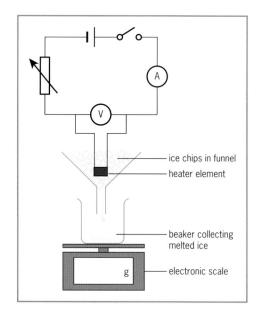

Figure 16.9 *Determining the specific latent heat of fusion of ice by an electrical method*

Precautions to minimise error

- Small chips of ice are used so that we can assume their temperature is 0 °C. (Larger chips may have colder temperatures at their centres).
- Before putting the ice in the funnel, it is quickly dabbed in a tissue so as to remove water from its surface.
- The heater element is always completely submerged so that it transfers thermal energy only to the ice.
- The current is kept constant during the experiment by adjusting the rheostat.

Source of error

- Thermal energy will be transferred to the ice from the atmosphere and the funnel.

The specific latent heat of vaporisation of water by an electrical method

- The apparatus is set up as shown in Figure 16.10 and the heater is switched on.
- *When the water is boiling*, the initial mass, m_1, is measured and recorded, and the stop watch is started.
- The readings of voltage, V, across the heater, and current, I, through it, are taken.
- After a few minutes, the new mass, m_2, and the time, t, are measured and recorded.

Assuming that all the electrical energy is used in boiling the water, the specific latent heat of vaporisation can be calculated from:

electrical energy = heat energy supplied to boil water

$$VIt = m_w l_v$$
$$VIt = (m_1 - m_2)\, l_v$$
$$\frac{VIt}{(m_1 - m_2)} = l_v$$

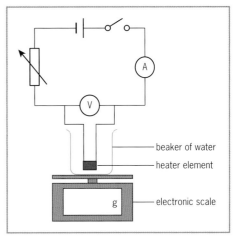

Figure 16.10 *Determining the specific latent heat of vaporisation of water by an electrical method*

Precautions to minimise error

- The water is allowed to boil for a few minutes before the mass measurement is made and the stop watch started, to ensure that all of it has reached boiling point.
- The heater is placed near the bottom of the water in order to produce convection currents which transfer thermal energy to the entire mass.
- The beaker can be lagged to prevent conduction of thermal energy to the surroundings.
- The beaker can be wrapped in shiny silver foil to prevent radiation of thermal energy to the atmosphere.

Source of error

- There will be thermal energy transferred to the environment.

Revision questions

1 Define:

   a latent heat

   b specific latent heat of fusion.

2 Describe a simple experiment to verify that the temperature of a liquid remains steady when it changes to a gas.

3 Sketch a temperature–time graph showing the conversion of ice at –4 °C to steam at 105 °C. Indicate on the graph where there are changes in the kinetic energy and potential energy of the molecules.

4 Using data from Table 15.1 and Table 16.1, determine the heat released when 2.0 kg of steam at 100 °C converts to water at 90 °C.

5 Describe how the specific latent heat of fusion of ice can be found using an electrical method.

17 Evaporation and boiling

Evaporation is the escape of molecules from the surface of a liquid.

Boiling is the escape of molecules from the body of a liquid and occurs only at a particular temperature for a given pressure.

Table 17.1 *Differences between boiling and evaporation*

Evaporation	Boiling
Occurs only at the surface of the liquid	Occurs throughout the body of the liquid
Occurs over a range of temperatures	Occurs at one temperature for a given pressure
Does not require an external heat source	Requires an external heat source

Cooling due to evaporation

During evaporation, the faster molecules escape from the surface of the liquid at a rate dependent on the temperature. Some may return to the liquid after rebounding from other molecules above the surface, but most will escape completely. The remaining liquid becomes cooler since the more energetic molecules absorb latent heat of vaporisation from the less energetic ones as they evaporate.

Factors affecting the rate of evaporation

The factors affecting the rate of evaporation can be explained by the kinetic theory, as follows.

1. *Temperature*: Molecules move faster at higher temperature and therefore possess more kinetic energy. They have a better chance of overcoming the attractive forces of the neighbouring molecules so that they may escape as a gas.

2. *Humidity*: If the humidity is high, molecules escaping from the surface are more likely to crash into other molecules and rebound to the liquid, thereby reducing the rate of evaporation. If the air becomes saturated with vapour, the rate of molecules entering the liquid is equal to the rate escaping from it.

3. *Wind*: The moving air removes evaporated molecules from above the surface, allowing other evaporating molecules to have a better chance of escaping completely without colliding and rebounding to the liquid.

4. *Surface area*: Evaporation is a surface phenomenon and therefore the larger the surface area, the greater is the chance for molecules of the liquid to escape.

Demonstrating cooling due to evaporation

A beaker of ether is allowed to rest in a small pool of water, as shown in Figure 17.1. Ether is a **volatile** liquid – it evaporates very easily. When the air above the liquid is saturated with vapour from the ether, there is less chance of evaporation occurring. However, by pumping dry air through the body of the ether, the following conditions for evaporation become favourable:

- the surface area between the liquid and the air is increased
- the air bubbling through the ether is unsaturated.

As the ether evaporates, it draws latent heat of vaporisation from the water around the beaker, causing the pool of water to rapidly freeze.

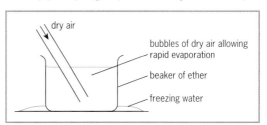

Figure 17.1 *Demonstrating cooling due to evaporation*

Refrigerator

At the evaporator

A volatile liquid – the **refrigerant** – is pumped up to an expansion valve, where it evaporates as it is sprayed through a fine nozzle (Figure 17.2). The latent heat necessary for evaporation of the refrigerant is absorbed by conduction from the food in the fridge.

At the condenser

The refrigerant gas is then pumped to the condenser where it is compressed and **condenses** back to a liquid, releasing the latent heat energy previously absorbed. Copper or aluminium fins are connected to the condenser so that the heat can quickly be conducted from the refrigerant and radiated to the surrounding air. The condenser should be in a well ventilated area so that the thermal radiation emitted can easily dissipate to the environment.

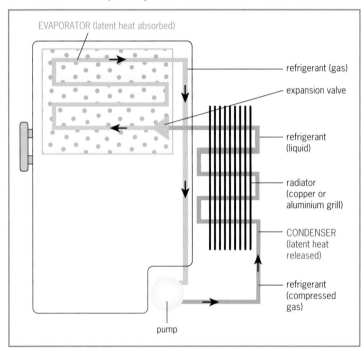

Figure 17.2 *A refrigerator*

Air conditioner

At the evaporator

Air from the room is circulated through the evaporator and then returned to the room by means of a fan (Figure 17.3). The liquid refrigerant is pumped to an expansion valve where it evaporates, removing latent heat from the surrounding air in the process.

At the condenser

The refrigerant gas is then pumped to the condenser where it is compressed and condenses back to a liquid, releasing the latent heat energy previously absorbed. This heat energy is conducted to the aluminium grill and then radiates to the surroundings. A fan produces *forced convection* of the hot air away from the unit, to the outside.

It is common to have the evaporator installed in the room and the condenser installed as a separate unit outside the building.

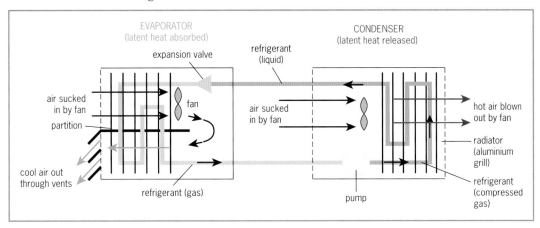

Figure 17.3 *An air conditioner*

Other phenomena involving latent heat

- *Earthenware vessels*: An earthenware vessel has very narrow **capillary** bores within its structure. Water placed in such a vessel is attracted through the capillaries to the outer surface where it evaporates, drawing latent heat from the container and its contents in the process.

- *Hurricanes*: The Sun provides energy for water to evaporate from the ocean and produce clouds. As the vapour condenses, the latent heat released powers the storm, driving the winds faster and faster towards the storm's eye and increasing the rate of evaporation. The region becomes covered in cloud and, as the large amount of condensation occurs, a tremendous amount of energy is released, producing hurricane-force winds.

- *Perspiration*: When we use excessive power, for example, when running or lifting heavy weights, our body temperature rises due to the higher rate of conversion of chemical energy. We then secrete perspiration which evaporates from our bodies, removing latent heat of vaporisation and cooling us. Dogs and cats also cool by evaporation, but since their bodies are almost totally covered by hair, they have wet nostrils and thick wet tongues to provide the cooling effect.

- *Spraying aerosols*: A can of insecticide, for example, becomes cold as its liquid contents are sprayed through the fine nozzle of the expansion valve. On expanding into the atmosphere under reduced pressure the liquid changes to gas, absorbing latent heat from the can and its remaining contents in the process.

Revision questions

1. State THREE differences between evaporation and boiling.

2. Use the kinetic theory to explain how the following affect the rate of evaporation of a liquid.

   temperature   humidity   wind   surface area

3. Briefly *describe* and *explain* how the refrigerant of an air conditioner removes heat energy from the air in a room and then releases it to the air outside.

18 Thermal energy transfer

Processes of thermal energy transfer

Conduction: *The transfer of thermal energy between two points in a medium by the relaying of energy between adjacent particles of the medium, with no net displacement of the particles.*

Convection: *The transfer of thermal energy between two points in a medium by the movement of the particles of the medium due to existing regions of different density.*

Radiation: *The transfer of thermal energy by means of electromagnetic waves.*

These processes occur to a greater or lesser degree in different media – see Table 18.1.

Table 18.1 *Thermal energy transfer through solids, liquids, gases and a vacuum*

Conduction	Occurs significantly in solids (to a greater extent in metals than in non-metals), less in liquids, and very little in gases. Cannot occur through a vacuum.
Convection	Occurs in liquids and gases. Cannot occur through a vacuum.
Radiation	Occurs readily through gases and through a vacuum.

Conduction

Conduction and the kinetic theory

Non-metals: Figure 18.1(a) shows what happens when one end of a non-metallic bar is warmed. The heat energy supplied converts to kinetic energy of the molecules which causes them to VIBRATE faster and with greater amplitude than before. They bombard their neighbours with greater force and higher frequency than before, passing on the increased vibration. In this manner, thermal energy is relayed between adjacent molecules to the other end of the bar. *The temperature of a substance is proportional to the kinetic energy of its particles* and therefore the temperature at the cooler end of the bar increases.

Metals: A similar process occurs in metals (Figure 18.1(b)). The cations (positively charged ions) receive the heat energy and VIBRATE faster and with greater amplitude than before, bombarding their neighbours with greater force and higher frequency, and so passing the vibration from particle to particle. Metals, however, also contain a 'sea' of **free electrons** which TRANSLATE between the cations. When these electrons are supplied with heat energy their kinetic energy increases, causing them to translate faster. On collision with a cation, the energy is transferred to it, increasing its vibration.

Since metals have two modes of conduction, whereas non-metals have only one, metals are better conductors.

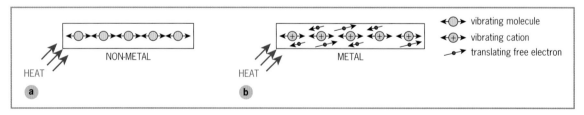

Figure 18.1 *Conduction in non-metals and metals*

Demonstrating conduction

Figure 18.2 shows rods of different materials, initially covered in wax, being heated by a water bath. The wax quickly melts from the copper, not as fast from the iron, and very slowly from the wood, indicating that copper is a very good conductor, but wood a good **insulator** (poor conductor).

Figure 18.3 shows a piece of ice wrapped in copper mesh and submerged in a test tube of water. The weight of the mesh keeps the ice at the bottom of the tube. The water, *heated at the top to avoid convection*, rapidly comes to a boil, but the ice remains solid for quite some time. This demonstrates that water is a very poor conductor.

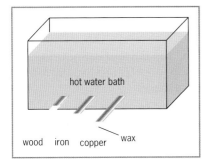

Figure 18.2 *Demonstrating conduction in solids*

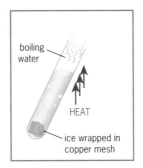

Figure 18.3 *Demonstrating that water is a poor conductor*

Convection

Convection and the kinetic theory

Figure 18.4 illustrates the process of convection. On warming a liquid or gas *from below*, the increase in thermal energy in its lower region gives the molecules increased kinetic energy, causing them to TRANSLATE more vigorously and to take up more space. The region therefore becomes less dense, resulting in its molecules rising and allowing cooler molecules from denser regions to fall in and take their place.

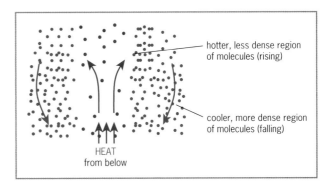

Figure 18.4 *Convection in liquids and gases*

Demonstrating convection

In liquids: Figure 18.5(a) shows a crystal of potassium permanganate (which is purple) added to a beaker of water. The beaker is heated from below the crystal and the coloured solution formed shows the path of the convection current. Alternatively, tiny flakes of aluminium can be used instead of the crystal. The flakes will be seen glittering as they travel the path of the convection current.

In gases: Heating the air below the hand-held fan of Figure 18.5(b) produces a convection current which causes it to spin.

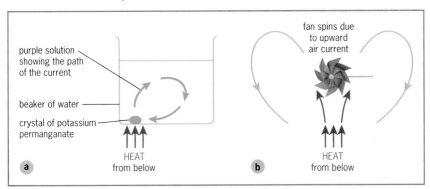

Figure 18.5 *Demonstrating convection in a liquid and in a gas*

Land and sea breezes

During the day: The Sun's *radiation* warms the land more than it warms the sea. The air above the land is then heated by *conduction*, becomes less dense and rises, allowing cool air from over the sea to take its place (Figure 18.6(a)). This creates a *convection* current and causes a cool onshore breeze from the sea. Coastal regions therefore do not experience extremely high temperatures during the day.

The air in contact with the ground further inland also becomes hot during the day but cannot rise because there is no cooler air nearby that can take its place. For this reason, deserts are usually found away from the coast, and during the day they experience very high temperatures.

During the night: The land loses heat by *radiation* at a higher rate than the sea. The surface of the land therefore becomes cooler than that of the sea. Air in contact with the sea is warmed by *conduction*. Warm *convection* currents rise from over the sea and cause a cool breeze to blow offshore from the land (Figure 18.6(b)). Coastal regions therefore do not experience extremely low temperatures during the night.

The air in contact with the land further inland also becomes cool during the night but cannot flow since there is no nearby warmer air rising that it may take the place of. For this reason, desert areas away from the coast experience very low temperatures during the night.

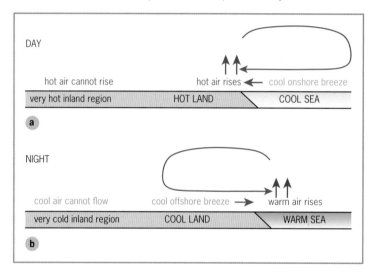

Figure 18.6 *Convection currents causing onshore and offshore breezes*

Radiation

- All bodies emit **infrared radiation**. This is a type of **electromagnetic wave** with wavelength greater (and frequency smaller) than light waves.
- Hotter bodies emit more infrared radiation than cooler bodies. The radiation is called **thermal radiation** or 'radiant energy'.
- Our bodies detect infrared radiation as warmth.
- Electromagnetic waves provide the only method of thermal energy transfer that *can occur through a vacuum*.
- The energy that an electromagnetic wave transmits is proportional to its frequency.

Demonstrating that radiant energy can propagate through a vacuum

The apparatus shown in Figure 18.7 demonstrates that infrared radiation can pass through a vacuum. The jar is first evacuated by means of the pump and the heater is then switched on. The coil begins to glow, and shortly after, the walls of the jar become warm. The energy therefore radiates through the vacuum, is absorbed by the glass, and is conducted through its wall to the outer surface.

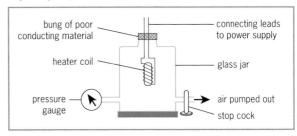

Figure 18.7 *Demonstrating that radiant energy can propagate through a vacuum*

Emitters and absorbers of thermal radiation

All bodies emit *and* absorb infrared radiation. Figure 18.8 illustrates that the temperature of a body relative to its surroundings determines whether it is a *net emitter* or *net absorber* at any particular time.

- Bodies that are hotter than their surroundings are net emitters of thermal radiation – they emit more radiant energy than they absorb.

- Bodies that are cooler than their surroundings are net absorbers of thermal radiation – they absorb more radiant energy than they emit.

- The surface of a body will reflect some of the radiation. A good absorber is a poor reflector, and a poor absorber is a good reflector.

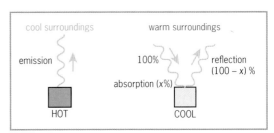

Figure 18.8 *Emitters and absorbers of radiation*

Factors affecting the absorption or emission of radiation

1. Texture of surface (rough, matt, dull/smooth, shiny, polished)

2. Colour of surface

3. Area of surface

Surfaces that are good absorbers are also good emitters. See Table 18.2.

Table 18.2 *Good absorbers and good emitters*

Matt / dull / rough / BLACK	Shiny / smooth / polished / SILVER (or WHITE)
good absorbers (poor reflectors)	poor absorbers (good reflectors)
good emitters	poor emitters

It is important to note that texture and colour do not determine whether a body is a net absorber or a net emitter. This depends on its temperature relative to the surroundings at the time.

- First determine if the body is a net absorber or net emitter *by considering its temperature relative to surrounding bodies.*

- Then examine the physical properties of its surface to determine how good an absorber or emitter it is.

A black surface is a better emitter of radiation than a white or silver surface.

Figure 18.9 shows two detectors of thermal radiation placed at equal distances from the surfaces being investigated. Both surfaces are at the temperature of the hot water. The detector facing the black surface gives a higher reading, indicating that the black surface is the better emitter of radiation.

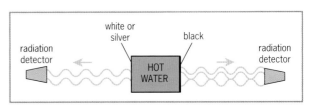

Figure 18.9 *Showing that a black surface is a better emitter than a white or silver surface*

A black surface is a better absorber of radiation than a white or silver surface.

Figure 18.10 shows an arrangement where an equal amount of radiant energy is incident on a black and on a white or silver surface. Corks are initially stuck to the outside of each plate with wax. The cork falls first from the plate which has its inner surface painted black; the wax there rapidly becomes hot and melts. The black surface is therefore the better absorber of radiation.

The experiment also shows that the white or silver surface is the better reflector, since less energy is transferred onto the white or silver plate to be conducted to the wax.

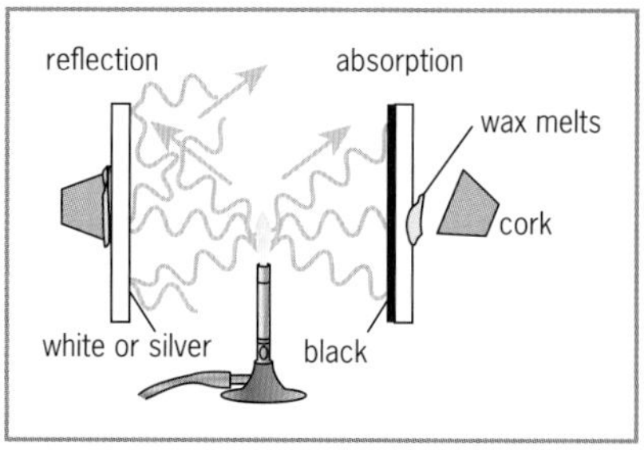

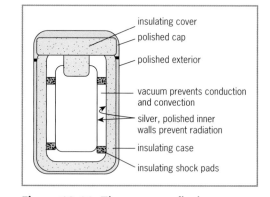

Figure 18.10 *Showing that a black surface is a better absorber of radiation than a white or silver surface*

Examples

- Two metal cans, one black and the other white, are filled with cool water and left in the yard exposed to the Sun's radiation. The cans are both net *absorbers* since they are cooler than their surroundings. The water in the black can warms up faster since the *black surface is the better absorber* of radiation.

- The cans are filled with boiling water and placed in the shade. They are now both net *emitters* since they are much hotter than their surroundings. The temperature of the water in the black can falls faster since the *black surface is a better emitter* of radiation.

Applications of thermal energy transfer processes

The vacuum flask

A **vacuum flask** has several features that reduce thermal energy transfer. See Figure 18.11.

- The vacuum *prevents transfer of thermal energy by conduction and convection*.

- The double-walled container which holds the food or drink is made of glass. Thermal energy transfer by *conduction* through the walls is therefore reduced because glass is a poor conductor.

- The inner, facing walls of the vacuum region are silver. If the contents of the flask are hot, thermal radiation will be emitted through the vacuum from the wall touching the contents. Since silver is a *poor emitter*, the extent of this radiation is minimised. On reaching the other silvered surface on the opposite side of the vacuum, the radiation will be *strongly reflected*. If the contents of the flask are cold, thermal energy entering the system will be similarly minimised.

- The cover, case and shock pads are made of good *insulating* material to prevent transfer of thermal energy by conduction.

- The outer wall of the case is polished. If the contents are hot, the thermal radiation emitted would be minimised since shiny surfaces are *poor emitters* of radiation. If the contents are cold, the radiation absorbed would be minimised since shiny surfaces are also *poor absorbers* of radiation.

Labels on figure: insulating cover, polished cap, polished exterior, vacuum prevents conduction and convection, silver, polished inner walls prevent radiation, insulating case, insulating shock pads

Figure 18.11 *The vacuum flask*

The glass greenhouse

The Sun's surface temperature is in excess of 6000 K and therefore it emits a large amount of high-frequency (short-wavelength) electromagnetic waves. This is mostly visible light, ultraviolet and short-wavelength infrared radiation. These waves are very energetic and easily enter a greenhouse through the glass walls, as shown in Figure 18.12(a). The contents of the greenhouse are then warmed and emit their own radiation. However, since their temperature is much lower than that of the Sun, the waves emitted are longer-wavelength infrared radiation. This is reflected by glass, so the greenhouse acts as a heat trap.

Another important feature of the greenhouse is that its roof and sides prevent the hot air from leaving by *natural convection*.

The greenhouse effect

The Earth's atmosphere behaves like the glass of the greenhouse, as shown in Figure 18.12(b). High-frequency radiation is emitted from the very hot surface of the Sun. This includes short-wavelength infrared waves and these easily penetrate the Earth's atmosphere and warm the planet.

The Earth's surface then emits its own radiation, but of longer wavelength, mainly longer-wavelength infrared. These waves are absorbed by certain gases in the atmosphere, called **greenhouse gases** – particularly carbon dioxide, water vapour and methane. When these gases are warmed they emit their own infrared radiation, much of it returning to Earth to produce **global warming**.

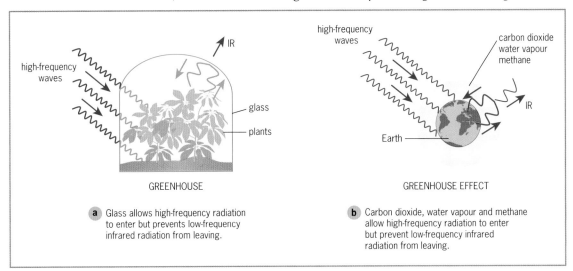

Figure 18.12 *The greenhouse and the greenhouse effect*

The solar water heater

The features of a solar water heater are illustrated in Figure 18.13.

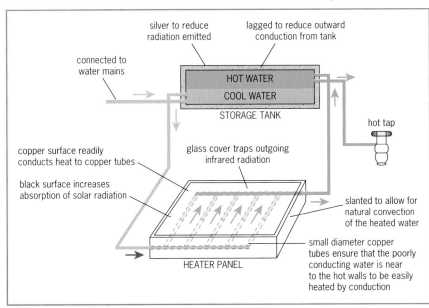

Figure 18.13 *The solar water heater*

Note the following about the solar water heater shown in Figure 18.13:

- All hot water exits and entries are at the top, and all cold water exits and entries are at the bottom of the tank or panel.
- Water is a poor conductor of thermal energy and therefore the hot water in the tank remains hot although it rests on the cooler water below.
- If the tank is too heavy for the roof, it may be placed on the ground. An electric pump will then be necessary to force the hot water downward from the heater panel.

Revision questions

1 Define:

   a conduction   **b** convection   **c** radiation

2 Use the kinetic theory to explain:

   a conduction in metals

   b convection in liquids.

3 Describe experiments to demonstrate each of the following.

   a Convection currents occur in a liquid.

   b Black surfaces are better absorbers of thermal radiation than white surfaces.

   c Thermal radiation can pass through a vacuum.

4 **a** State THREE features of a vacuum flask that prevent thermal energy transfer.

   b Explain how each feature mentioned in part a achieves its purpose.

5 Describe and explain the greenhouse effect.

6 For EACH of the features (i to vi) of the solar water heater listed below:

   a state the PROCESS of thermal energy transfer involved

   b explain how the feature makes the associated process more efficient.

    i Glass cover on the heater panel

    ii Copper tubes in the heater to contain the water

    iii Matt black surface in contact with the tubes in the panel

    iv Storage tank placed above the heater panel

    v Lagging around the storage tank

    vi Silver outer surface of the storage tank

Exam-style questions – Chapters 10 to 18

Structured questions

1 **a)** Distinguish between the heat capacity of a body and the specific heat capacity of a substance. **(2 marks)**

b) An immersion heater of power 600 W provides energy to 500 g of water initially at 30 °C until 200 g of it converts to steam. Calculate:

   i) the heat capacity of the water **(2 marks)**

   ii) the time taken to bring the water to boiling point **(2 marks)**

   iii) the latent heat supplied **(2 marks)**

   iv) the time for which the water was boiling. **(2 marks)**

   (Specific heat capacity of water = 4200 J kg^{-1} K^{-1}; specific latent heat of vaporisation of water = 2.3×10^6 J kg^{-1})

c) **i)** Define *temperature*. **(1 mark)**

   ii) Name TWO types of thermometer and state the thermometric property that each utilises. **(4 marks)**

   Total 15 marks

2 **a)** Complete Table 1 by giving the name of the law that corresponds to the relation outlined in the first column between the pressure (*P*), volume (*V*) and absolute temperature (*T*) of a fixed mass of gas.

Table 1

Relation	Law
$V \propto T$ (*P* constant)	
$P \propto \dfrac{1}{V}$ (*T* constant)	
$P \propto T$ (*V* constant)	

(3 marks)

b) **i)** 10 cm^3 of air in a syringe is at a temperature of 30 °C and a pressure of 8.0×10^4 Pa. Calculate the new pressure if the air is compressed to 5.0 cm^3 and the temperature is kept constant. **(2 marks)**

   ii) Use the kinetic theory of matter to explain the increase in pressure in part b) i). **(2 marks)**

   iii) Use Newton's second law of motion to explain why the molecules of a gas exert a force on the walls of the container that encloses them. **(2 marks)**

c) The graph shown in Figure 1 shows the temperature of a mass, *m*, of water as it is heated.

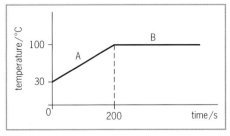

Figure 1

    i)   Calculate the mass, *m*, given that the power of the heater is 300 W and the specific heat capacity of water is 4200 J kg^{-1} °C^{-1}. **(3 marks)**

    ii) Calculate the time for the same heater to melt 400 g of ice at 0 °C if the specific latent heat of fusion of ice is 3.4×10^5 J kg^{-1}. **(3 marks)**

Total 15 marks

Extended response questions

3   **a)** Describe an experiment to determine the specific latent heat of vaporisation of water using the apparatus shown in Figure 2. You must indicate by means of an equation how you would arrive at your result. **(6 marks)**

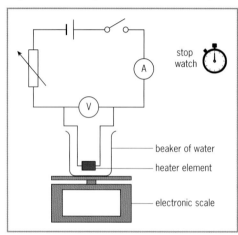

stop watch

A

V

beaker of water

heater element

electronic scale

Figure 2

    b) In an experiment like that in part a), a power of 1.0 kW was supplied and it took 10 minutes to boil off 250 g of water, when at 100 °C. Determine:

        i)   the specific latent heat of vaporisation of water **(3 marks)**

        ii) the latent heat supplied. **(3 marks)**

    c) The value calculated in part b) i) would be different from the true value.

        i)   Suggest a reason why this may be so. **(1 mark)**

        ii) Deduce whether the calculated value is greater or lesser than the true value. **(2 marks)**

Total 15 marks

4   **a)** Coastal regions generally have their temperatures moderated during the day by cool onshore breezes. Explain this phenomenon. **(6 marks)**

    b) Solar radiation reaches the panels of a water heater system at an average rate of 800 W m^{-2} between 6am and 6pm. The system has 8 panels, each with an area of 0.50 m^2, and is capable of transferring 60% of the received radiation to the water. Determine:

        i)   the total receiving area of the panels **(1 mark)**

        ii) the solar power reaching the system's panels between 6am and 6pm. **(2 marks)**

        iii) the solar power transferred to the water **(2 marks)**

        iv) the time taken to raise the temperature of 250 kg of water by 40 °C. **(4 marks)**

    (Specific heat capacity of water = 4200 J kg^{-1} K^{-1})

Total 15 marks

19 Wave motion

Types of waves

A **pulse** is a single *disturbance that propagates from one point to a next.* As the pulse passes, as in the rope or slinky spring in Figure 19.1, for example, each particle mimics the vibration at the source.

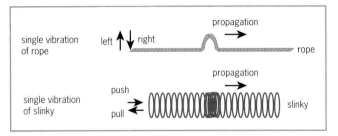

Figure 19.1 *A pulse in a rope and in a slinky*

A **wave** is a continuous stream of regular disturbances.

Transverse and longitudinal waves

Waves may be classified as being either transverse or longitudinal.

A **transverse wave** *is one that has vibrations perpendicular to its direction of propagation.*

Examples of transverse waves

- The wave produced in a rope or slinky lying on a horizontal surface and vibrated from one end, perpendicularly to its length (see Figures 19.2 and 19.3).
- The wave produced in water by an object vibrated perpendicularly into and out of its surface.
- An electromagnetic wave, for example light.

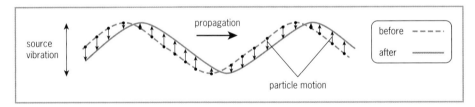

Figure 19.2 *Particle motion in a transverse wave*

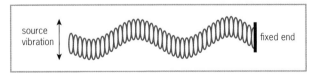

Figure 19.3 *Transverse wave in a slinky*

A **longitudinal wave** *is one that has vibrations parallel to its direction of propagation.*

Longitudinal waves are characterised by regions of high pressure (**compressions**) and regions of low pressure (**rarefactions**), indicated by C and R in Figures 19.4 and 19.5.

Examples of longitudinal waves

- The sound wave produced in a solid, liquid or gas (see Figure 19.4).
- The wave produced in a slinky lying straight on a horizontal surface and vibrated parallel to its length from one end (see Figure 19.5).

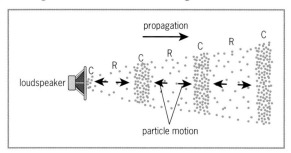

Figure 19.4 *Particle motion and pressure variation in a longitudinal sound wave*

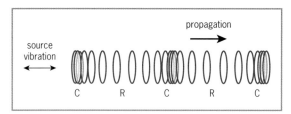

Figure 19.5 *Longitudinal wave in a slinky*

Progressive and stationary waves

Waves may also be classified is either being progressive or stationary.

Progressive waves are those that transfer energy from one point to the next.

Stationary waves do not transfer energy. These waves are not on the CSEC syllabus.

Wave parameters

- **Amplitude**, *a*: *The amplitude of a wave is the maximum displacement of the vibration or oscillation from its mean position.*

  See Figure 19.6.

  If the amplitude of a light wave increases, the light becomes *brighter*.

  If the amplitude of a sound wave increases, the sound becomes *louder*.

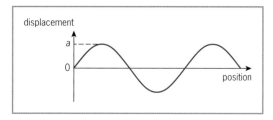

Figure 19.6 *Amplitude, a*

- **Phase**: *Points in a progressive wave are **in phase** if the distance between them along the direction of propagation is equal to a whole number of wavelengths, λ: 0λ, 1λ, 2λ, and so on.*

  See Figure 19.7.

  When points are in phase in a progressive wave they have the same displacement, direction and speed in their vibrations.

*Points in a wave are **in antiphase** (exactly out of phase), when the distance between them along the direction of propagation is equal to $\frac{1}{2}\lambda$, $1\frac{1}{2}\lambda$, $2\frac{1}{2}\lambda$, and so on.*

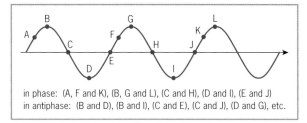

in phase: (A, F and K), (B, G and L), (C and H), (D and I), (E and J)
in antiphase: (B and D), (B and I), (C and E), (C and J), (D and G), etc.

Figure 19.7 *Phase and antiphase*

- **Wavelength**, λ: *The wavelength is the distance between successive points in phase in a wave.*

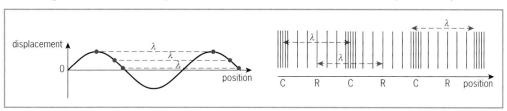

Figure 19.8 *The wavelength λ of a transverse and a longitudinal wave*

- **Period**, *T*: *The wave period is the time for one complete vibration.*
  In Figure 19.9 the period is 200 ms = 0.2 s.
- **Frequency**, *f*: *The wave frequency is the number of complete vibrations per second.*

$$T = \frac{1}{f} \quad \text{and} \quad f = \frac{1}{T}$$

T must be in seconds (s) for *f* to be in hertz (Hz).

If $T = 0.2\,\text{s}$ then $f = \dfrac{1}{0.2} = 5\,\text{Hz}$.

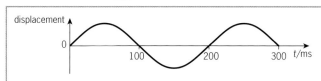

Figure 19.9 *A displacement–time graph for a wave*

The frequency of a light wave determines its *colour*. Red has the lowest frequency and violet the highest frequency of the visible spectrum.

The frequency of a sound wave determines its *pitch*. A bass note has a low frequency and a treble note has a high frequency.

- **Wavefront**: This is a line *perpendicular to the propagation* of a wave on which all points are in phase. Wavefronts are generally taken through crests of transverse waves and through compressions of longitudinal waves, as illustrated in Figure 19.10. Figure 19.11(a) shows the reflection of plane wavefronts at a barrier.

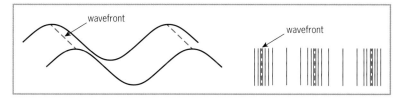

Figure 19.10 *Wavefronts of transverse and longitudinal waves*

- **Speed**, *v*: This is the rate at which the wavefronts of a wave propagate, and it depends on the medium of propagation. At a boundary between media the speed changes and the wave undergoes **refraction** (Figure 19.11(b)).

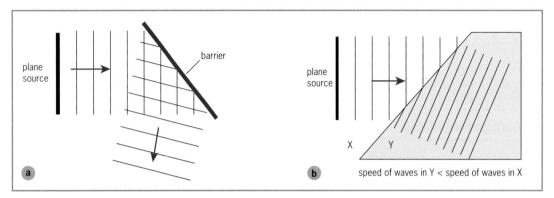

Figure 19.11 *Reflection and refraction of plane wavefronts*

Variation of the speed of waves

The speed of light is *greater in media of lesser density*. Light therefore travels fastest in a vacuum or in air and slower in water or glass.

The speed of sound is *greater through gases of lesser density*. Molecules of lesser mass respond more readily to vibrations than those of greater mass. Sound therefore travels faster through air than through carbon dioxide.

The speed of sound is *greatest through solids*, less in liquids and least in gases. The *closer packing* of the particles and the *rigidity of the bonds* in a solid allows vibrations to transfer more readily. See Table 19.1.

The speed of sound through gases is *greater at higher temperatures* because the *increased kinetic energy* allows the vibrations to be passed on more readily.

The speed of a water wave is *greater across a deeper region*.

Table 19.1 *Speed of sound in steel, water and air*

	steel	water	air at 0 °C
Speed/m s^{-1}	5100	1500	330

General wave equations

$$v = \lambda f \qquad v = \frac{\lambda}{T}$$

$$\frac{v_1}{v_2} = \frac{\lambda_1}{\lambda_2} = \frac{\sin \theta_1}{\sin \theta_2} = \frac{\eta_2}{\eta_1}$$

where η represents the **refractive index** of a medium (see Chapter 24), and θ_1 and θ_2 are as shown in Figure 19.12.

Figure 19.12 shows in detail the change in direction of wavefronts when the wave is refracted. Note the following:

- θ_1 and θ_2 are the angles (of incidence and refraction respectively) between RAYS and the NORMAL or between WAVEFRONTS and the INTERFACE.

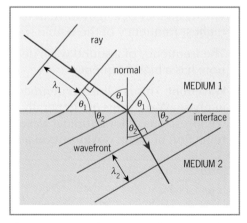

Figure 19.12 *Change in direction of waves on refraction*

- The speed, v, wavelength, λ, and $\sin \theta$, all *change by the same proportion* when the wave goes into a new medium. If v doubles, then λ and $\sin \theta$ also double. The angle θ will not double, but will increase.

- T and f *do not change* when a wave passes from one medium to the next.

- When using the equations in calculations it is a good idea to use relevant letters as subscripts rather than numbers – for example, v_w for the speed in water and v_g for the speed in glass. This reduces errors due to incorrect substitution into an otherwise correct equation.

- In the third equation above, the ratio of refractive indices has its subscripts inverted relative to the other three ratios.

Example 1

Calculate the wavelength of the broadcast from a radio station which emits waves of frequency 104.1 MHz, given that the speed of the wave is 3.0×10^8 m s^{-1}.

$$v = \lambda f$$
$$3.0 \times 10^8 = \lambda \times 104.1 \times 10^6$$
$$\frac{3.0 \times 10^8}{104.1 \times 10^6} = \lambda$$
$$2.9 \, \text{m} = \lambda$$

Example 2

A water wave has a speed of 3.0 m s^{-1} and its crests are 5.0 m apart. It approaches a reef at an angle of incidence of 60°. On passing over it, the distance between its crests reduces to 4.0 m. Determine for the wave:

a   the frequency in the deeper water

b   the period in the deeper water

c   the frequency as it passes over the reef (shallow)

d   the period as it passes over the reef

e   the speed as it passes over the reef

f   the angle of refraction on reaching the reef

g   the refractive index on travelling from the deep to the shallow.

a $$v = \lambda f$$
$$3.0 = 5.0f$$
$$\frac{3.0}{5.0} = f$$
$$0.60 \, \text{Hz} = f$$

b $$T = \frac{1}{f} = \frac{1}{0.60}$$
$$T = 1.67 \, \text{s} \ (1.7 \, \text{s to 2 sig. fig.})$$

c   0.60 Hz (frequency does not change)

d   1.7 s (period does not change)

e   Using s for 'shallow' and d for 'deep':
$$\frac{v_s}{v_d} = \frac{\lambda_s}{\lambda_d}$$
$$\frac{v_s}{3.0} = \frac{4.0}{5.0}$$
$$v_s = \frac{4.0}{5.0} \times 3.0$$
$$v_s = 2.4 \, \text{m s}^{-1}$$

f

$$\frac{\sin \theta_s}{\sin \theta_d} = \frac{\lambda_s}{\lambda_d}$$

$$\frac{\sin \theta_s}{\sin 60} = \frac{4.0}{5.0}$$

$$\sin \theta_s = \frac{4.0}{5.0} \times \sin 60$$

$$\theta_s = 44°$$

g When referring to refractive index of one medium relative to the next, the second medium must be in the numerator.

$$\frac{\eta_s}{\eta_d} = \frac{\lambda_d}{\lambda_s}$$

$$\frac{\eta_s}{\eta_d} = \frac{5.0}{4.0}$$

$$\frac{\eta_s}{\eta_d} = 1.25$$

Graphs of waves

Displacement–position graph

A displacement–position graph relates the displacement of each point in a wave to the distance or position from some reference point at ONE INSTANT IN TIME (the time is held fixed). See Example 3.

Example 3

Figure 19.13 shows a wave of speed 32 m s^{-1} at an instant in time. Determine:

a the amplitude   **b** the wavelength   **c** the frequency   **d** the period

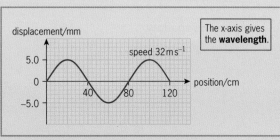

The x-axis gives the **wavelength**.

Figure 19.13

a Amplitude = 5.0 mm

b Wavelength = 80 cm or 0.80 m

c Frequency f:

$$v = \lambda f$$

$$f = \frac{v}{\lambda} = \frac{32}{0.80} = 40 \text{ Hz}$$

d Period T:

$$T = \frac{1}{f} = \frac{1}{40} = 0.025 \text{ s}$$

Displacement–time graph

A displacement–time graph relates the displacement of ONE POINT in the wave as time continues (the position is held fixed). See Example 4.

Figure 19.14 shows a wave of speed 40 m s^{-1}. Determine:

a the amplitude of particle P   **b** the displacement of particle P   **c** the period

d the frequency   **e** the wavelength

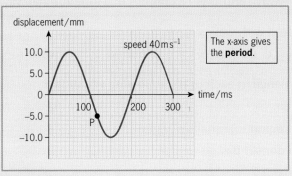

The x-axis gives the **period**.

Figure 19.14

a Amplitude of P = 10.0 mm

b Displacement of P = –5.0 mm

c Period = 200 ms or 0.200 s

d Frequency f:

$$f = \frac{1}{T} = \frac{1}{0.200} = 5.00 \text{ Hz}$$

e Wavelength λ:

$$v = \lambda f$$

$$\lambda = \frac{v}{f} = \frac{40}{5.00} = 8.0 \text{ m}$$

Important notes

- Displacement–position and displacement–time graphs of waves have the shape of transverse waves, but they can represent *both transverse and longitudinal waves*. Recall that graphs are a mathematical means of relating two variables – they are not pictures.

- Pressure–position and pressure–time graphs always represent *longitudinal* waves. Recall that these waves have regions of high and low pressure – compressions and rarefactions.

- The mean value on the vertical axis of a pressure–time graph of a sound wave (see Figure 19.15) is *not zero*, as it is with a graph of displacement.

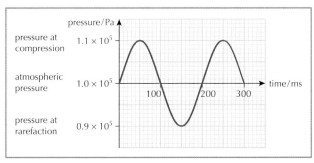

Figure 19.15 *Pressure–time graph of a sound wave*

1 What is meant by each of the following terms describing waves?

   a longitudinal wave

   b transverse wave

   c progressive wave

2 Give TWO examples of a transverse wave and TWO examples of a longitudinal wave.

3 Define the following terms associated with waves:

   a wavelength   **b** amplitude   **c** frequency   **d** period   **e** wavefront

4 How does the speed of the wave change in each of the following situations?

   a Light wave travels from glass to air.

   b Water wave travels from a deep region to a shallow region.

   c Sound wave travels from air to a denser gas.

   d Sound wave travels from air to water.

5 Give reasons for your answers to 4c and 4d above.

6 Calculate the frequency of blue light in air given that its wavelength and speed are 4.0×10^{-7} m and 3.0×10^8 m s^{-1} respectively.

7 The speed of a wave reduces from 40 m s^{-1} to 32 m s^{-1} on entering a second medium. The angle of incidence is 30° and the period of vibration is 0.40 s. Determine for the wave:

   a the frequency

   b the wavelength in the first medium

   c the wavelength in the second medium

   d the angle of refraction.

8 The wave shown in the graph of Figure 19.16 has a speed of 4.0 m s^{-1}. Determine:

   a its period   **b** its frequency   **c** its amplitude   **d** its wavelength

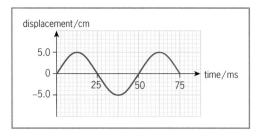

Figure 19.16

20 Sound waves

Production and propagation

Production: Sound waves are produced by mechanical vibrations.

Propagation: They can only travel through a material medium (solid, liquid or gas). Each particle of the medium passes on the vibration to the one adjacent to it.

Sound cannot propagate through a vacuum.

Figure 20.1 shows an electric bell suspended in a sealed glass jar. With the bell switched on, observers can see it and hear it ringing. As the air is pumped out, the sound level diminishes to almost zero, but the bell is still seen to be functioning. This occurs because there is no material medium between the bell and the glass jar to transmit the vibrations.

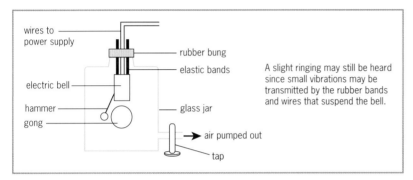

Figure 20.1 *Sound cannot propagate through a vacuum*

Pitch and loudness (volume)

Figure 20.2 shows three sound waves, A, B and C. They have the *same speed* because they are in the same medium.

*A greater frequency wave produces a sound of higher **pitch**.*

- A and B have the same wavelength and the same speed, so they must also have the same frequency and pitch.

$$f = \frac{v}{\lambda}$$

- A has a smaller wavelength than C but the same speed, so the frequency and pitch of A must be greater.

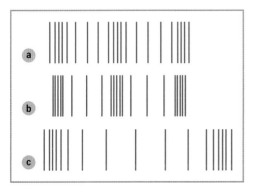

Figure 20.2 *Comparing pitch and volume from wavefront diagrams*

A tuning fork (Figure 20.3) gives a sound of a fixed frequency and pitch, dependent on its dimensions and on the material from which it is made.

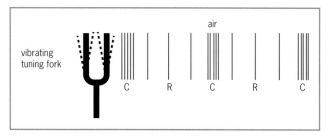

Figure 20.3 *A tuning fork is a two pronged, U-shaped fork made of an elastic metal. When struck, it vibrates with a particular frequency, creating compressions and rarefactions in the air.*

A greater amplitude wave gives a higher volume (louder) sound.

- In Figure 20.2, the volume of B is greater than that of A. The compressions and rarefactions of B have greater and lesser pressures respectively than those of A. This greater *change* in pressure between the compressions and rarefactions of B causes the ear drum to be pushed and pulled with greater amplitude, and therefore produces a louder sound.

Pitch and loudness (volume) from a displacement–time graph

The graph of Figure 20.4 shows a varying sound produced by a signal generator. Recall that amplitude governs the volume and frequency governs the pitch.

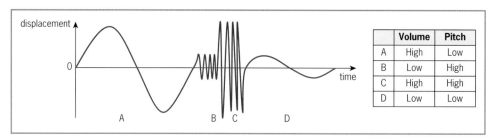

	Volume	Pitch
A	High	Low
B	Low	High
C	High	High
D	Low	Low

Figure 20.4 *Comparing pitch and volume from a graph*

Classification of frequencies of sound

Frequency below 20 Hz: **infrasound**.

Frequency 20 Hz to 20 kHz: the **audible range** of the average human. As one grows older the upper limit gradually reduces to about 16 kHz.

Frequency above 20 kHz: **ultrasound**.

Uses of ultrasound

- *Communicating*: Dolphins communicate by emitting and receiving ultrasonic vibrations.
- *Measuring distance*: Bats determine distances by emitting ultrasound and assessing the time in which the echoes return. Depth sounding (see the next page) uses a similar technique.
- *Diagnostic imaging*: Ultrasound is partly reflected when it strikes the boundary between different materials. Doctors use a probe to direct ultrasonic waves into the patient. The reflected waves, received by the same probe, are analysed by a computer to produce an image on a screen. Pre-natal scanning, as well as the examination of internal organs, can be carried out by this technique. Ultrasonic waves are relatively safe in comparison to X-rays, which have the risk of producing cancer.

- *Materials testing*: Flaws in solid objects such as metal castings can also be detected by ultrasound probes.
- *Cleaning*: Small objects such as electronic components may be sprayed with a cleanser and then subjected to ultrasonic waves. The vibrations easily remove the dirt and grease.

Estimating the speed of sound in air using echoes

Observers, A and B, stand about 50 m from a tall, hard, smooth, vertical wall (Figure 20.5). Observer A claps two blocks of wood at such a rate that the returning echo coincides with each succeeding clap. Observer B measures the time, t, for the sound to go to the wall and back 20 times.

The velocity of sound is found from:

$$v = \frac{d}{t}$$

$$v = \frac{20(2x)}{t}$$

Note:

- The error due to reaction time is greatly reduced by measuring the total time for 20 echoes to return.
- The features of the wall produce a strong, undiffused echo.
- The observers should not be too close to the wall because it would then be difficult to differentiate between a clap and its succeeding echo.

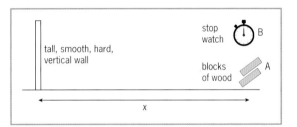

Figure 20.5 *Estimating the speed of sound using echoes*

Other uses of echoes

Thunder cloud proximity

Thunder and lightning occur simultaneously. Due to the extremely high speed of light it can be assumed that an observer sees lightning as soon as it is produced. Sound travels much slower and it generally takes a few seconds for us to hear the thunder. The speed of sound is approximately 330 m s^{-1}, so *it takes about* 3 *seconds to travel* 1 km. An observer who counts the seconds between seeing the flash and hearing the sound can estimate the distance from the thunder cloud (in km) by *dividing the count by* 3.

Depth sounding

Ultrasonic waves are used to determine the depth of water. Pulses of ultrasound are emitted by a transmitter, T, as shown in Figure 20.6, and a timer is started simultaneously. A receiver, R, detects the reflected pulses and records the time. A computer then calculates the depth, x, of the water from:

$$v = \frac{2x}{t}$$

where t is the measured time and v is the velocity of sound in water, which is 1500 m s^{-1}.

$$1500 = \frac{2x}{t}$$
$$\frac{1500t}{2} = x$$
$$750t = x$$

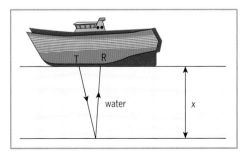

Figure 20.6 *Depth sounding using echoes*

Behaviour of sound waves

Evidence that sound waves reflect

The echo produced when a loud sound is made in front of a cliff is evidence that sound waves reflect.

Evidence that sound waves refract

Sounds are more audible at night. The air in contact with the ground is cooler at this time. A sound wave travelling upwards will increase in speed as it enters layers of warmer air (see Chapter 19). The wavefronts therefore separate more, taking up the shape shown in Figure 20.7. Since rays (lines of propagation) are always perpendicular to wavefronts, the sound ray *refracts* along a curved path, returning to the surface of the Earth and allowing more sound energy to reach the observer.

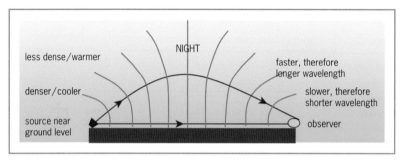

Figure 20.7 *Evidence that sound waves refract*

Evidence that sound waves diffract

Figure 20.8 shows a small sound-proof cabin, initially completely closed, and in the middle of a large open region of flat land. The music from a loudspeaker in the cabin will not be heard outside. If a window is opened, an observer at A will hear the music even if he/she is not in the direct line of sight of the loudspeaker.

It is not possible for the sound to reflect to the observer from objects outside, since the land is flat. The direction of the sound wave spreads as it passes through the window, a phenomenon known as **diffraction**. Diffraction is discussed in Chapter 22.

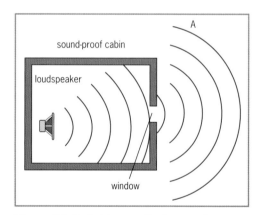

Figure 20.8 *Evidence that sound waves diffract*

Evidence that sound waves interfere

A signal generator, connected to loudspeakers as shown in Figure 20.9, emits a note of constant frequency. Speakers S_1 and S_2 are **coherent sources**, meaning they emit waves in phase or with some constant phase difference.

An experimenter walking along the line AB will observe alternate points where he/she hears no sound and then a loud sound. Where the waves from S_1 and S_2 meet the experimenter in phase, a loud note is heard, and where they meet exactly out of phase, nothing is heard. Sound waves therefore exhibit the phenomenon of **interference**. Interference is discussed in Chapter 22.

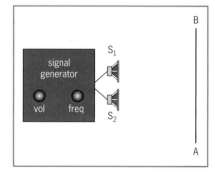

Figure 20.9 *Demonstrating that sound waves interfere*

Example 1

A thunder clap is heard 5.0 s after the flash of lightning is seen. How far away is the thunder cloud, if the speed of sound is 350 m s^{-1}?

$$v = \frac{d}{t}$$

$$350 = \frac{d}{5.0}$$

$$350 \times 5.0 = d$$

$$1750 \text{ m} = d$$

Example 2

A man standing 700 m from the face of a tall cliff fires a rifle. He hears the returning echo 4.0 s later. Determine the speed of sound in the region.

$$v = \frac{d}{t}$$

$$v = \frac{2x}{t} \text{ (distance to cliff and back is 2x)}$$

$$v = \frac{2(700)}{4.0}$$

$$v = 350 \text{ m s}^{-1}$$

Example 3

Observers A and B stand together in front of a tall, smooth, vertical wall. Person A claps two blocks of wood at such a rate that each returning echo is synchronised with the succeeding clap. Person B starts a stop watch and times the period for the return of 20 echoes. If the speed of sound is 350 m s^{-1}, and B records a time of 8.0 s, determine the distance of the observers from the wall.

$$v = \frac{d}{t}$$

$$v = \frac{20(2x)}{t} \text{ (distance to wall and back (2x) is travelled 20 times)}$$

$$350 = \frac{40x}{8.0}$$

$$\frac{350 \times 8.0}{40} = x$$

$$70 \text{ m} = x$$

Revision questions

1. Describe how sound propagates through a medium.

2. What can be said of the volume and the pitch of note A relative to note B, if A has a lesser frequency but greater amplitude than B?

3. Construct a table to contrast the frequencies associated with ultrasound, the audible range of sound, and infrasound.

4. State TWO uses of ultrasound.

5. A pulse of ultrasound is transmitted from beneath a boat and the echo returns after 0.20 s. What is the depth of the ocean at the location, if the speed of sound in water is 1500 m s^{-1}?

6. A crash of thunder is heard 3.0 s after a flash of lightning is seen. Determine the distance from the thunder cloud, if the speed of sound in air is 350 m s^{-1}.

7. Explain, with the aid of a diagram, why sounds emitted at ground level are more audible at night.

8. Describe, with the aid of a diagram, how you could demonstrate that sound waves can exhibit interference.

21 Electromagnetic waves

Electromagnetic waves are a group of transverse waves consisting of an electric field and a magnetic field which vibrate perpendicular to each other and to their direction of propagation.

This is depicted in Figure 21.1.

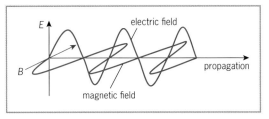

Figure 21.1 *An electromagnetic wave*

General properties of electromagnetic waves

- They are all transverse waves.
- They travel at the *same speed* of 3.0×10^8 m s^{-1} through a vacuum or through air.
- They can propagate through a vacuum.
- They consists of varying electric and magnetic fields.

As for all waves, electromagnetic waves can:

- reflect
- refract
- diffract
- exhibit the phenomenon of interference
- transfer energy.

Wavelengths and frequencies of the electromagnetic spectrum

Each category of electromagnetic energy contains waves of a particular frequency range and wavelength range. Together they make up the **electromagnetic spectrum**, as shown in Figure 21.2. Their production is outlined in Table 21.1.

Within the category of visible light, each smaller frequency range is detected as a different colour. In order of increasing frequency, these colours of the **visible spectrum** are *red, orange, yellow, green, blue, indigo, violet* (ROYGBIV).

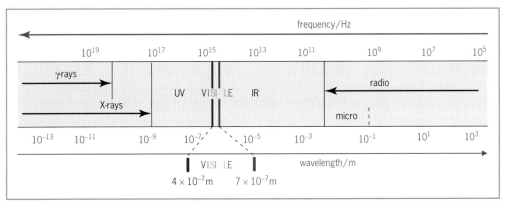

Figure 21.2 *Wavelengths and frequencies of the electromagnetic spectrum*

Table 21.1 *Production of electromagnetic waves*

Type	Relative wavelength	Produced by
radio		Radio transmitters – metal rods (aerials) that emit radio waves when electric current oscillates within them
infrared		All bodies above temperature 0 K (–273 °C)
visible light (ROYGBIV)		Bodies above 1100 °C
ultraviolet		Very hot bodies, such as the Sun (6000 °C), welding torches, electric sparks, lightning
X and gamma		X – High-speed electrons bombarding metal targets Gamma – Changes in nuclei of unstable atoms

Uses of electromagnetic waves

Radio waves and microwaves

- Radio and television broadcasting
- Cell phone communication
- Warming food

Infrared radiation (IR)

- Ovens, toasters and heat radiators: IR is detected by our nerves as heat.
- Remote controls: When a button on the control is pressed, an IR beam pulses with a unique code to carry out a particular function.
- Fibre-optic cables in telecommunication systems including the internet: IR is absorbed less than visible light by the glass fibres and can therefore transmit information over longer distances before the need for amplification.
- Heat-seeking missiles: These are able to follow aircraft by using sensors to detect the IR emitted from engines.
- Treatment of certain muscular disorders.
- Infrared cameras: These produce images showing regions of different temperatures. Bodies at higher temperatures emit higher-frequency waves. The radiation is detected by infrared sensors and passed to a computer program which produces a visible image of the variations in temperature.
- Some animals can detect IR emitted from the bodies of their prey and can therefore hunt in the dark.

Ultraviolet radiation (UV)

Fluorescence is the process whereby high-frequency radiation such as UV is absorbed by certain substances and is then emitted as visible light of lower frequency.

- Detergents contain fluorescent substances so that clothes washed with them look 'whiter than white' – they absorb UV from the Sun and then emit the energy as visible light waves.

- Bank notes have a marking made from a fluorescent substance which becomes visible when UV is incident on them. This helps to discourage the circulation of fraudulent bank notes.

- Fluorescent lighting tubes contain mercury vapour which emits UV radiation when a current is passed through it. The UV is absorbed by a fluorescent coating on the inside of the tube which then emits the energy as visible light. See Figure 21.3.

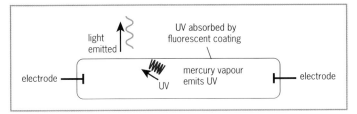

Figure 21.3 *A fluorescent lighting tube*

X-rays

- Medical imaging of dense materials such as bones or tumours within flesh
- Security scanning of passengers and luggage
- X-ray crystallography: a method of investigating the structure of crystals

Gamma-rays

- Cancer therapy
- Imaging using a gamma camera
- Tracers
- Sterilisation

See also Chapter 34.

Revision questions

1. State FOUR properties of electromagnetic waves.

2. Five groups of electromagnetic waves are:

   visible light   X and gamma   infrared   ultraviolet   radio and microwaves

   a List the groups in order of increasing frequency.

   b What is the range of wavelengths of the visible spectrum?

   c Which colour has the shortest wavelength?

   d Which GROUP has the longest wavelength?

   e State ONE source and ONE use of EACH group.

22 Light waves

Rival theories of light

At the beginning of the 18th century there were two rival classical theories of the nature of light – the **wave theory** and the **corpuscular (particle) theory**.

Wave theory – Huygens

In 1690 Huygens suggested that light was a longitudinal wave, capable of propagating through a material called the *aether* which he believed filled *all space*. This material medium justified why light can pass through a vacuum despite the fact that it was supposedly a longitudinal wave, as is sound.

Huygens proposed that each point along a wavefront, such as A in Figure 22.1, acts as a source of new 'wavelets'. After a short time, *t*, each of these secondary wavelets has advanced by the same amount and a new wavefront, B, is formed from the envelope of the individual wavelets from sources on wavefront A. After a time 2*t*, the wavefront C is the envelope of all the wavelets produced from sources on wavefront B. The advancing wavefront is therefore always perpendicular to the direction of propagation of the wave.

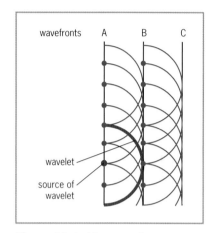

Figure 22.1 *Huygens' wave theory*

Particle (corpuscular) theory – Newton

Newton proposed in 1704 that light was 'shot out' from a source as particles. He believed that the mass of the source diminished as it releases these particles.

- At that time, the diffraction of light had not been observed and Newton argued that since light does not diffract, it cannot be a wave.

- Also at that time, it was not known that light travels faster in air than in water. Newton's corpuscular theory suggested that it should be faster in water.

His argument could not explain why the velocity of light is not higher when coming from bodies of higher temperature. According to accepted theory, higher temperature suggests that the 'particles' should have more kinetic energy.

Wave theory – Young

Young showed experimentally in 1802 that light from two very narrow slits can produce a pattern of bright and dark fringes on a screen (see later in the chapter). He argued that this was the result of the 'principle of superposition' of light acting as *waves*. However, Newton's corpuscular theory still lived on, mainly due to his reputation as a dominant physicist and mathematician.

Wave theory – Foucault

Foucault showed experimentally in 1850 that light travelled faster in air than in water, contrary to what Newton's corpuscular theory suggested. This seemed at the time to be the deciding factor that tilted the balance in favour of the wave nature of light.

Wave–particle duality – Planck and Einstein

Max Planck in 1900 put forward the **quantum theory** which combined the wave and particle theories.

In 1905 Einstein showed that the phenomenon of *photoelectric emission* cannot be explained by wave theory, but only by particle theory. On the other hand, particle theory could not explain phenomena such as diffraction and interference, which were clearly due to waves.

Einstein had also shown that there is an equivalence between matter and energy in accordance with his famous equation, $\Delta E = \Delta mc^2$ (see Chapter 34).

Today we accept the quantum theory which considers light as particle-like as well as wave-like in nature – each wave pulse is a *packet (particle) of energy*, known as a **photon**.

Diffraction and interference

Diffraction

Diffraction is the spreading of a wave as it passes an edge or goes through a gap.

Speed, wavelength, frequency and period *do not change* as a result of diffraction.

The smaller the wavelength relative to the gap, the lesser is the diffraction (Figure 22.2). The wavelength of light waves is extremely small – approximately 5×10^{-7} m for yellow light. This is much smaller than most gaps commonly encountered and therefore the diffraction of light is not usually observed – we say that 'light travels in a straight line'. Light will diffract, however, if it passes through an extremely small gap.

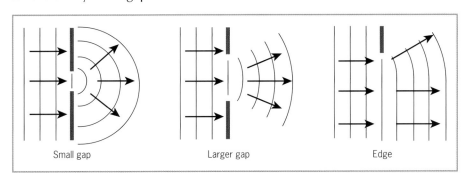

Small gap   Larger gap   Edge

Figure 22.2 *Diffraction through gaps and around edges*

- Radio waves have the largest wavelengths of the electromagnetic wave group and therefore diffract considerably. This makes them suitable for radio, television and cell phone communication as well as for radar tracking, because they can diffract around hills and buildings on their route to and from receivers and transmitters.

- In the case of sound waves, bass notes have larger wavelengths than treble notes and therefore diffract more. Similarly, red light has a larger wavelength than blue light and diffracts more.

Interference

Interference is the phenomenon which occurs at a point where two or more waves superpose on each other (add) to produce a combined vibration of amplitude lesser or greater than any of the individual waves.

Constructive interference occurs where two or more waves superpose *in phase* to create a vibration greater than that of either of the individual waves. For a transverse wave, this is can be where two crests or two troughs meet; for a longitudinal wave, it can be where two compressions or two rarefactions meet.

Destructive interference occurs where two or more waves superpose *out of phase* to create a vibration less than either of the individual waves. For a transverse wave, this can be where a crest meets a trough; for a longitudinal wave, it can be where a compression meets a rarefaction.

- The resulting displacement at the point of constructive or destructive interference is the *sum of the displacements* of the individual waves at that point.
- Displacement is a **vector** quantity and can have positive and negative values.

Each wave shown in Figure 22.3 has an amplitude of 5.0 mm. The plane wavefronts represent crests of identical water waves (transverse waves) produced by plane sources S_1 and S_2. The circular wavefronts represent compressions of identical sound waves (longitudinal waves) produced by point sources S_3 and S_4. Determine the displacement, s, of each of the marked points A to F at the instant shown.

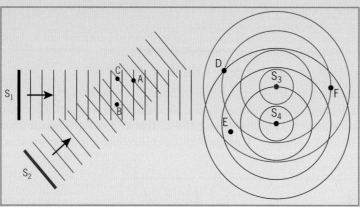

Figure 22.3

A: Constructive interference; crest meets crest

$s = 5.0$ mm $+ 5.0$ mm $= 10.0$ mm

B: Constructive interference; trough meets trough

$s = -5.0$ mm $+ -5.0$ mm $= -10.0$ mm

C: Destructive interference; crest meets trough

$s = 5.0$ mm $+ -5.0$ mm $= 0$ mm

D: Constructive interference; compression meets compression

$s = 5.0$ mm $+ 5.0$ mm $= 10.0$ mm

E: Constructive interference; rarefaction meets rarefaction

$s = -5.0$ mm $+ -5.0$ mm $= -10.0$ mm

F: Destructive interference; compression meets rarefaction

$s = 5.0$ mm $+ -5.0$ mm $= 0$ mm

Coherence

Vibrations are **coherent** if they are *in phase or have a constant phase difference*. They must therefore have the *same frequency*. To produce a pattern that demonstrates complete constructive and destructive interference, the following conditions must be met:

- The sources must be coherent.
- The waves produced must have the same amplitude and shape.

To produce an interference pattern for light waves, a single lamp must be used in front of two narrow gaps (S_1 and S_2, as shown in Figure 22.4). If two bulbs were used, they would emit waves randomly and disarrange the pattern. However, if the single source emits randomly, sources S_1 and S_2 will still be coherent.

Young's double-slit experiment demonstrating the interference of light waves

Figure 22.4 shows waves from a monochromatic source diffracting through a narrow slit, S, and then undergoing further diffraction through two other narrow slits, S_1 and S_2, about 0.5 mm apart. The emerging wavefronts progress towards a translucent screen where they superpose and form an interference pattern of bright and dark **fringes**. The experiment should be performed in a poorly lit room.

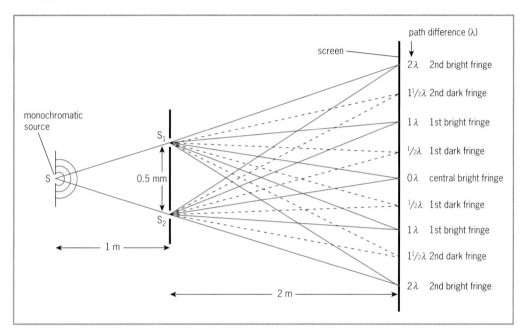

Figure 22.4 *Young's double-slit experiment*

A sodium vapour lamp emits only yellow light and is a suitable **monochromatic** source. Alternatively, a filament lamp emitting white light can be used if a colour filter is placed in front of it. Without the filter, however, the various frequencies would produce overlapping fringes and the uniform pattern will not be observed.

S_1 and S_2 are coherent sources since they depend on a *common primary source*, S. They emit waves which are in phase, or have some constant phase difference, to produce the pattern of bright and dark fringes observed.

Bright fringes

When the waves from S_1 and S_2 meet the screen *in phase*, their path difference is a whole number of wavelengths, 0λ, 1λ, 2λ, 3λ, and so on. They undergo *constructive interference* and a bright fringe is formed.

Dark fringes

When the waves from S_1 and S_2 meet the screen *exactly out of phase*, their path difference is $\frac{1}{2}\lambda$, $1\frac{1}{2}\lambda$, $2\frac{1}{2}\lambda$, and so on. They undergo *destructive interference* and a dark fringe is formed.

Evidence for the wave nature of light

Young's double-slit experiment provides evidence for the wave nature of light, since interference is a phenomenon of waves.

Young's experiment in relation to sound waves

The experiment can be carried out using sound waves as shown in Chapter 20, Figure 20.9.

Revision questions

1. Briefly describe Huygens' wave theory of light.

2. Which scientist proposed a particle theory of light?

3. a Which theory of light was backed by the experiment performed by Young?

   b How does Young's experiment support the theory mentioned in part a?

4. a Which theory was backed by the experiment performed by Foucault?

   b How does Foucault's experiment support the theory mentioned in part a?

5. a Name TWO 20th century scientists responsible for the quantum theory.

   b What does the quantum theory suggest?

6. a What is meant by the term *diffraction*?

   b What condition is required for strong diffraction?

   c Why is the diffraction of light waves not generally observed?

7. a What is meant by the term *interference*?

   b Sketch wavefronts to show how waves from two plane sources can interfere. Mark a point C and a point D where there is *constructive* and *destructive* interference, respectively.

   c If the amplitude of each wave in part b is 2 mm, what is the amplitude at each marked point?

8. This question is about Young's double-slit experiment.

   a Why is it not possible to use two separate lamps as the light sources?

   b Why is it not possible to use a source of white light without a colour filter if complete destructive interference is to be observed?

   c What can you say about the path difference between waves that produce a bright fringe on the screen?

23 Light rays and rectilinear propagation

*A **ray** of light is the direction in which light propagates.*

*A **beam** of light is a stream of light energy.*

Shadows

Shadow produced by a point source of light

Light travels in straight lines and therefore a shadow is formed when an opaque object obstruct its path (Figure 23.1).

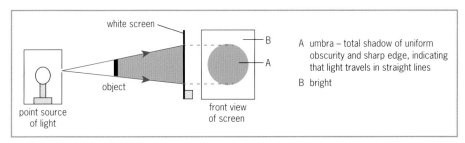

Figure 23.1 *Shadow produced by a point source of light*

Shadow produced by an extended source of light

A lamp in a box with a large hole acts as an extended source of light. The hole can be interpreted as several point sources, each casting a shadow which overlaps with the shadows from the other neighbouring point sources. There is an **umbra** and a **penumbra**, as shown in Figure 23.2.

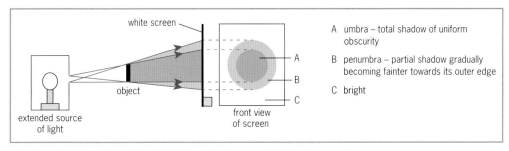

Figure 23.2 *Shadow produced by an extended source of light*

Eclipse of the Moon

The Moon is a non-luminous body and is therefore seen from the Earth by reflection of light from the Sun. The orbit of the Moon usually passes outside of the Earth's shadow, but at times it travels through the cone of shadow, as shown in Figure 23.3. When this happens, light from the Sun can no longer reach the Moon and there is a **lunar eclipse**. The full Moon is eclipsed (obscured). It can take more than 1½ hours before it emerges from the other edge of the shadow.

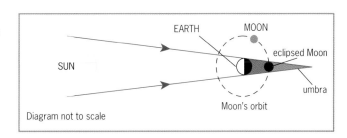

Figure 23.3 *Eclipse of the Moon*

Eclipse of the Sun

At times the orbit of the Moon can pass directly through the line joining the Sun to the Earth, as in Figure 23.4. When this occurs, the Moon's umbra reaches the Earth's surface over a small region, from which a *total* **solar eclipse** can be observed. People in the penumbra will observe a *partial* eclipse.

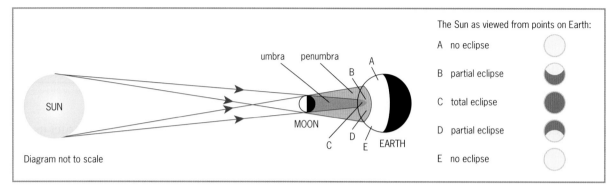

Figure 23.4 *Eclipse of the Sun*

The pinhole camera

When an object is placed in front of the **pinhole camera** shown in Figure 23.5, an inverted image is formed on the translucent screen. Since light travels in a straight line, rays from any point on the object have only one possible path into the box, and consequently only one point at which they meet the screen. A *focused, real, inverted* image is therefore always produced.

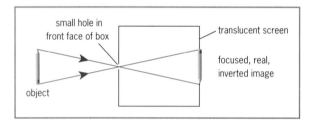

Figure 23.5 *Formation of an image by a pinhole camera*

- The image becomes smaller on increasing the distance of the object from the box, because the rays enter at a smaller angle.
- The image becomes larger on increasing the depth of the box, because the rays spread more before reaching the screen.
- If the hole in the front face is made larger, the image becomes:

  a blurred due to the formation of several overlapping images

  b brighter due to the increased light intensity entering the box.

1   Define:

   a a ray of light   **b** a beam of light

2   State the property of light responsible for the formation of shadows.

3   Draw ray diagrams to represent the formation of each of the following.

   a The shadow produced by a point source of light

   b An eclipse of the Moon (lunar eclipse)

   c An eclipse of the Sun (solar eclipse)

4   Draw ray diagrams to show the formation of the image in a pinhole camera for each of the following cases.

   a The camera focusing an image of an object

   b The effect on the image of increasing the size of the hole

   c The effect on the image of moving the object further from the camera

   d The effect on the image of making the box deeper

24 Reflection and refraction

Reflection

Laws of reflection

- *The incident ray, the reflected ray and the normal, at the point of incidence, are on the same plane.*
- *The angle of incidence is equal to the angle of reflection* (Figure 24.1).

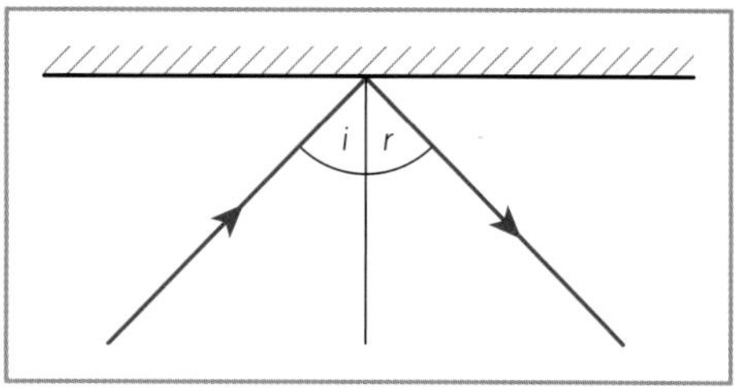

Figure 24.1 *The laws of reflection*

Characteristics of the image formed in a plane mirror

1. Same size as object

2. Same distance perpendicularly behind the mirror as the object is in front

3. Virtual

4. Laterally inverted

Virtual means not real – the image cannot be formed on a screen, and light does not come from where the image appears to be.

Laterally inverted means reversed side to side, so that the image of a word placed to face a mirror is reversed as shown:

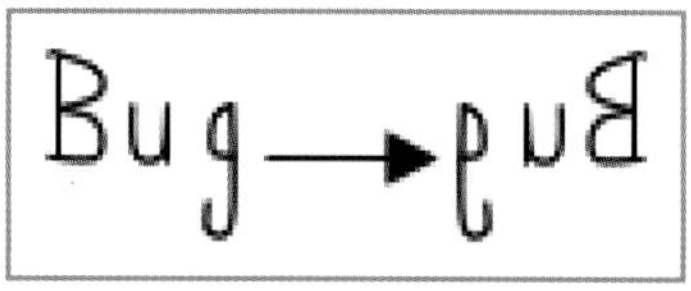

Reflection ray diagrams using point objects

- Draw a line to represent the mirror and place a small dot to represent the point object in its correct position to scale on the diagram.
- Place the point image in the diagram the same distance perpendicularly behind the mirror as the point object is in front. A faint construction line, perpendicular to the mirror, is useful here.
- Draw an eye at the location from which the image is viewed.
- Draw two rays *from the image* to the edges of the eye (use broken lines behind the mirror).
- Draw two more rays, this time *from the object*, to where the first two rays intersect the mirror.

See Figure 24.2 for some examples.

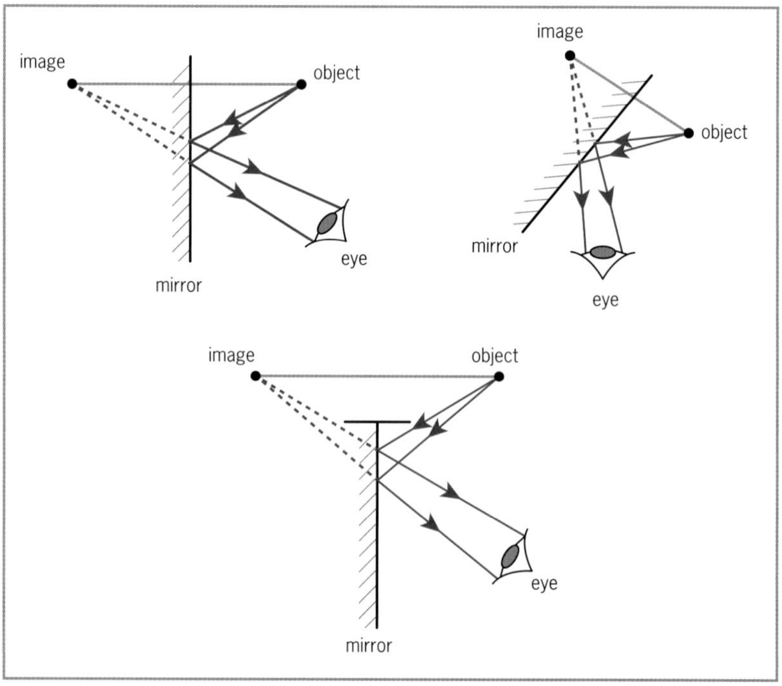

Figure 24.2 *Examples of reflection ray diagrams*

Refraction

Laws of refraction

- *The incident ray, the refracted ray and the normal, at the point of incidence, are on the same plane.*
- *The ratio $\dfrac{\sin i}{\sin r}$ is a constant for a given pair of media, where i is the angle of incidence and r is the angle of refraction.* This is **Snell's law**, see Figure 24.3.

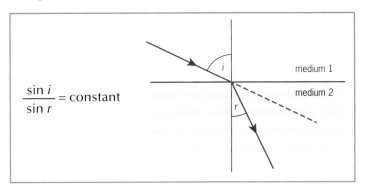

$$\frac{\sin i}{\sin r} = \text{constant}$$

Figure 24.3 *Snell's law of refraction*

Refractive index, η

*For light travelling from one medium to another, the ratio $\dfrac{\sin i}{\sin r}$ is the **refractive index** of the second medium relative to the first $\left(\dfrac{\eta_2}{\eta_1}\right)$.*

$$\frac{\eta_2}{\eta_1} = \frac{\sin i}{\sin r}$$

For light travelling from one medium to another, the ratio

$$\frac{\text{speed in medium of incidence}}{\text{speed in medium of refraction}}$$

is also equal to the refractive index of the second medium relative to the first:

$$\frac{\eta_2}{\eta_1} = \frac{v_i}{v_r}$$

Table 24.1 Refractive indices of common materials

Material	Refractive index, η
air	1.0
water	1.3
glass	1.5

Deviation on passing from one medium to another

When light enters a second medium perpendicular to its interface (Figure 24.4(a)):

- it does not deviate – the angles of incidence and refraction are both zero
- its *speed is greater in the less optically dense medium.*

When light enters a *more optically dense* medium other than perpendicularly (Figure 24.4(b)):

- it refracts *towards the normal,* that is the angle between the ray and the normal decreases
- its speed decreases.

When light enters a *less optically dense* medium other than perpendicularly (Figure 24.4(c)):

- it refracts *away from the normal*, that is the angle between the ray and the normal increases
- its speed increases.

Figure 24.5 shows light being deviated as it passes through triangular prisms.

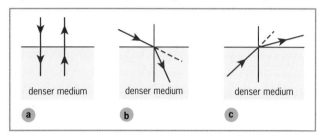

Figure 24.4 *Deviation of light passing between media of different optical density*

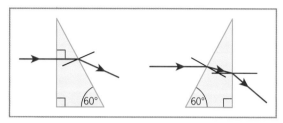

Figure 24.5 *Deviation through triangular prisms*

Refraction ray diagrams using point objects in the denser medium

The rules for drawing these ray diagrams are basically the same as for reflection diagrams. Figure 24.6 shows how they can be applied.

- Draw a line to represent the interface between the media and place a small dot to represent the point object in its correct position on the diagram.
- Place the point image in the diagram. An estimate will be sufficient here unless the exact position is given. An imaginary line connecting the object and the image is perpendicular to the interface. The image is closer to the interface than is the object.
- Draw an eye at the location from which the image is viewed.
- Draw two rays *from the image* to the edges of the eye (use broken lines before they reach the interface).
- Draw two more rays, this time *from the object*, to where the first two rays intersect the interface.

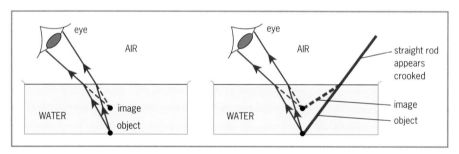

Figure 24.6 *Examples of refraction ray diagrams*

Refraction through a rectangular glass block

Figure 24.7 shows the path of a ray through a rectangular glass block. The *net deviation, D, is zero* since the clockwise deviation, d_1, is equal in magnitude to the anticlockwise deviation, d_2. The emergent ray is parallel to the incident ray and therefore the angle of emergence is equal to the angle of incidence.

There is a *lateral displacement, x*.

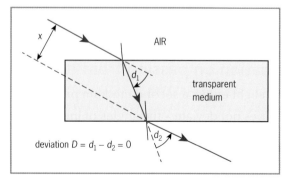

Figure 24.7 *Refraction through a rectangular transparent block*

Calculations

Figure 24.8 shows the type of diagram that is helpful when tackling a refraction problem.

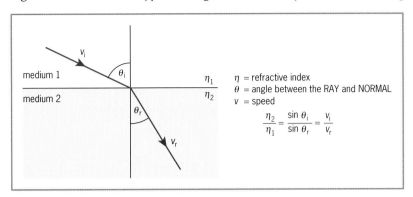

Figure 24.8

The relation shown in Figure 24.8 can also be written as:

$$\frac{\eta_y}{\eta_x} = \frac{\sin \theta_x}{\sin \theta_y} = \frac{v_x}{v_y}$$

where x and y represent the two media. It is helpful to use subscripts relevant to the media in order to reduce errors of substitution, for example v_g for the speed in glass or η_w for the refractive index of water. Note that the ratio of refractive index has its subscripts reversed when compared with the others ratios.

Example 1

(Speed of light in air = 3.0×10^8 m s^{-1}; use the data for refractive indices from Table 24.1.)

Light enters water from the air above at an angle of incidence of 60°. Determine:

a the angle of refraction

b the speed of light in water.

a $\dfrac{\sin \theta_w}{\sin \theta_a} = \dfrac{\eta_a}{\eta_w}$

$\dfrac{\sin \theta_w}{\sin 60} = \dfrac{1}{1.3}$

$\sin \theta_w = \dfrac{\sin 60}{1.3}$

$\theta_w = 42°$

b $\dfrac{v_w}{v_a} = \dfrac{\eta_a}{\eta_w}$

$\dfrac{v_w}{3.0 \times 10^8} = \dfrac{1}{1.3}$

$v_w = \dfrac{3.0 \times 10^8}{1.3} = 2.3 \times 10^8 \text{ m s}^{-1}$

Example 2

Determine the angle of incidence on the glass surface shown in Figure 24.9.
(Use the data for refractive indices from Table 24.1.)

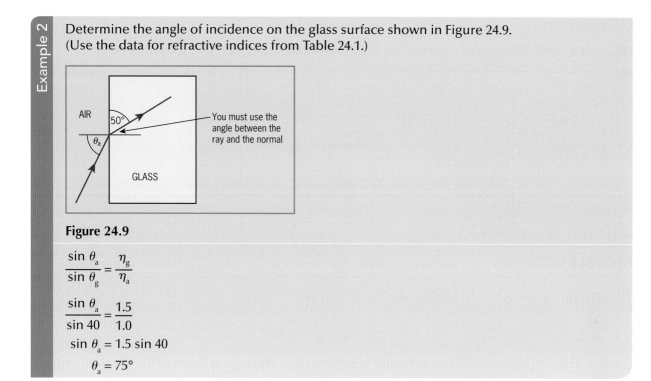

AIR

You must use the angle between the ray and the normal

GLASS

Figure 24.9

$$\frac{\sin \theta_a}{\sin \theta_g} = \frac{\eta_g}{\eta_a}$$

$$\frac{\sin \theta_a}{\sin 40} = \frac{1.5}{1.0}$$

$$\sin \theta_a = 1.5 \sin 40$$

$$\theta_a = 75°$$

Dispersion

*The **dispersion** of white light is the separation of white light into its constituent colours.*

Figure 24.10(a) shows the set-up of an experiment originally done by Newton. A narrow beam of white light from a double slit collimator is incident on a glass prism. On entering the prism, the light waves refract and each colour is deviated differently. Red refracts least, and violet most. The beam therefore separates, and the emerging light forms a visible spectrum on a white screen: red, orange, yellow, green, blue, indigo, violet (ROYGBIV). Newton was first to demonstrate that white light can be separated in this manner. Note that a wide incident beam will produce several overlapping spectra which will recombine to form white light.

A rainbow is produced when white light is dispersed in this way by water droplets in the sky.

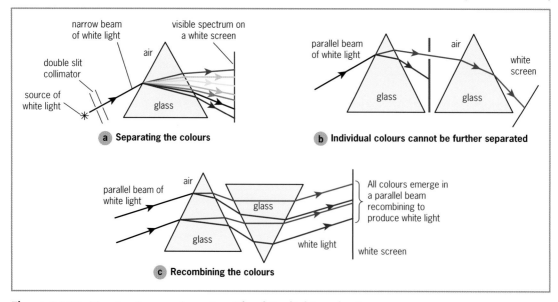

a **Separating the colours**

b **Individual colours cannot be further separated**

c **Recombining the colours**

Figure 24.10 *Newton's experiments with white light and prisms*

Newton made a number of changes to the experiment in order to prove that the origin of the coloured light was *not within the prism*. He:

- changed the size of the slits of the collimator
- used prisms of different types
- altered the distance between the light source and the prism
- isolated a colour and showed that it was not affected by another prism (Figure 24.10(b))
- added a second prism to show that the colours can be recombined (Figure 24.10(c)).

Newton's experiments proved that white light was a combination of light of different colours. His approach is to be commended since he *experimented* rather than simply *theorised*.

Critical angle and total internal reflection

Figure 24.11 shows that light directed into a medium of lesser optical density (smaller refractive index) is partly reflected and partly refracted. At small angles of incidence the reflected ray is weak and the refracted ray is strong. As the angle of incidence increases, the angle of refraction also increases, and the reflected ray becomes slightly stronger. At a certain angle of incidence, c, the refracted ray passes just along the surface, and for angles greater than this **critical angle**, there is **total internal reflection**.

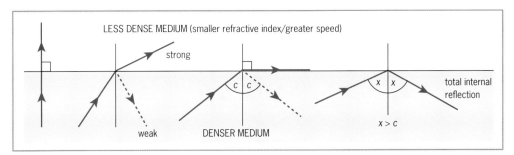

Figure 24.11 *Critical angle, c, and total internal reflection for incident angles greater than c*

Two ways to define critical angle

- *The **critical angle** of a material is the largest angle at which a ray can approach an interface with a medium of smaller refractive index and be refracted into it.*
- *The **critical angle** of a material is the smallest angle at which a ray can approach an interface with a medium of smaller refractive index and be totally internally reflected by it.*

Conditions necessary for total internal reflection

- The ray must approach the second medium from one of greater refractive index, that is from one in which its speed is less.
- The angle of approach must be greater than the critical angle.

The mirage

During the day the temperature of the air directly above the surface of a road increases due to conduction of heat from the asphalt. A ray of light from low in the sky will refract away from the normal as it enters the hotter, less dense air (Figure 24.12). The deviation continues until the ray is totally reflected just above the road. It is then continuously refracted towards the normal as it enters the cooler, denser, air above. An observer receiving this ray will see a virtual image of the sky and may interpret it as a pool of water.

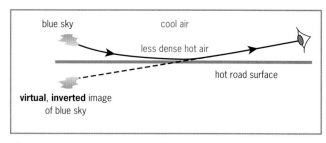

Figure 24.12 *Formation of a mirage*

Viewing from above a water surface

Figure 24.13 shows a light source at the bottom of a large swimming pool. When viewed from above, one would see light leaving the water from within a circle of a certain diameter, d. Rays reaching the surface outside of this circle are totally internally reflected, because their angles of incidence are greater than the critical angle ($x > c$ and $y > c$).

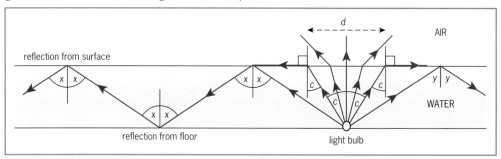

Figure 24.13 *Viewing a light on a swimming pool floor from above the water surface*

Relation between critical angle and refractive index

If one of the media is air, as in Figure 24.14, then the relation is:

$$\sin c = \frac{1}{\eta}$$

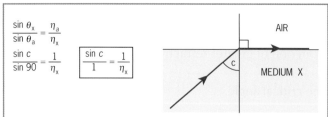

Figure 24.14 *Relation between critical angle and refractive index*

If neither medium is air, or if the question involves wavelength or velocity, then this general relation is used:

$$\frac{\eta_y}{\eta_x} = \frac{\sin \theta_x}{\sin \theta_y} = \frac{v_x}{v_y}$$

One of the angles is 90° and the other is the critical angle, c. The critical angle is always in the medium in which the wave travels with lesser speed – for light, this is the more optically dense medium.

Note that, if the critical angle or the refractive index of a material is referred to without mention of the second medium, it can be assumed that it is relative to air.

The light bulb under the water in Figure 24.15 produces an illuminated disc on the water surface of diameter 20 m. The refractive index of water is 1.33.

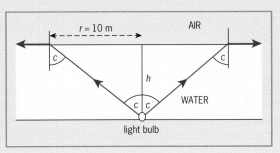

Figure 24.15

Calculate:

a the critical angle of water   **b** the depth of the water

a $\sin c = \dfrac{1}{\eta}$

   $\sin c = \dfrac{1}{1.33}$

   $c = 48.8° = 49°$ to 2 sig. fig.

b $\tan c = \dfrac{r}{h}$

   $\tan 48.8 = \dfrac{10}{h}$

   $h = \dfrac{10}{\tan 48.8}$

   $h = 8.8$ m

Applications of total internal reflection

Optical fibres

Light entering through one end of a thin, transparent, glass fibre will mainly be totally internally reflected until it emerges from the other end (Figure 24.16(a)). This is the principle of an **optical fibre**.

Scratches on the outside of the fibre could cause light to exit through the sides. A cladding of a different type of glass is placed around the core in order to protect it (Figure 24.16(b)). Since the light is transmitted through the core, scratches on the outside of the cladding are unimportant. For total internal reflection, the refractive index of the cladding *must be less* than that of the core.

Figure 24.16 *An optical fibre*

Optical fibres have the following uses:

- **Telecommunications**: Electronic communications for cable TV, telephone and the internet are largely transmitted by means of light pulses in fibre-optic cables.

- **Endoscopes**

    1. Diagnostic imaging: Light is transmitted into the patient through a bundle of optical fibres. The reflected light then returns through another bundle of fibres connected to a video camera which displays the image on a screen.

    2. Therapy: Tumours in solid organs are difficult to remove by surgery. A laser beam can be directed to destroy such tumours by means of optical fibres.

Reflecting prisms

A mirror reflects only about 90% of the light incident on it. Utilising total internal reflection in optical devices allows 100% of the radiation to be reflected and therefore produces a stronger image. Right-angled, isosceles-triangular glass prisms are used in many optical instruments, such as periscopes and binoculars, to reflect light (see Figure 24.17).

When light enters the prism perpendicularly through one of the shorter sides, it meets the opposite wall at 45°. This is more than the critical angle of glass (42°), and therefore there is total internal reflection.

In Figure 24.17, all angles angles are either 90° or 45°. The medium around the prisms is air.

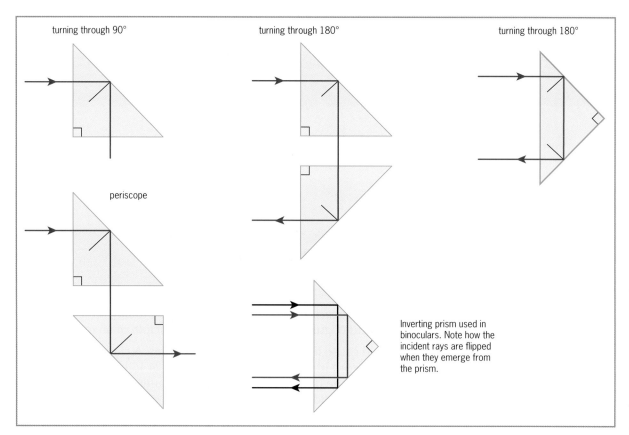

Figure 24.17 *Reflecting prisms*

Revision questions

Use this data:

speed of light in air = 3.0×10^8 m s^{-1} refractive index of glass = 1.5   refractive index of air = 1.0

speed of light in water = 2.3×10^8 m s^{-1} refractive index of water = 1.3

1 State the laws of reflection.

2 A point object is 3.0 cm in front of a plane mirror. Sketch a ray diagram using TWO rays from the object to indicate how an eye can view the image in the mirror.

3 State FOUR characteristics of the image formed in a plane mirror.

4 State the laws of refraction.

5 Light enters water from air at an angle of incidence of 40°. Determine the angle of refraction.

6 What phenomenon of light is associated with each of the following?

a Glare is produced by the white sands of Caribbean beaches.

b The depth of the water above a coral reef appears less than it actually is when viewed from a fishing boat above.

7 Light travelling in air enters a liquid of refractive index 1.4. Determine its speed in the liquid.

8 Sketch a diagram to show a ray of light passing obliquely through opposite faces of a rectangular glass block. Indicate the angle of deviation as it enters and leaves the block and comment on the net deviation and the lateral displacement of the ray.

9 With the aid of a diagram, explain the formation of a mirage.

10 Sketch a ray diagram to show why a straight pencil appears crooked when partly immersed in a bowl of water. Your diagram should include TWO rays from the lowest point on the pencil.

11 Sketch a diagram to show how white light can be dispersed using a triangular glass prism.

12 State a natural phenomenon that demonstrates the dispersion of white light.

13 Name the scientist who concluded that white light is a mixture of several colours.

14 Determine the critical angle of glass of refractive index 1.5.

15 Determine the refractive index of a material that has a critical angle of 35°.

16 For light travelling in glass towards water, calculate the maximum angle of approach for which there can be refraction into the water.

17 The speed of light in medium M is 1.8×10^8 m s^{-1}. Determine the critical angle of medium M with respect to air.

18 A bright bulb is at the bottom of a swimming pool of depth 2.0 m. Calculate the diameter of the disc through which light emerges at the surface. (HINT: First calculate the critical angle of water.)

19 State TWO uses of optical fibres.

20 Sketch a diagram showing how a ray of light can be reflected by a single right-angled isosceles glass prism (critical angle 42°), through

a 90°   **b** 180°

25 Lenses

- A **lens** is a piece of specially shaped transparent material that can form focused images of objects.
- A **convex** or **converging lens** is one that is thicker at its centre. It can converge parallel rays of light to produce a real image.
- A **concave** or **diverging lens** is one that is thinner at its centre. It can diverge parallel rays of light to produce a virtual image.
- The **optical centre**, O, of a lens (see Figure 25.1) is the point at the centre of the lens through which all rays pass without deviation.
- The **principal axis** of a lens is the line that passes through its optical centre and is perpendicular to the faces of the lens.
- The **principal focus**, F, of a lens is the point on the principal axis through which all rays parallel and close to the axis converge, or from which they appear to diverge, after passing through the lens.
- The **focal length**, f, of a lens is the distance between its optical centre and its principal focus.
- The **focal plane** of a lens is the surface perpendicular to its principal axis and containing its principal focus.

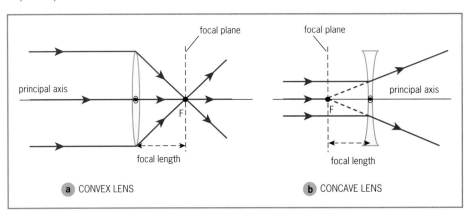

Figure 25.1 *Terms used with lenses*

Parallel rays focus on the focal plane even if they are not parallel to the principal axis – see Figure 25.2.

In order to determine where the rays focus, draw an incident ray *straight through* the optical centre to a point on the focal plane. Then connect the other parallel rays, after passing through the lens, to the same point.

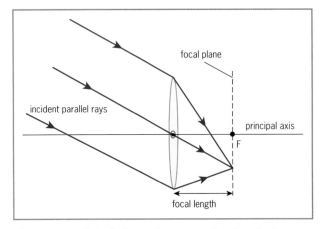

Figure 25.2 *Parallel rays focus on the focal plane*

Magnification

Magnification, m, is the ratio of the size of the image to the size of the object.

$$\text{magnification} = \frac{\text{image height}}{\text{object height}} \qquad m = \frac{I}{O}$$

$$\text{magnification} = \frac{\text{distance of image from lens}}{\text{distance of object from lens}} \qquad m = \frac{v}{u}$$

Therefore

$$\frac{I}{O} = \frac{v}{u}$$

An object of height 2.0 cm, placed 40 cm in front of a convex lens, produces an image of height 8.0 cm. Determine:

a   the magnification   b   the distance of the image from the lens

a $m = \dfrac{I}{O}$

   $m = \dfrac{8.0 \text{ cm}}{2.0 \text{ cm}}$

   $m = 4.0$

b $m = \dfrac{v}{u}$

   $4.0 = \dfrac{v}{40 \text{ cm}}$

   $v = 4.0 \times 40 \text{ cm} = 160 \text{ cm}$

Determining the focal length of a converging lens

A converging lens is mounted as shown in Figure 25.3. The distance between the lens and the object (a small gap with crossed wires) is altered until a sharp image is observed next to the object. Light from the object almost retraces its path after reflection from the mirror, and the *parallel* beam focuses at the principal focus. The distance between the centre of the lens and the object is therefore the focal length of the lens.

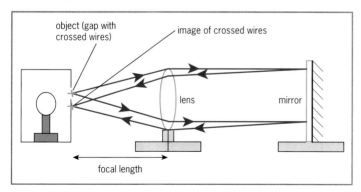

Figure 25.3 *Determining the focal length of a converging lens*

Real and virtual images

Real images are those produced at a point to which light rays converge.

Virtual images are those produced at a point from which light rays appear to diverge.

See Tables 25.1 and 25.2.

Table 25.1 *Examples of real and virtual images*

Examples of real images	Examples of virtual images
image produced on the retina	image produced in a mirror
image produced in a camera	image produced by a convex lens acting as a magnifying glass
image produced on the screen at the cinema	image produced by a concave lens

Table 25.2 *Features of real and virtual images of real objects produced by a lens*

Real images formed by lenses	Virtual images formed by lenses
can be formed on a screen	cannot be formed on a screen
are produced by the convergence of rays	are produced due to the divergence of rays
are located on the side of the lens opposite to the object	are located on the same side of the lens as the object
are inverted	are erect

Constructing scale diagrams

Convex lenses

1. Draw two perpendicular lines to represent the principal axis and the lens.

2. Place points, F, to scale in position, to represent the principal foci.

3. Draw the object to scale, in size and position, to stand on the principal axis.

4. Draw lines to represent the following rays *from the top of the object*:

- parallel to the principal axis, and then through F after passing through the lens
- straight through the optical centre.

5. Where the rays cross represents the top of the image. Draw the image from the principal axis to this point.

See the examples in Figure 25.4. The points 2F have been included in these diagrams to provide a better understanding of how the position of the object affects the characteristics of the image. These points, however, are unnecessary for the construction of the scale drawing.

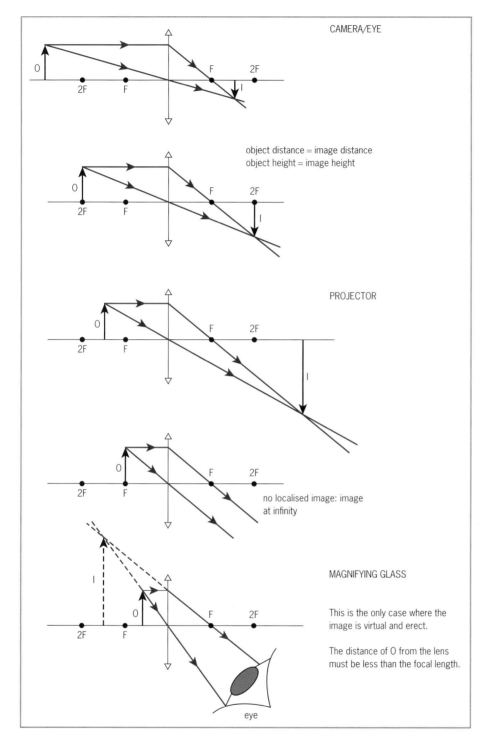

Figure 25.4 *Ray diagrams for several object positions relative to a convex lens*

Concave lenses

The method used is similar to that for convex lenses with one exception; the ray which is parallel to the principal axis until reaching the lens is then divergent, appearing to come from F on the same side of the lens as the object.

See the examples in Figure 25.5.

Characteristics of the image formed in a concave lens

- Smaller than the object
- Closer to the lens than is the object
- Virtual
- Erect

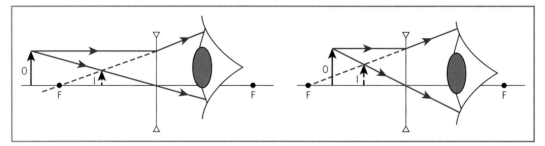

Figure 25.5 *Ray diagrams with a concave lens*

Important rays for lens diagrams

Figure 25.6 summarises the rays used to construct image positions.

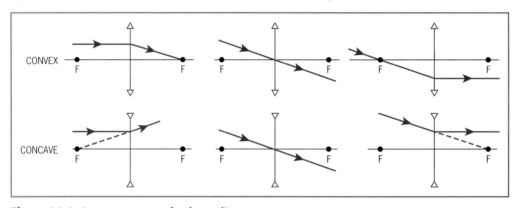

Figure 25.6 *Important rays for lens diagrams*

The lens formula

$$\frac{1}{u} + \frac{1}{v} = \frac{1}{f}$$

u = distance of object from lens: + if real, − if virtual

v = distance of image from lens: + if real, − if virtual

f = focal length: + for convex, − for concave

Look back to Table 25.2 for features of real and virtual images of real objects produced by a lens.

Example 2

A needle is placed with its length perpendicular to the principal axis of a convex lens of focal length 10 cm. Determine the *nature* and *orientation* of the image, as well as its *position relative to the lens*, when it is placed at each of the following points:

a 25 cm from the lens   **b** 4.0 cm from the lens

a $\dfrac{1}{u} + \dfrac{1}{v} = \dfrac{1}{f}$

$\dfrac{1}{25} + \dfrac{1}{v} = \dfrac{1}{10}$

$\dfrac{1}{v} = \dfrac{1}{10} - \dfrac{1}{25}$

$\dfrac{1}{v} = 0.060$

$v = \dfrac{1}{0.060} = 16.7 \text{ cm} = 17 \text{ cm to 2 sig. fig.}$

Since *v* is positive, the image is real, inverted and on the side of the lens opposite to that of the object.

b $\dfrac{1}{u} + \dfrac{1}{v} = \dfrac{1}{f}$

$\dfrac{1}{4.0} + \dfrac{1}{v} = \dfrac{1}{10}$

$\dfrac{1}{v} = \dfrac{1}{10} - \dfrac{1}{4.0}$

$\dfrac{1}{v} = -0.15$

$v = \dfrac{1}{-0.15} = -6.7 \text{ cm}$

Since *v* is negative, the image is virtual, erect and on the same side of the lens as the object.

Example 3

A concave lens of focal length 12 cm is placed 16 cm in front of a thin rod placed perpendicular to its principal axis. Determine the *nature*, *orientation* and *position relative to the lens*, of the image it produces.

$\dfrac{1}{u} + \dfrac{1}{v} = \dfrac{1}{f}$

$\dfrac{1}{16} + \dfrac{1}{v} = \dfrac{1}{-12}$ (focal length of concave lens is negative)

$\dfrac{1}{v} = \dfrac{1}{-12} + \dfrac{1}{-16}$

$\dfrac{1}{v} = -\dfrac{7}{48}$

$v = -6.9 \text{ cm to 2 sig. fig.}$

Since *v* is negative, the image is virtual, erect and on the same side of the lens as the object.

Revision questions

1. Define each of the following with respect to lenses:
   a convex lens
   b concave lens
   c focal length
   d principal focus
   e optical centre.

2. Draw ray diagrams to show how an image is formed by PARALLEL RAYS on the focal plane of a converging lens for each of the following situations.
   a Rays parallel to the principal axis
   b Rays not parallel to the principal axis

3. An object of height 5.0 cm is placed 20 cm in front of a converging lens and produces an image which is 50 cm from the other side of the lens. Determine:
   a the height of the image   b the magnification

4. Define the following, giving TWO examples of how each may be formed:
   a a real image   b a virtual image

5. State TWO differences between the properties of the images produced by an object placed in front of a convex lens at a distance greater than its focal length and closer than its focal length.

6. An object of height 2.0 cm is placed in front of a convex lens of focal length 20 cm. Construct scale diagrams to determine the *nature*, *size* and *position* of the image when the object stands perpendicular to the principal axis at the following distances from the lens. (The vertical and horizontal scales in your diagrams may be different.)
   a 50 cm   b 10 cm

7. An object of height 3.0 cm stands perpendicular to the principal axis, 7.0 cm in front of a concave lens of focal length 10 cm. Construct a scale diagram to determine the *nature*, *size* and *position* of the image.

8. An ant is 5.0 cm in front of a convex lens of focal length 12 cm. State the nature of the image formed and determine its position.

9. If the lens in question 8 is replaced by a concave one, what is the new nature and position of the image?

Exam-style questions – Chapters 19 to 25

Structured questions

1 **a) i)** List FOUR types of electromagnetic wave, in order of increasing wavelength. **(2 marks)**

  ii) Complete Table 1 of the sources and uses of two types of electromagnetic wave.

Table 1

Type of wave	Source	Use
radio		
gamma		

  (4 marks)

  iii) Which of the waves in Table 1 diffracts least? **(1 mark)**

  b) Calculate the wavelength, in a vacuum, of X-rays of frequency 1.5×10^{17} Hz. **(2 marks)**

  (Velocity of electromagnetic waves in a vacuum $= 3.0 \times 10^8$ m s^{-1})

  c) A ray of yellow light from a sodium vapour lamp travels in air until it enters a prism of critical angle 39°. The angle of refraction in the prism is 33°. Determine:

  i) the refractive index of the material of the prism with respect to yellow light **(3 marks)**

  ii) the angle of incidence on the prism. **(3 marks)**

  Total 15 marks

2 **a) i)** State the laws of reflection of light. **(2 marks)**

  ii) List THREE characteristics of the image formed in a plane mirror. **(3 marks)**

  b) The wave shown in Figure 1 has a velocity of 4.0 m s^{-1}. Determine its:

  i) amplitude **(1 mark)**

  ii) period **(1 mark)**

  iii) frequency **(2 marks)**

  iv) wavelength. **(2 marks)**

  v) Comment on whether the wave would diffract slightly or extensively when passing through a gap of width 25 m. **(2 marks)**

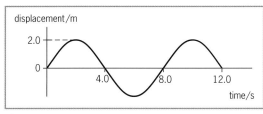

  Figure 1

  c) Sketch a diagram showing the form of a transverse water wave. Identify the following on the diagram:

  i) the direction of vibration of the water particles **(1 mark)**

  ii) the direction of progression of the wave. **(1 mark)**

  Total 15 marks

Extended response questions

 3

a) Describe, with the aid of a diagram, the Young's double slit experiment which produces an interference pattern of light waves. **(6 marks)**

b) Rihanna and Mechka, two dedicated CSEC students, stand 60 m in front of a tall, vertical cliff of rock. Rihanna claps two wooden blocks at such a rate that the returning echo coincides with each succeeding clap. Mechka times the interval for 20 echoes to return and finds it to be 7.0 s.

i) Determine the speed of sound from this data. **(5 marks)**

ii) Predict how this result would change if the blocks were clapped with greater force, producing a louder sound. **(1 mark)**

iii) The teenagers then see a flash of lightning, and 6.0 seconds later a loud crash of thunder startles them. How far are the girls from the thunder cloud? **(3 marks)**

Total 15 marks

 4

a) Describe an experiment to determine the focal length of a converging lens. **(6 marks)**

b) A thin nail is placed 20 cm in front of the plane of a converging lens of focal length 15 cm. The nail stands perpendicular to the principal axis of the lens.

i) Determine the distance from the lens at which a screen can be placed to produce a focused image of the nail. **(3 marks)**

ii) Is the image real or virtual? **(1 mark)**

iii) Is the image erect or inverted? **(1 mark)**

The height of the nail is 5.0 cm. Calculate:

iv) the magnification **(2 marks)**

v) the height of the image. **(2 marks)**

Total 15 marks

26 Static electricity

Introduction to electric charges

- All matter contains positive and negative **electric charges**.
- In liquids and gases, the positive and negative charges can be mobile.
- In metals, the negative charges (**electrons**) can be mobile and the positive charges remain fixed.
- **Neutral** bodies have the same amount of positive and negative charge and these therefore cancel. When sketching diagrams of charged bodies, usually only the excess charge of any region is shown.
- *Electron flow is opposite in direction* to **conventional current** flow (see Chapter 27).
- The term **earth** refers to a large body that can provide electrons to, or take electrons from, another body and still be considered neutral.
- **Electrostatic induction** is the process by which electrical properties are transferred from one body to another without physical contact.

Charging by friction

Figure 26.1 shows a glass rod and a polythene rod being rubbed by a dry cloth.

Electrons transfer from the surface of the glass rod onto the cloth, leaving the glass with excess positive charge and the cloth with excess negative charge.

Electrons transfer from the cloth onto the surface of the polythene rod leaving the polythene with excess negative charge and the cloth with excess positive charge.

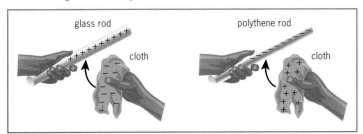

Figure 26.1 *Charging by friction*

Demonstrating attraction and repulsion

Two balls, each about 6 mm in diameter and made of compressed aluminium foil, are each suspended by a thin nylon thread. One ball is allowed to momentarily touch the positive terminal, and the other, the negative terminal, of a battery. The balls become charged, positively and negatively respectively, by contact.

A glass rod, charged positively by friction, is brought near to each of the balls (Figure 26.2). It will be observed that the positive rod attracts the negative ball but repels the positive one.

Similar charges repel.
Unlike charges attract.

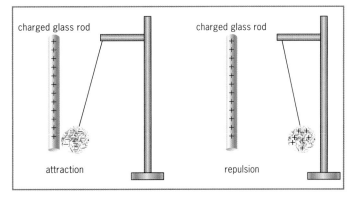

Figure 26.2 *Similar charges repel and unlike charges attract*

A charged body can attract an uncharged one

A charged polythene rod brought near to a small piece of paper will attract the paper as shown in Figure 26.3. Electrons in the paper are repelled by the negatively charged polythene, leaving a net positive charge on the side of the paper nearest to the rod. Since the positive charges of the paper are close to the negative polythene, the attraction is strong and the paper jumps onto the rod.

In humid Caribbean regions the paper will not stick to the rod for long. Electrons from the rod will conduct to the paper through the layer of moisture that coats the rod, and the positive charge on the paper reduces so that the attraction is insufficient to support its weight.

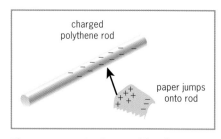

Figure 26.3 *A charged body can attract an uncharged one*

Charging a metal dome by induction

A metal dome can be charged negatively by **induction** using a positively charged rod. See Figure 26.4.

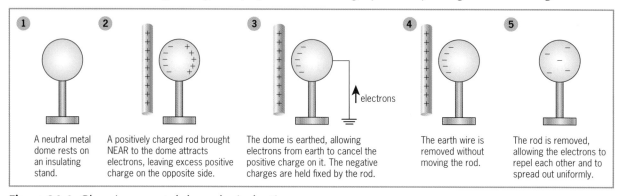

1	2	3	4	5
A neutral metal dome rests on an insulating stand.	A positively charged rod brought NEAR to the dome attracts electrons, leaving excess positive charge on the opposite side.	The dome is earthed, allowing electrons from earth to cancel the positive charge on it. The negative charges are held fixed by the rod.	The earth wire is removed without moving the rod.	The rod is removed, allowing the electrons to repel each other and to spread out uniformly.

Figure 26.4 *Charging a metal dome by induction*

The final charge on the dome is *opposite* to the inducing charge. By a similar procedure, a negatively charged rod can be used to charge the dome positively.

This is different from charging a metal dome by contact – see Figure 26.5.

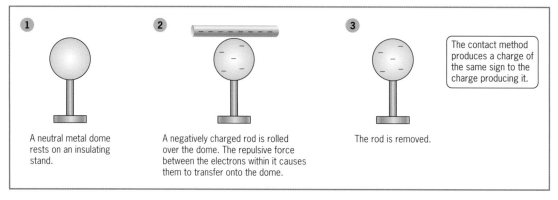

1	2	3	
A neutral metal dome rests on an insulating stand.	A negatively charged rod is rolled over the dome. The repulsive force between the electrons within it causes them to transfer onto the dome.	The rod is removed.	The contact method produces a charge of the same sign to the charge producing it.

Figure 26.5 *Charging a metal dome by contact*

Hazards of static charge

Lightning

A cloud becomes charged due to friction between layers of air and water molecules rising and falling within it. The base of the cloud usually becomes negatively charged and the top positively charged, as shown in Figure 26.6. Sparks occur between opposite charges within the cloud.

The negative charge on the base of the cloud repels electrons further into the ground below, resulting in a net positive charge accumulating at the surface of the Earth. When the potential difference (see Chapter 27) between the base of the cloud and the surface of the Earth is sufficiently large, electrons and negatively charged ions (heavier charged particles) will rush from the cloud to the ground. These high-speed particles crash into air molecules, knocking electrons out of them and creating pairs of oppositely charged ions. The result is an avalanche of positive and negative ions, which rush to the cloud and the Earth respectively. The discharge current can be as high as 20 000 A. Electrical energy transforms into heat and light energy (lightning) which transforms further into sound energy as the air rapidly expands, increasing the pressure and producing a sonic shock wave – thunder.

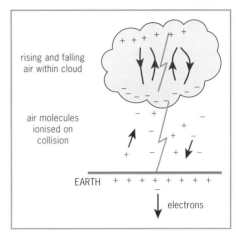

Figure 26.6 *Lightning*

Charges from fabric in the seats of vehicles

The occupants of a vehicle usually become charged by friction with the fabric of the seats, especially in dry regions. When someone gets out of a vehicle to operate a gasoline pump, a spark may jump between the person's body and the metal nozzle of the hose, producing a flash fire through the flammable vapour. It is therefore advisable to discharge oneself immediately on exiting the vehicle by touching the metal body of the car.

Useful applications of static charge

Lightning conductors

Figure 26.7 shows a lightning conductor protecting a tall building from the danger of a lightning strike. The negative charge on the base of a nearby cloud induces opposite charge at the spikes, by repelling electrons down the copper strip and into the ground. The positive charge at the spikes is very *concentrated due to their sharp curvature* and this **ionises** nearby air molecules by ripping electrons from them. The positive and negative ions produced, rush to the base of the cloud and to the spikes respectively, cancelling the charges there, and reducing the potential difference to a safe value.

Even if the cloud did spark to the rods, the discharge would be less violent and would pass readily to the ground through the thick copper strip, instead of through the building.

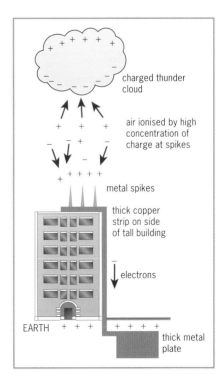

Figure 26.7 *A lightning conductor*

Dust precipitators

Figure 26.8 shows how an **electrostatic precipitator** prevents smoke, containing dust and carbon particles, from polluting the environment. A **cathode** in the form of an electric grid at a potential of about –40 kV ionises the gases in the chimney. As the rising smoke passes through the ionised region, electrons stick to the smoke particles, making them negative. They are then attracted to a positive metal **anode** on the side of the chimney. The anode is periodically struck so that the dust particles can fall into a trough and be collected for disposal.

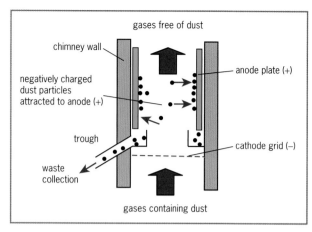

Figure 26.8 *Electrostatic dust precipitator*

Electrostatic spraying

Spray painting, for example of vehicles, can take advantage of electrostatic charging. As the paint passes through a nozzle (Figure 26.9) it becomes charged positively by friction. The positive droplets then induce opposite charge on the metal to be painted and are attracted to it. To increase the attraction, the metal can be connected to a negative potential.

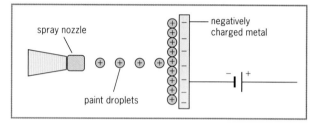

Figure 26.9 *Electrostatic spray painting*

Advantages:

* Similarly charged drops repel each other, spreading uniformly and giving good coverage.

* The drops are opposite in charge to the metal and therefore stick well to it.

* Shadow regions also receive the paint since the electric field can redirect the drops.

Insecticides, herbicides and fertilisers can be applied in a similar way. The chemical is charged and sprayed as a fine mist onto the plants, where it sticks firmly to the leaves and stems due to the opposite charge it induces.

Photocopiers

Figure 26.10 illustrates the role of electrostatic charge in the action of a photocopier.

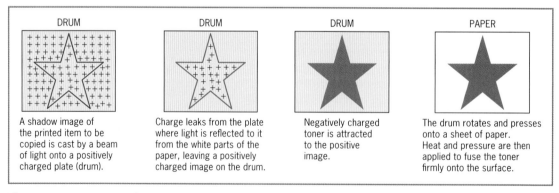

Figure 26.10 *How a photocopier works*

Electric fields

*An **electric field** is the region in which a body experiences a force due to its charge.*

The *direction of an electric field* at a point is the direction of the force caused by the field on a *positive charge* placed at the point.

Field lines

Field lines may be used to represent the strength and direction of electric (or magnetic) fields.

Important properties of field lines:

* The lines *never touch*.
* There is a *longitudinal tension* within a line.
* There is a *lateral repulsion* between lines that are close to each other.
* The field is *uniform* where the lines are evenly spaced and parallel.
* Electric field lines are directed *from positive charge to negative charge*.

Obtaining a uniform electric field

A uniform electric field will exist in the central region between charged metal plates, as shown in Figure 26.11. The field lines there are evenly spaced and parallel.

Near to the edges of the region, the field is not uniform. Field lines near to the top will be pushed upward due to the lateral repulsion from lines below, and field lines near to the bottom will be pushed downward due to the lateral repulsion from lines above.

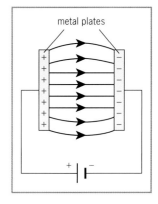

Figure 26.11 *A uniform electric field in the central region between charged metal plates*

Electric fields around and between charged bodies

Figures 26.12 and 26.13 illustrate electric fields for several arrangements of charges.

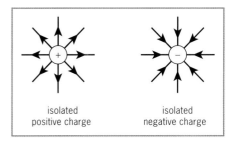

Figure 26.12 *Electric field lines around isolated point charges*

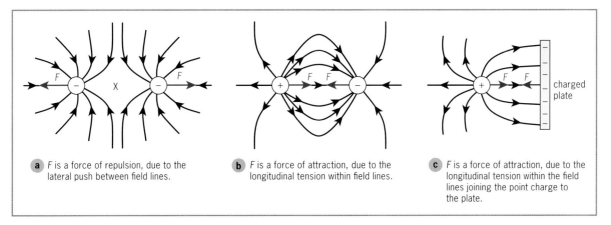

a *F* is a force of repulsion, due to the lateral push between field lines.

b *F* is a force of attraction, due to the longitudinal tension within field lines.

c *F* is a force of attraction, due to the longitudinal tension within the field lines joining the point charge to the plate.

Figure 26.13 *Electric field lines around and between charged bodies*

- The point **X** in Figure 26.13(a) is a **neutral point** – the field strength there is zero.
- Field lines do not necessarily point along the direction of force. In Figure 26.13(b) two oppositely directed forces are along the same field line.

Revision questions

1   Describe and explain what happens, in terms of the movement of charges, in each of the following cases.

   a A glass rod is rubbed with a cloth.

   b The rod in part a is then brought near to a small piece of uncharged paper.

2   A neutral metal dome supported by an insulated stand can be charged using a polythene rod which has been rubbed by a cloth. Describe and explain, in terms of the movement of charges, how this may be done by each of the following methods:

   a induction method   **b** contact method

3   Describe and explain:

   a the formation of lightning

   b how a lightning conductor can protect a tall building.

4   Draw diagrams to show the electric field in the following regions:

   a between two oppositely charged parallel plates

   b around a negatively charged particle

   c between and around two oppositely charged particles

   d between and around two similarly charged particles.

27 Current electricity

Conductors and insulators

Conductors are materials through which electrical charges can flow freely.

* Metals contain **free electrons** which have broken away from their atomic orbits and are not bound to any particular atom.
* Graphite (a non-metal) is a good conductor and is widely used for 'make and break' contacts in electrical circuits. As in metals, the mobile free charges are electrons.
* Solutions of ionic substances, as well as molten ionic substances, have mobile positive and negative **ions**, which move in opposite directions when connected in an electrical circuit.

Insulators are materials in which electrical charges do not flow freely.

* Non-metallic solids are usually good insulators, because most of them do not contain free charges.

Semiconductors are a class of materials with conductivity in a range between that of good conductors and good insulators.

An understanding of charge carriers in semiconductors is beyond the scope of this syllabus.

Table 27.1 *Examples of conductors, semiconductors and insulators*

Good conductors	Semiconductors	Insulators
silver, gold, copper, aluminium, graphite	silicon, germanium	glass, mica, quartz, rubber, plastic

Conventional current and electron flow

Current is the rate of flow of charge.

$$I = \frac{Q}{t} \qquad\qquad Q = It$$

I = current, Q = charge, t = time

The **coulomb**, C, is the SI unit of charge.

The **ampere**, A, is the SI unit of current.

The current is 1 ampere when the rate of flow of charge is 1 coulomb per second through a point.

Since $Q = It$,

$$1\,C = 1\,A \times 1\,s \qquad\qquad 1\,C = 1\,A\,s$$

Note that if the number of particles (N) is known, together with the charge on each particle (q), then the total charge Q is given by $Q = Nq$.

Conventional current is in the direction in which a POSITIVE charge would move if free to do so. It is the direction of the electric field.

Electron flow is the flow of NEGATIVE charge and is therefore opposite to the direction of conventional flow.

A charge of 20 μC flows past a point in a time of 4.0 ms. Determine:

a the current

b the number of electrons that flow past the point, given that the charge on an electron is -1.6×10^{-19} C.

a $I = \dfrac{Q}{t}$

$I = \dfrac{20 \times 10^{-6}}{4.0 \times 10^{-3}}$

$I = 5.0 \times 10^{-3}$ A or 5.0 mA

Note that the negative sign in front of the charge of the electron is ignored in calculating the size of the current.

b $\qquad Q = Nq$

$20 \times 10^{-6} = N \times 1.6 \times 10^{-19}$

$\dfrac{20 \times 10^{-6}}{1.6 \times 10^{-19}} = N$

$1.25 \times 10^{14} = N$

Alternating and direct current

*An **alternating current** (ac) is a current that repeatedly reverses direction with time.*

*A **direct current** (dc) is a current that does not change direction with time.*

The voltage, V (see Chapter 28), follows a similar pattern to the current. Figure 27.1 shows some examples of how the voltage might vary with time, t.

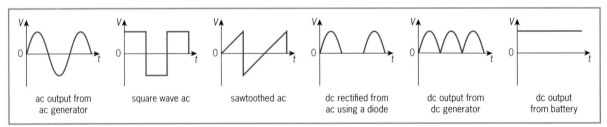

| ac output from ac generator | square wave ac | sawtoothed ac | dc rectified from ac using a diode | dc output from dc generator | dc output from battery |

Figure 27.1 *Examples of ac and dc voltage variation*

For ac:

- *the **frequency**, f, is the number of complete oscillations or cycles per second.* Its unit is Hz (1 Hz = 1 s⁻¹)

- *the **period**, T, is the time taken for one complete oscillation or cycle.* Its unit is s.

$$f = \frac{1}{T}$$

Determine the period of a 50 Hz ac electrical mains supply.

$T = \dfrac{1}{f} = \dfrac{1}{50 \text{ Hz}} = 0.02$ s

Revision questions

1 Define the following electrical terms:

    a conductor   **b** insulator   **c** current

2 Give TWO examples of each of the following:

    a conductors   **b** insulators   **c** semiconductors

3 Differentiate between each of the following:

    a alternating current and direct current

    b conventional current and electron flow.

4 Sketch *V–t* graphs of each of the following:

    a output from an ac generator

    b output from a battery.

5 Calculate the frequency of an ac supply whose period is 16.7 ms.

6 Calculate the current in a discharge of 8.0×10^3 C that occurs during a time of 4.0 ms.

28 Electrical quantities

Table 28.1 *Common electrical quantities*

Quantity	Common symbol	SI unit	
power	P	watt	W
energy	E	joule	J
voltage	V	volt	V
current	I	ampere	A
charge	Q	coulomb	C
time	t	second	s

Electromotive force and potential difference in a circuit

*The **electromotive force** (**emf**) of a cell is the energy used (or work done) in transferring unit charge around a complete circuit, including through the cell itself.*

$$\text{electromotive force} = \frac{\text{energy}}{\text{charge}}$$

Electrical components offer resistance and therefore energy is needed to drive charges through them.

*The **potential difference** (**pd**) between two points in a circuit is the energy used (or work done) in transferring unit charge between those points.*

$$\text{potential difference} = \frac{\text{energy}}{\text{charge}}$$

Since potential difference and electromotive force are both voltages, we can write in symbols (see Table 28.1) for each:

$$V = \frac{E}{Q} \quad \text{or} \quad E = QV$$

where E is the **electrical potential energy**.

*The **volt**, V, is the SI unit of voltage. 1 V is the potential difference existing between two points when 1 J of energy is required per 1 C of charge transferred between those points.*

Current flows from points of higher potential to points of lower potential through the circuit outside the cell. Chemical reactions of the cell then enable it to return to the higher potential. See Figure 28.1, where X and Y are components in the circuit. A cell of emf 1.5 V raises the potential at one end of the string of components such that it is 1.5 V higher than at the other end of the components. The greater the emf, the higher the potential would be raised, and the greater would be the rate of flow of charge through the components, X and Y. Figure 28.1 shows that:

The emf in a circuit is equal to the sum of pds in the circuit.

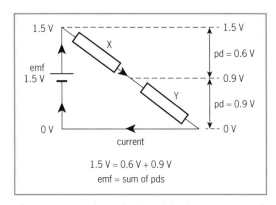

Figure 28.1 *The relationship between emf and pd in a circuit*

Electrical power

*Electrical **power** is the rate of transfer of electrical energy.*

$$\text{power} = \frac{\text{energy}}{\text{time}}$$

$$P = \frac{E}{t}$$

$$P = \frac{VQ}{t} \quad (\text{since } E = VQ)$$

$$P = VI \quad (\text{since } \frac{Q}{t} = I)$$

The unit of power is the **watt**, W, and $1\ \text{W} = 1\ \text{J s}^{-1}$.

Example 1

A current of 4.0 mA flows in a resistor for a time of 48 µs. There is a pd of 4.0 kV between the ends of the resistor. Determine:

a   the charge that passes through the resistor

b   the energy used by the resistor

c   the power used by the resistor.

a $Q = It$

    $Q = 4.0 \times 10^{-3} \times 48 \times 10^{-6} = 1.92 \times 10^{-7}\ \text{C}$

b $E = VQ$

    $E = 4.0 \times 10^3 \times 1.92 \times 10^{-7} = 7.68 \times 10^{-4}\ \text{J}$

c $P = VI$

    $P = 4.0 \times 10^3 \times 4.0 \times 10^{-3} = 16\ \text{W}$

    Alternatively:

    $P = \frac{E}{t}$

    $P = \frac{7.68 \times 10^{-4}}{48 \times 10^{-6}}$

    $P = 16\ \text{W}$

Example 2

4.0×10^{12} electrons flow between two electrodes in a discharge tube in a time of 5.0 ms. (Electron charge $= -1.6 \times 10^{-19}$ C; electron mass $= 9.1 \times 10^{-31}$ kg.) Determine:

a   the total charge that flows

b   the current

c   the energy used if the pd between the electrodes is 2.0 kV

d   the energy transformation occurring as the electrons leave the cathode, accelerate across the tube, and strike the anode

e   the electrical potential energy of a single electron leaving the cathode

f   the maximum kinetic energy acquired by an electron on reaching the anode

g   the maximum speed acquired by a single electron in the tube.

a $Q = Nq$

$Q = 4.0 \times 10^{12} \times -1.6 \times 10^{-19} = -6.4 \times 10^{-7}$ C

b $Q = It$

$$I = \frac{Q}{t}$$

$$I = \frac{6.4 \times 10^{-7}}{5.0 \times 10^{-3}}$$

$I = 1.28 \times 10^{-4}$ A $= 1.3 \times 10^{-4}$ A to 2 sig. fig.

In calculating the size of the current, or energy, the negative sign on the charge is ignored.

c $E = QV$

$E = 6.4 \times 10^{-7} \times 2.0 \times 10^{3}$

$E = 1.28 \times 10^{-3}$ J $= 1.3 \times 10^{-3}$ J to 2 sig. fig.

d electrical potential energy ⟶ kinetic energy ⟶ thermal energy

e For ONE electron:

$E = qV$

$E = 1.6 \times 10^{-19} \times 2.0 \times 10^{3} = 3.2 \times 10^{-16}$ J

f For ONE electron, electrical potential energy transforms to kinetic energy, so maximum kinetic energy $= 3.2 \times 10^{-16}$ J.

g Kinetic energy $E_k = \frac{1}{2}mv^2$, so

$$\frac{2E_k}{m} = v^2$$

$$v = \sqrt{\frac{2(3.2 \times 10^{-16})}{9.1 \times 10^{-31}}}$$

$v = 2.7 \times 10^{7}$ m s^{-1}

Importance of conserving electrical energy

Electricity plays an important role in our everyday lifestyle.

- It can readily be transformed into other types of energy such as heat, light, sound and kinetic.
- It can be transmitted easily over long distances.

Caribbean territories depend heavily on energy from fossil fuels. Due to pollution (including greenhouse gas emissions that lead to global warming – see Chapter 18), limited oil reserves, fluctuating fuel costs and rising health care costs, it is important that we utilise alternative sources of energy and become more **energy efficient**. Alternative sources of energy are discussed in Chapter 8.

Becoming more energy efficient at home

- Install high-efficiency, certified electrical appliances and LED lighting.
- Install photovoltaic (PV) panels to produce electrical energy from solar radiation.
- Install solar water heaters to produce thermal energy from solar radiation.
- Only wash full loads in the washing machine.
- Dry clothes by hanging on lines or racks rather than by using electric dryers.
- Switch off electrical equipment when not in use.
- Save on gasoline by car-pooling and ensuring that the engine is tuned.

- Ensure that your home is designed for efficiency, by having
    a) double glazed windows, especially in rooms that use air conditioning
    b) proper insulation of roofs and ceilings
    c) walls built with hollow blocks (air is a poor thermal conductor)
    d) hoods on windows and curtains to block excessive solar radiation
    e) walls painted white to reflect excessive solar radiation.

Revision questions

1 Define:

   a electromotive force   **b** potential difference

2 20 J of energy transfers 80 mC of charge between two points in a time of 5.0 ms. Calculate:

   a the pd between the points

   b the current

   c the power used

   d the number of charged particles transferred (the charge on each particle is 1.6×10^{-19} C).

3 **a** State TWO reasons why electrical energy is such an important type of energy in our everyday lives.

   b State FOUR ways by which we can be more energy efficient at home.

29 Circuits and components

Figure 29.1 shows the circuit symbols for some common components.

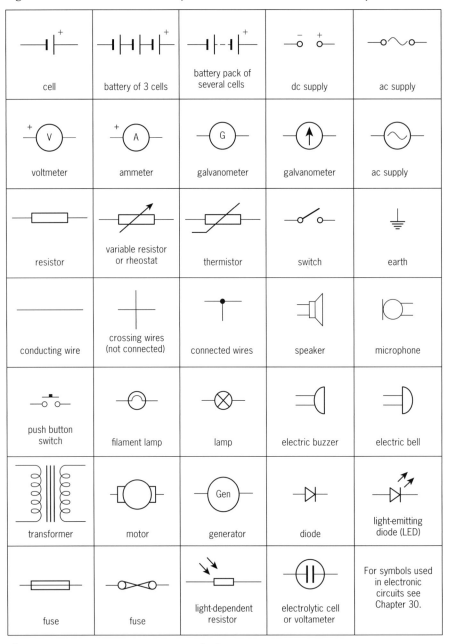

Figure 29.1 *Common circuit symbols*

Some important electrical components

- **Voltmeter**: A device that measures the potential difference between two points
- **Ammeter**: A device that measures the current flowing through a point
- **Galvanometer**: A device that detects, measures, and determines the direction of very small electric currents
- **Resistor**: A component that opposes the flow of current
- **Rheostat**: A variable resistor whose resistance can be altered, usually by means of a slider control

- **Light-dependent resistor** (**LDR**): A resistor whose resistance decreases with increased light intensity
- **Thermistor**: A resistor whose resistance changes with temperature (generally decreases with increased temperature)
- **Diode**: A device that normally allows current to flow through it in one direction only
- **Light-emitting diode** (**LED**): A diode that emits light when a current flows through it in a particular direction
- **Fuse**: A metallic resistance wire placed in series with a device, which protects a circuit from excessive current by becoming hot, melting and disconnecting it
- **Circuit breaker**: An electromagnetic switch which protects a circuit from excessive current by disconnecting it
- **Transformer**: A device that increases (steps up) or decreases (steps down) an alternating voltage

Series and parallel circuits

Figure 29.2(a) shows a **series circuit**. The ammeter A_1 is measuring the current through the diode, lamp and variable resistor. Figure 29.2(b) shows a **parallel circuit**. Ammeter A_2 is measuring the current through the diode only. Part of the current from the cell is passing through the thermistor.

For some components, such as ammeters, voltmeters and diodes, the **polarity** of their terminals must be considered when connecting a circuit. The + terminals are marked in Figure 29.2. The + terminal (or pole) of the battery must always connect with the + marking on the instrument or component.

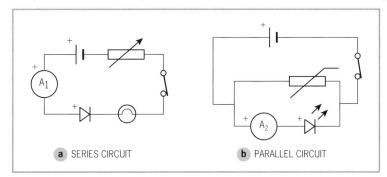

Figure 29.2 *Series and parallel circuits*

Cells

Primary and secondary cells

A **primary cell** is a source that converts chemical energy to electrical energy by a non-reversible chemical reaction.

$$A + B \longrightarrow C + D + \text{electrical energy}$$

A **secondary cell** (also known as an **accumulator** or storage cell) is a source that converts chemical energy to electrical energy, *and* electrical energy to chemical energy, by a *reversible* chemical reaction.

$$A + B \longrightarrow C + D + \text{electrical energy}$$
$$\text{electrical energy} + C + D \longrightarrow A + B$$

To charge a secondary cell, current must flow through it in a direction opposite to that in which it normally delivers current during discharge.

discharging: chemical energy $\longrightarrow$ electrical energy
charging: electrical energy $\longrightarrow$ chemical energy

The zinc-carbon dry cell – a primary cell

Figure 29.3 shows a zinc-carbon dry cell.

- Ammonium chloride (the **electrolyte**) reacts with the zinc, producing electricity.
- The manganese oxide and carbon mixture is used to *prevent polarisation*. Polarisation causes the collection of hydrogen bubbles around the carbon rod, and these bubbles would add to the unwanted *internal resistance* of the cell.

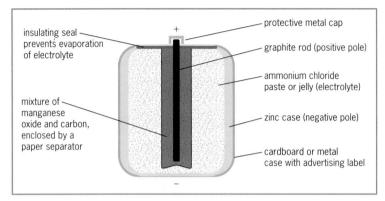

Figure 29.3 *The zinc-carbon dry cell*

The lead-acid accumulator – a secondary cell

This type of cell is **rechargeable** and is capable of delivering higher currents than the zinc-carbon cell. Its structure is not a requirement of the CSEC syllabus.

Advantages of zinc-carbon dry cell over lead-acid accumulator

1. Small and light, whereas the accumulator is large and heavy.

2. Can be inverted without spillage because its electrolyte is in the form of a paste.

3. Batteries of various voltages can easily be made by packing the cells in series or in parallel.

4. Less costly.

Advantages of lead-acid accumulator over zinc-carbon dry cell

1. Can produce much larger currents because the electrolyte is liquid and the electrode plates have large surface areas for reaction.

2. Has a much lower internal resistance.

3. Can be recharged.

Table 29.1 summarises the features of the two types of cell.

Table 29.1 *Comparison of zinc-carbon cell and lead-acid cell*

	Zinc-carbon cell	Lead-acid cell
Rechargeability	not rechargeable	rechargeable
Terminal voltage	1.5 V	2.0 V
Internal resistance	high (0.5 Ω)	low (0.01 Ω)
Maximum current	a few amps (works well up to about 1 A)	> 400 A
Electrolyte	ammonium chloride paste	dilute sulfuric acid
Portability	small and light	large and heavy

Other types of cell

- **Alkaline cells** have potassium hydroxide as their electrolyte. They are not generally rechargeable.
- **Lithium-ion cells** are rechargeable cells used in laptop computers, cell phones and digital cameras.

Charging an accumulator from the ac mains

Figure 29.4 shows how an accumulator can be charged from the ac mains supply.

- The charging current must be *driven into the positive terminal* of the accumulator.
- A *step-down transformer* is used to reduce the voltage (see Chapter 32).
- The *variable resistor* adjusts the pd across the battery to be just above 12 V.
- A *diode* is used to **rectify** the ac to dc (see Chapter 30).

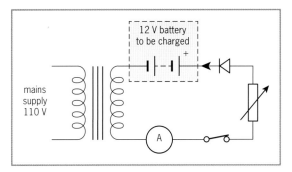

Figure 29.4 *Charging an accumulator*

Amp-hours (A h)

The CHARGE stored in a cell or battery is sometimes stated, usually given in the unit A h.

Since $Q = It$,

1 A h = 1 A (60 × 60) s = 3600 A s = 3600 C

Creating a battery by joining cells

Series connection

If each cell has an emf of 1.5 V,

total emf of battery = 1.5 V + 1.5 V + 1.5 V = 4.5 V

Parallel connection

If each cell has an emf of 1.5 V,

total emf of battery = 1.5 V

The advantage of connecting similar cells in parallel is that they will last longer, because each has to produce only *a portion of the total current output* of the battery.

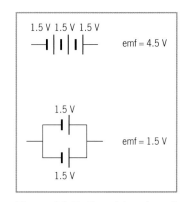

Figure 29.5 *Combined emf of cells in series and in parallel*

A 12 V battery storing a charge of 80 A h is connected to a lamp that uses 6.0 W. Determine:

a the charge stored, in coulombs

b the current

c the maximum time for which the average current calculated in part b can flow.

a $Q = It = 80 \times 60 \times 60 = 288\ 000\ C = 288\ kC$

b $P = VI$

$6.0 = 12I$

$I = \dfrac{6.0}{12}$

$I = 0.5\ A$

c $Q = It$

$288\ 000 = 0.5t$

$t = \dfrac{288\ 000}{0.5}$

$t = 576\ 000\ s$ or $576\ 000 \div (60 \times 60) = 160$ hours

Alternatively, using charge in A h,

$Q = It$

$80 = 0.5t$

$\dfrac{80}{0.5} = t$

$t = 160$ hours

Resistance

Resistance is a measure of the opposition provided to an electrical current; it is the ratio of the pd across a conductor to the current through it.

A **resistor** is a device having resistance.

Explanation of resistance

When electrons flow through a conductor, they are *obstructed by vibrating atoms* in their paths. These atoms therefore decrease the rate of flow of the electrons and hence the current.

Effect of length and cross-sectional area on resistance

The resistance, R, of a conducting wire is proportional to its length, l, and inversely proportional to its cross-sectional area, A:

$$R \propto \frac{l}{A}$$

Adding resistors

In series

$$R = R_1 + R_2 + R_3 \ ....$$

In parallel

$$\frac{1}{R} = \frac{1}{R_1} + \frac{1}{R_2} + \frac{1}{R_3} \ ....$$

In the special case of TWO resistors in parallel:

$$R = \frac{\text{product}}{\text{sum}} \qquad\qquad R = \frac{R_1 \times R_2}{R_1 + R_2}$$

- When resistors are connected in parallel, their total resistance is less than any of the resistors.
- If two identical resistors are placed in parallel, their combined resistance is *half* the value of either of the individual resistors. If each is of resistance 5.0 Ω, then the total resistance is 2.5 Ω.

Example 2

Find the combined resistance of each of the following.

a 3 Ω and 2 Ω in series   **b** 3 Ω and 2 Ω in parallel   **c** 2 Ω, 4 Ω and 8 Ω in parallel

a $R = 3 + 2 = 5\ \Omega$

b $R = \dfrac{3 \times 2}{3 + 2} = \dfrac{6}{5}$

$R = 1.2\ \Omega$

c $\dfrac{1}{R} = \dfrac{1}{2} + \dfrac{1}{4} + \dfrac{1}{8} = \dfrac{7}{8}$

$R = \dfrac{8}{7}\ \Omega$ (invert)

Example 3

Find the combined resistance between X and Y in each arrangement in Figure 29.6.

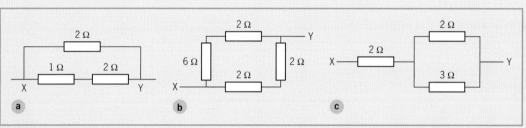

Figure 29.6

a $R = \dfrac{3 \times 2}{3 + 2}$

$R = 1.2\ \Omega$

b $R = \dfrac{8 \times 4}{8 + 4} = \dfrac{32}{12}$

$R = 2\dfrac{2}{3}\ \Omega$ or 2.7 Ω

c $R = 2 + \dfrac{2 \times 3}{2 + 3} = 2 + 1.2$

$R = 3.2\ \Omega$

Ideal ammeters and voltmeters

- **Ammeters** *are connected in series* with a component in order to measure the current *through it*. They must therefore have negligible resistance so as not to affect the very current they are measuring. *An ideal ammeter has zero resistance.*

- **Voltmeters** *are connected in parallel* with a component in order to measure the potential difference *across it*. Current will divert and flow through the voltmeter, leaving a smaller current through the component. The voltmeter should therefore have a very high resistance to keep this diversion to a minimum. *An ideal voltmeter has infinite resistance.*

Ohm's law and *I–V* characteristic curves

Ohm's law

Provided the temperature and other physical conditions remain constant, the current, I, through a conductor is proportional to the pd, V, between its ends.

$$V = IR$$

The equation shows that *V* is proportional to *I*, and the constant of proportionality is *R*, the resistance of the conductor.

I–V relationships

If a material is an **ohmic conductor**, a graph of *I* against *V*, or *V* against *I*, is a *straight line through the origin.*

The relationship between the current, *I*, through a component such as a resistor and the potential difference, *V*, across it, can be investigated using the circuit shown in Figure 29.7(a). The more complex circuit of Figure 29.7(b) may be used by your teacher for investigating filament lamps and diodes. (Lamps and diodes behave differently at low voltages from how they behave at higher voltages and the circuit of Figure 29.7(a) is unable to produce voltages across the component close to zero.)

- An initial pair of readings of *I* and *V* is taken.
- By adjusting the rheostat (variable resistor), other pairs of values of *I* and *V* are obtained.
- The connection between the terminals of the battery and the circuit is then reversed and the process is repeated.
- A graph of *I* against *V* is plotted.

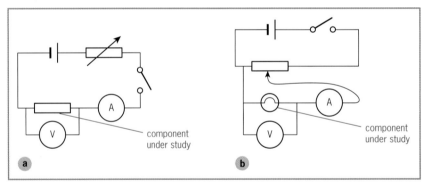

Figure 29.7 *Investigating I–V relationships*

Graphs of *I* against *V*, called '*I–V* characteristics' are shown in Figure 29.8 for a metallic conductor, a filament lamp, a semiconductor diode, and an aqueous solution of copper sulfate with copper electrodes.

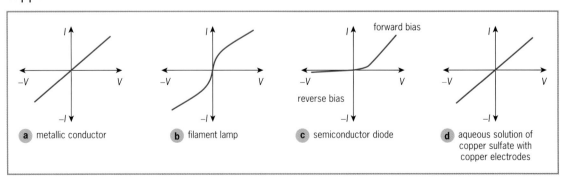

Figure 29.8 *I–V characteristics for different components*

- Figure 29.8(a) and (d): For conductors that obey Ohm's law, the gradient of an *I–V* graph is the inverse of the resistance. (The gradient of a *V–I* graph is the resistance.)
- Figure 29.8(b): As the voltage is increased across the lamp, the electrons are pulled with greater force and collide more vigorously with the cations of the metallic filament. Their kinetic energy transforms into thermal energy, causing the vibration of the cations to increase. The increased vibration blocks the path of the electrons to a greater extent than previously and the resistance rises.
- Figure 29.8(c): When the diode is **forward biased** (its polarity such that it conducts), a small initial voltage is needed before a current flows. When it is **reverse biased**, conduction is almost zero.

Current and voltage in complete circuits

The following rules apply.

Current

1. Series circuit (Figure 29.9(a)): The current is the same at all points in the circuit.

2. Parallel circuit (Figure 29.9(b)): The sum of the currents in the branches is equal to the total current outside the branch.

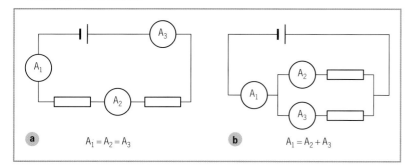

Figure 29.9 *Current in series and parallel circuits*

Voltage (potential difference)

3. Series circuit (Figure 29.10(a)): The sum of the potential differences across the individual resistors is equal to the total potential difference across the group.

4. Parallel circuit (Figure 29.10(b)): The potential difference across each resistor is the same, and this is equal to the potential difference across the group.

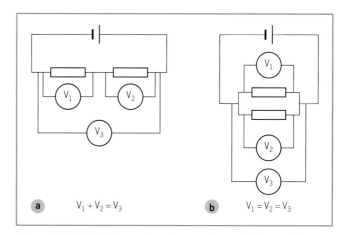

Figure 29.10 *Voltage in series and parallel circuits*

Calculations on complete circuits

- When using formulae, V, I and R must pertain to the *same component* or *group of components*. Subscripts may be used to identify the components. In the Examples that follow, if no subscript is used, V, I and R pertain to *totals*.

- emf = sum of pds in the circuit

- A double-ended arrow (see the following Examples) should be placed across ALL the resistors as a reminder of the components that can be used in a formula involving the emf or total pd.

Example 4

Determine for the circuit in Figure 29.11:

a the current from the battery

b the pd across A

c the pd across B

d the pd between X and Y.

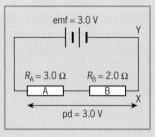

Figure 29.11

a $V = IR$

$3.0 = I(3.0 + 2.0)$

$3.0 = 5.0I$

$\dfrac{3.0}{5.0} = I$

$I = 0.60\ \text{A}$

b $V_A = I_A R_A$

$V_A = 0.60 \times 3.0 = 1.8\ \text{V}$

c $V_B = I_B R_B$

$V_B = 0.60 \times 2.0 = 1.2\ \text{V}$

d $V_{XY} = I_{XY} R_{XY}$

$V_{XY} = 0.60 \times 0 = 0\ \text{V}$

Example 5

Determine for the circuit in Figure 29.12:

a the total resistance

b the current from the battery

c the pd between X and Y

d the pd across A

e the pd across B

f the current in A

g the current in B.

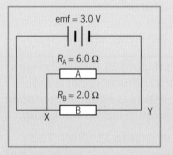

Figure 29.12

a $R = \dfrac{\text{product}}{\text{sum}}$

$R = \dfrac{6.0 \times 2.0}{6.0 + 2.0}$

$R = \dfrac{12.0}{8.0} = 1.5\ \Omega$

b $V = IR$

$3.0 = I \times 1.5$

$\dfrac{3.0}{1.5} = I$

$I = 2.0\ \text{A}$

c $V_{XY} = 3.0\ \text{V}$ (emf = total pd)

d $V_A = 3.0$ V (see rule 4 for pd in parallel circuits)

e $V_B = 3.0$ V (see rule 4 for pd in parallel circuits)

f $V_A = I_A R_A$

$3.0 = I_A \times 6.0$

$3.0 = 6.0 I_A$

$\dfrac{3.0}{6.0} = I_A$

$I_A = 0.50$ A

g $V_B = I_B R_B$

$3.0 = I_B \times 2.0$

$\dfrac{3.0}{2.0} = I_B$

$I_B = 1.5$ A

Alternatively:

$I = I_A + I_B$

$2.0 = 0.50 + I_B$

$I_B = 1.5$ A

Example 6

Calculate the current in resistor B of Figure 29.13.

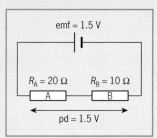

emf = 1.5 V

$R_A = 20\ \Omega$ $R_B = 10\ \Omega$

A   B

pd = 1.5 V

Figure 29.13

Note that the 1.5 V *cannot* be used with the 10 Ω, because 1.5 V is the total voltage but 10 Ω is not the total resistance. Using 1.5 V with the *total resistance* of 30 Ω will give the total current. Since this is a series circuit, *the current is the same everywhere*, $I = I_A = I_B$.

$V = IR$

$1.5 = I(20 + 10)$

$1.5 = I \times 30$

$\dfrac{1.5}{30} = I$

$I_B = I = 0.05$ A

Example 7

Determine for the circuit in Figure 29.14:

a the total resistance

b the current from the battery

c the pd between X and Y

d the pd between Y and Z

e the pd across A

f the pd across B

g the pd across C

h the current in A

i the current in B

j the current in C.

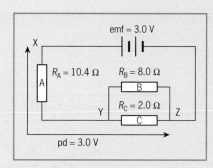

X

emf = 3.0 V

$R_A = 10.4\ \Omega$ $R_B = 8.0\ \Omega$

A   B

Y $R_C = 2.0\ \Omega$ Z

C

pd = 3.0 V

Figure 29.14

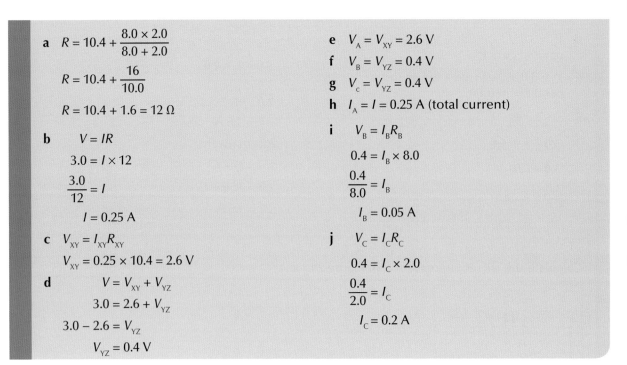

a $R = 10.4 + \dfrac{8.0 \times 2.0}{8.0 + 2.0}$

$\quad R = 10.4 + \dfrac{16}{10.0}$

$\quad R = 10.4 + 1.6 = 12\ \Omega$

b $\quad V = IR$

$\quad 3.0 = I \times 12$

$\quad \dfrac{3.0}{12} = I$

$\quad I = 0.25\ \text{A}$

c $V_{XY} = I_{XY}R_{XY}$

$\quad V_{XY} = 0.25 \times 10.4 = 2.6\ \text{V}$

d $\quad V = V_{XY} + V_{YZ}$

$\quad 3.0 = 2.6 + V_{YZ}$

$\quad 3.0 - 2.6 = V_{YZ}$

$\quad V_{YZ} = 0.4\ \text{V}$

e $V_A = V_{XY} = 2.6\ \text{V}$

f $V_B = V_{YZ} = 0.4\ \text{V}$

g $V_C = V_{YZ} = 0.4\ \text{V}$

h $I_A = I = 0.25\ \text{A}$ (total current)

i $\quad V_B = I_B R_B$

$\quad 0.4 = I_B \times 8.0$

$\quad \dfrac{0.4}{8.0} = I_B$

$\quad I_B = 0.05\ \text{A}$

j $\quad V_C = I_C R_C$

$\quad 0.4 = I_C \times 2.0$

$\quad \dfrac{0.4}{2.0} = I_C$

$\quad I_C = 0.2\ \text{A}$

Energy and power in complete circuits

Table 29.2 shows the equations used to calculate these quantities.

Table 29.2 *Energy and power in complete circuits*

Power = $\dfrac{\text{energy}}{\text{time}}$	Energy = power × time
$P = VI$	$E = VIt$
$P = I^2R$	$E = I^2Rt$
$P = \dfrac{V^2}{R}$	$E = \dfrac{V^2t}{R}$

Example 8

Determine for the circuit in Figure 29.15:

a the power used by resistor A

b the energy used by resistor B in 5 minutes

c the power delivered by the battery.

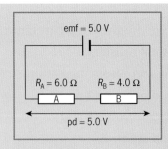

Figure 29.15

a Note that the 5.0 V is not the pd across A and therefore cannot be used with the resistance of A.

$$V = IR$$

$$5.0 = I \times (6.0 + 4.0)$$

$$\frac{5.0}{10.0} = I$$

$$I = 0.50 \text{ A}$$

$$P_A = (I_A)^2 R_A$$

$$P_A = 0.50^2 \times 6.0 = 1.5 \text{ W}$$

b $E_B = I_B^2 R_B t$

$$E_B = 0.50^2 \times 4.0 \times (5 \times 60) = 300 \text{ J}$$

c $P = VI$

$$P = 5.0 \times 0.50 = 2.5 \text{ W}$$

Determine for the circuit in Figure 29.16:

a the pd across A

b the current in B

c the power used by A

d the power used by B

e the total power used by both resistors

f the power delivered by the battery

g the energy used by B in 3.0 minutes

h the energy delivered by battery in 10 minutes.

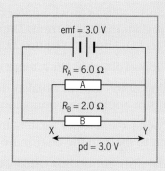

Figure 29.16

a $V_A = 3.0 \text{ V}$

b $V_B = I_B R_B$

$$3.0 = I_B \times 2.0$$

$$\frac{3.0}{2.0} = I_B$$

$$I_B = 1.5 \text{ A}$$

c $P_A = \frac{V_A^2}{R_A}$

$$P_A = \frac{3.0^2}{6.0} = 1.5 \text{ W}$$

d $P_B = \frac{V_B^2}{R_B}$

$$P_B = \frac{3.0^2}{2.0} = 4.5 \text{ W}$$

e $P = 1.5 \text{ W} + 4.5 \text{ W} = 6.0 \text{ W}$

f Power delivered by battery = power used by resistors = 6.0 W

g $E_B = \frac{V_B^2 t}{R_B}$

$$E_B = \frac{3.0^2 (3 \times 60)}{2.0} = 810 \text{ J}$$

h $P = \frac{E}{t} \quad \therefore E = Pt$

$$E = 6.0 \times (10 \times 60) = 3600 \text{ J}$$

Electricity in the home

Advantages of parallel connection of domestic appliances

- Appliances can be switched on and off without affecting each other. If, instead, they were connected in series, switching off one would switch off all.

- Appliances can be designed to operate on a single voltage. This voltage is about 115 V in Barbados and Trinidad. If appliances were connected in series, they would have to share the 115 V and would each have a smaller pd across their terminals.

Fuses

A **fuse** is a short piece of thin wire which is placed in a circuit in series with one or more devices. When too high a current flows, it melts and breaks the circuit, preventing damage to the devices. An appropriate fuse should melt at a current slightly greater than that which the circuit takes under normal operation. This value is known as the **current rating**, in A, of the fuse. See also 'Fuses in plugs or appliances' below.

Thickness of wires

High-powered electrical appliances, such as water heaters, fridges, cookers and washing machines, should use thick wires because they need high currents – the currents they draw are proportional to the power they consume.

Distribution box

- A LIVE and a NEUTRAL wire enter the distribution box from the electrical power company, delivering alternating current. There is a fuse or circuit breaker in each live wire. The international colour code is shown in Figure 29.17, together with a distribution box.
- If the supply voltage is 115 V, there is a pd of 115 V between each live and neutral wire leaving the box.
- The rating of the fuse or breaker depends on the *total possible current* that should flow when all the lights or appliances connected to it are being used.
- Since cookers and water heaters usually take large currents they have a fuse or breaker specially assigned to them in the distribution box.
- An actual distribution box usually has many more wires exiting. A separate fuse or circuit breaker may be connected to the supply for each room in the building.

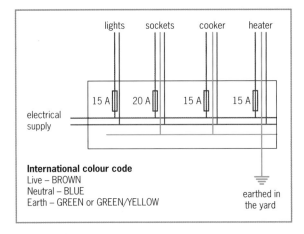

Figure 29.17 *Distribution box and colour code for wiring*

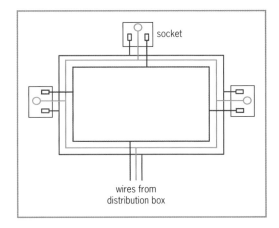

Figure 29.18 *Ring-mains circuit with sockets*

Ring-mains circuit (socket circuit)

This is illustrated in Figure 29.18.

- The circuit uses thick wires because they carry current to several sockets.
- If the supply voltage is 115 V, each socket will provide a pd of 115 V because they are all in parallel.
- If the socket is viewed with the EARTH at the top and centred, then the LIVE is on the right.

Function of the earth wire

A **short circuit** can occur if a piece of metal bridges the gap between a circuit and the metal case of a device. If there is no earth wire and the case is touched, current may pass from it through the person to the ground. Since some of the resistance is now bypassed, the current is larger than before, so the person will *receive an electrical shock* and the fuse will blow.

Figure 29.19 shows an electric toaster resting on insulating supports. To avoid electrical shock, an **earth wire** is connected between the case of the toaster and the ground in the yard (see Figure 29.17). Under normal conditions (Figure 29.19(a)) current flows in the *live* and *neutral* wires only. If there is a short circuit inside the toaster and some of the resistance is bypassed, a large current will flow via the *live* and *earth* wires (Figure 29.19(b)), and the fuse (or breaker) will blow (or trip).

- No current flows in the earth wire unless a malfunction occurs.
- When current flows in the earth wire, the neutral wire is bypassed.
- The short circuit should be fixed before the fuse is replaced (or the breaker reset).

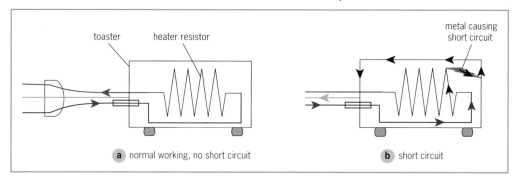

Figure 29.19 *The function of the earth wire*

Placement of fuses, breakers and switches in the live wire

- Fuses 'blow' or breakers 'trip' when there is

  a) a short circuit in the appliance so that current flows in the live and earth wires, or

  b) a power surge for reasons external to the appliance so that excess current flows in the live and neutral wires.

  By placing fuses or breakers in the *live* wire, the appliance is protected for both situations.

- Switches should also always be placed in the live wire. If a switch in the 'off' position is in the neutral wire connected to a lamp, of course no current can flow. If, however, an attempt is made to change the lamp and the live terminal is touched, the person can receive an electric shock. By placing the switch in the *live* wire, once it is in the 'off' position, no current can reach any of the terminals of the appliance.

Fuses in plugs or appliances

A fuse in the plug of the appliance or in the appliance itself can offer better protection than the fuse in the distribution box. Its rating should only be *slightly higher* than the current normally taken by the appliance. Say the device requires 2.5 A for normal operation, a fuse with a rating of 3 A will be more suitable than the larger fuse in the distribution box, which will not blow unless the current rises to a much higher value.

Adverse effects of connecting electrical appliances to an incorrect or fluctuating supply

- Appliances are normally designed to operate on ac frequencies of either 50 Hz or 60 Hz. If operated on an incorrect frequency they are likely to malfunction or even be damaged.
- If an appliance is supplied with a voltage higher than it is designed for, overheating due to excessive current may result in it being destroyed.
- If a motor is supplied with a voltage that is too low, the current in its coils will rise (due to reasons beyond the scope of this syllabus) and the device can be damaged due to overheating.

Revision questions

1 Sketch a circuit diagram containing a switch, a battery of two cells in series, and a LDR in series with two lamps which are in parallel. Insert a voltmeter to measure the pd across the LDR, and an ammeter to measure the current through one of the lamps.

2 **a** What is the difference between a primary cell and a secondary cell?

b Draw a diagram of a zinc-carbon dry cell.

c How are hydrogen bubbles prevented from accumulating around the anode of a zinc-carbon dry cell?

d List THREE advantages and THREE disadvantages of the zinc-carbon dry cell relative to a lead-acid accumulator.

e Construct a table showing the differences between a zinc-carbon dry cell and a lead-acid accumulator with respect to the following:

   i terminal voltage   **ii** maximum current   **iii** internal resistance   **iv** portability

   v rechargeability   **vi** electrolyte

3 Draw a circuit diagram illustrating how a 12 V accumulator may be charged by a 120 V ac supply.

4 A battery storing a charge of 60 A h discharges completely with an average current of 5.0 A.

a How much charge in coulombs is stored before discharge?

b How long does the discharge take?

5 **a** Define *resistance*.

b How does the length and cross-sectional area of a resistor affect its resistance?

c Determine the total resistance of each of the following arrangements:

   i two 8 Ω resistors in series   **iii** four 2 Ω resistors in parallel.

   ii two 8 Ω resistors in parallel

6 **a** Sketch graphs of current against voltage for each of the following:

   i a metallic resistor at constant temperature

   ii a filament lamp   **iii** a semiconductor diode.

b State which of the components in part a are *ohmic* conductors.

c State how the resistance of the filament lamp changes with increasing voltage, and give an explanation of the change in terms of the kinetic theory.

7 Two 10 Ω bulbs connected in parallel are joined in series to a 5.0 Ω resistor. A 5.0 V battery is connected across the arrangement. Draw a diagram of the circuit and determine the following:

a the total resistance   **d** the pd across the parallel section

b the current from the battery   **e** the power used by the 5.0 Ω resistor

c the pd across the 5.0 Ω resistor   **f** the power used by each bulb.

8 **a** State TWO reasons for using parallel connection of domestic appliances.

b What is the purpose of a fuse or circuit breaker?

c In which wire from an ac supply should a fuse always be placed?

d In which wire from an ac supply should a switch always be placed?

e Describe and explain the function of an earth wire in a domestically wired system.

f Describe the adverse effects of connecting electrical appliances to incorrect or fluctuating voltages.

30 Electronics

Rectification

Rectification is the process of converting alternating current (ac) to direct current (dc).

Half-wave rectification is the process of converting ac to dc by preventing one half of each cycle from being applied to the load.

An **oscilloscope** is an instrument that produces graphs of voltage against time, allowing the observation and measurement of varying electrical signals (Figure 30.1).

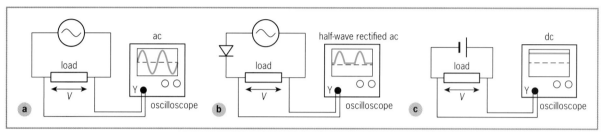

Figure 30.1 *Displaying voltages using an oscilloscope*

- In Figure 30.1(a) an alternating voltage is applied to a load.
- In Figure 30.1(b) a diode is placed in the circuit. The diode allows current to flow through it in only one direction. In the half of the cycle when there is no current in the load resistor, there can be no potential difference across it ($V = IR$).
- Note how ac rectified to dc by a diode differs from the dc of a battery shown in Figure 30.1(c).

Logic gates

Digital electronics is based on circuits that can exist in one of two possible states. The two possible states can be represented by the numbers (digits) 1 and 0. Electronic systems represent these two **logic states** as a 'high' and a 'low' voltage, respectively, by the use of electronic pulses.

Since there are only two states, 1 and 0, the circuits function on **binary** decision making. An example of a *decision making* situation could be an **AND** decision. Imagine that your mother says you will be rewarded if you are polite AND helpful; we specify that

      polite / helpful / rewarded are each represented by 1

      impolite / unhelpful / not rewarded are each represented by 0

The possible outcomes are shown in a **truth table** (Table 30.1).

Table 30.1 *Truth table for AND decision*

input		output
polite	helpful	rewarded
0	0	0
0	1	0
1	0	0
1	1	1

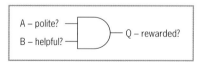

Figure 30.2 *AND gate*

*A **logic gate** is an idealised or physical electronic device that processes one or more input states (low or high, logic states 0 or 1) to produce a single output state (low or high, logic states 0 or 1).*

Figure 30.2 summarises the AND decision making, using the symbol for an **AND gate** – a logic gate used in electronic circuitry for carrying out an AND decision. It has two inputs (A and B) and a single output (Q).

Table 30.2 shows a range of different logic gates and their corresponding truth tables. The inputs to the gates are on the left of the symbol, and the output at the right.

Table 30.2 *Logic gates and their truth tables*

Gate	AND		NAND		OR		NOR		NOT	
Circuit symbol										
	input	**output**	**input**	**output**	**input**	**output**	**input**	**output**	**input**	**output**
Truth table	0 0	0	0 0	1	0 0	0	0 0	1	0	1
	0 1	0	0 1	1	0 1	1	0 1	0	1	0
	1 0	0	1 0	1	1 0	1	1 0	0	This gate simply switches the logic state	
	1 1	1	1 1	0	1 1	1	1 1	0		

Note that:

AND: TWO 1s produce a 1; OTHERWISE, the output is 0

NAND: TWO 1s produce a 0; OTHERWISE, the output is 1

OR: ANY 1s produce a 1; OTHERWISE, the output is 0

NOR: ANY 1s produce a 0; OTHERWISE, the output is 1

NOT: 1 produces a 0; 0 produces a 1

Constructing truth tables for a combination of gates

The following Example shows the construction of a truth table for a combination of logic gates. The number of inputs determines the number of possible combinations of input states to the circuit.

For example:

TWO inputs $\longrightarrow 2^2 = 4$ different combinations (4 rows in truth table)

THREE inputs $\longrightarrow 2^3 = 8$ different combinations (8 rows in truth table, as in the following Example)

An easy way to set up the input part of the table is shown in Table 30.3.

• The least significant input column (P in this case) has its values alternating 0, 1, 0, 1, 0, 1, 0, 1.

• The column immediately preceding it (F) has its values changing 0, 0, 1, 1, 0, 0, 1, 1.

• The third column (T) has its values changing 0, 0, 0, 0, 1, 1, 1, 1.

The output from each gate is determined by considering its inputs together with the rule for that gate.

An alarm (A) is to sound (logic 1) if the temperature (T) in a piece of machinery rises above 500 °C (logic 1) while its pistons are oscillating with a frequency (F) greater than 20 Hz (logic 1). It is also to sound if the oil pressure (P) is low (logic 1). Draw a truth table and a suitable circuit.

The combination of gates will have inputs T, F and P, and output A.

The requirement is that if (T = 1 AND F = 1) OR P = 1 then A = 1

This can be written as:

$$(T \text{ AND } F) \text{ OR } P = A$$

Table 30.3 shows all combinations of inputs and the resulting outputs. The X column holds the value of the output of the AND gate which then acts, together with P, as the input to the OR gate.

The logic circuit is shown in Figure 30.3.

Table 30.3

inputs				output
T	F	P	X	A
0	0	0	0	0
0	0	1	0	1
0	1	0	0	0
0	1	1	0	1
1	0	0	0	0
1	0	1	0	1
1	1	0	1	1
1	1	1	1	1

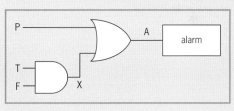

Figure 30.3

Impact of electronic and technological advances in society

Pros

- Businesses get a competitive edge when they use advanced technologies.
- The global pooling of information increases the rate of research and development.
- Improved transport through airplanes and trains, as well as better communicating devices such as cell phones and computers, has led to more efficient business transactions and to an increase in social contact.
- Better machinery leads to increased and improved productivity.
- Electronic banking has facilitated the process of financial transactions.

Cons

- Incorrect information is common on the internet.
- Individuals can be addicted to social networking to such an extent that their productivity decreases.
- Excessive virtual communication may lead to lack of real communication and to a fall in social skills.
- Exposure to movies with immoral sexual content and violence can eventually lead to some persons accepting these acts as the norm.
- Hackers can intrude on computers and manipulate information such as bank accounts.
- More efficient machinery can result in a decrease in available jobs.

Revision questions

1 **a** What is meant by *half-wave rectification*?

  b Describe how ac can be converted to dc using half-wave rectification.

  c Sketch graphs to show how each of the following vary with time:

  i   domestic supply ac voltage

  ii domestic supply ac voltage converted to dc by a diode

  iii voltage output from a battery.

2 Draw the truth table for each of the following logic gates.

  a AND   **b** OR   **c** NAND   **d** NOT

3 A warning light is to glow on a motor cycle if the key is placed in the ignition (logic 1) while either the tyre pressure is below 80 PSI (logic 1) or the oil level is low (logic 1). The warning light glows when logic 1 is input to it. Draw a truth table and a circuit appropriate to this application.

4 Discuss the pros and cons of the impact of electronic and technological advances on society today.

31 Magnetism

Magnetic materials are those which are attracted or repelled by magnets. Examples are iron, nickel and cobalt, and some materials containing these elements, such as steel and magnadur.

A bar of magnetic material is comprised of tiny atomic magnetic **dipoles** (atoms that behave as magnets, having a north pole and a south pole). If the bar is *unmagnetised*, these dipoles are arranged in such a way that their associated magnetic fields are not experienced outside the material. In the presence of a strong magnetic field, however, the dipoles align with it, and the bar becomes magnetised with a north pole (N) and a south pole (S).

Forces between magnetic poles

- *Similar magnetic poles repel* and *unlike magnetic poles attract.*
- The force between magnets diminishes rapidly with increased separation of the magnets.

Magnetic induction

Magnetic induction is the process by which magnetic properties are transferred from one body to another without physical contact.

Figure 31.1 shows the arrangement of atomic dipoles as a bar magnet is placed onto the door of a fridge (N poles represented by arrow heads). The dipoles of the fridge door are initially disarranged, but when a pole of the magnet is brought near, it attracts opposite poles. The *induced* S pole created on the fridge then attracts the N pole of the magnet.

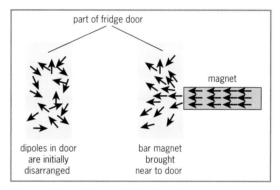

Figure 31.1 *Magnetic induction*

Testing for polarity

A magnet is freely suspended by means of a string (Figure 31.2). One end of the body (X) under test is brought close to one of the known poles of the magnet.

If there is attraction, X may be either of the following:

a) a previously unmagnetised piece of magnetic material whose nearby end has been magnetised by induction, with opposite polarity to the inducing pole

b) a magnet whose nearby pole is of opposite polarity to that of the suspended magnetic pole attracting it.

If there is repulsion, X must be a magnet whose nearby pole is of similar polarity to that of the suspended magnetic pole repelling it.

The only true test for the polarity of a magnet is REPULSION.

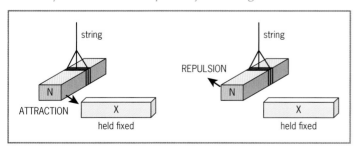

Figure 31.2 *Testing for polarity*

Permanent and temporary magnets

Steel forms **permanent magnets** ('hard magnets'). Other permanent magnetic materials are magnadur, alnico, ticonal and alcomax. Permanent magnets are used in directional compasses and in loudspeakers.

Iron forms **temporary magnets** ('soft magnets'). Other temporary magnetic materials are mumetal and stalloy. Temporary magnetic materials are used in **electromagnets** (see Chapter 32), which are used for lifting metal objects and are also important components in electric bells, magnetic relays and electromagnetic circuit breakers.

Magnetic fields

*A **magnetic field** is the region in which a body experiences a force due to its magnetic polarity.*

The *direction of a magnetic field* is the direction of motion of a *free N pole* placed in the field.

Magnetic fields lines

A magnetic field is a **vector** quantity and can be represented by lines labelled with arrows to indicate its direction. Important features of magnetic field lines are:

- They *never cross or touch*.
- There is a *longitudinal tension* within each line, causing it to behave as a stretched elastic band.
- There is a *lateral repulsion* between lines that are close 'side by side'.
- The field is *uniform* where the lines are parallel, in the same direction, and evenly spaced.
- The field is stronger where the lines are more concentrated.
- They are directed *from a N pole to a S pole*.

Forces between bar magnets explained in terms of magnetic field lines

Forces of attraction exist between dissimilar poles due to the longitudinal tension within the field lines joining them (Figure 31.3).

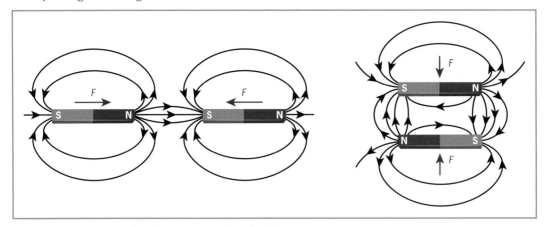

Figure 31.3 *Longitudinal tension within field lines*

Forces of repulsion exist between similar poles due to the lateral push between the field lines passing close to each other (Figure 31.4).

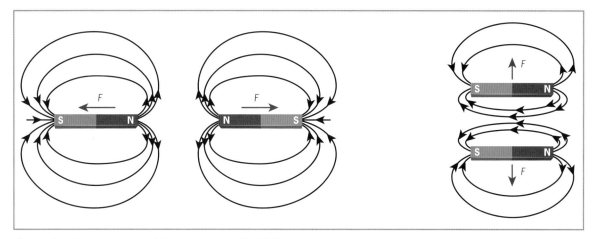

Figure 31.4 *Lateral repulsion between field lines*

Mapping the magnetic field of a bar magnet using a plotting compass

The magnet is placed at the centre of a large sheet of paper and its perimeter is outlined. The ends of the magnet are marked and a plotting compass is positioned near to the N pole. The positions of the head and tail of its magnetised needle are marked by dots on the paper, as shown in Figure 31.5. The compass is advanced such that its tail now lies over the dot where the head was previously, and the new position of the head is marked. This is continued until the dots reach the other end of the magnet or extend off the paper. The dots are joined by a *smooth* line with an *arrow* to indicate the direction of the field. The process is repeated to produce several other field lines.

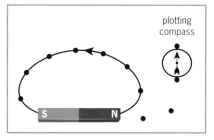

Figure 31.5 *Plotting the magnetic field of a bar magnet*

Mapping the magnetic field of a bar magnet using iron filings

The magnet is stuck to the work bench by a piece of tape and a sheet of card is placed over it. Iron filings are sprinkled onto the card. When the card is tapped gently, the filings indicate the pattern of the magnetic field, as shown in Figure 31.6.

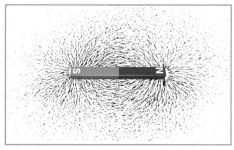

Figure 31.6 *Magnetic field shown by iron filings*

A uniform magnetic field

A uniform magnetic field exists in the central region between plane, facing magnetic poles, as shown in Figure 31.7. The field lines there are evenly spaced and parallel. Near the edges of the poles, the field lines curve due to lateral repulsion from lines closer to the centre.

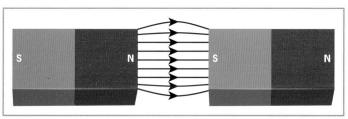

Figure 31.7 *Uniform magnetic field*

The Earth's magnetic field

The core of the Earth contains iron and nickel and therefore behaves as a magnet. A directional compass will point along the magnetic field lines towards the north pole of the Earth, which is towards the S pole of the magnet within the core (Figure 31.8).

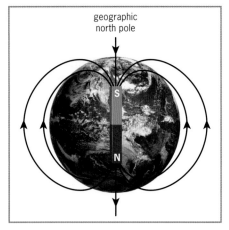

Figure 31.8 *The Earth's magnetic field*

Identifying the poles of a magnet using the Earth's magnetic field

If a magnet is hung from a string it will align itself with the Earth's magnetic field, as shown in Figure 31.9. It behaves as a compass, with its N pole facing north.

In the northern hemisphere, the N pole *declines* (points down) towards the Earth; in the southern hemisphere, the N pole *inclines* (points up) away from the Earth. You can see that this is following the direction of the field lines in Figure 31.8.

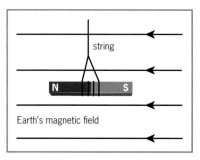

Figure 31.9 *Identifying the poles of a magnet using the Earth's magnetic field*

Revision questions

1   State how a magnetic material may be identified.

2   When the pole of a magnet is placed next to a body X, there is attraction. What does this indicate about the nature of X?

3   When the pole of a magnet is placed next to a body Y, there is repulsion. What does this indicate about the nature of Y?

4   State TWO temporary magnetic materials and TWO permanent magnetic materials.

5   Define:

   a a magnetic field   **b** the direction of a magnetic field

6   Draw magnetic field diagrams to show two bar magnets:

   a attracting each other   **b** repelling each other

7   Draw an arrangement that may be used to set up a uniform magnetic field. Your diagram should include magnetic field lines.

8   Describe how the poles of a bar magnet may be identified using the Earth's magnetic field.

32 Electromagnetism

Magnetic fields and electric currents

Electric currents create magnetic fields. The patterns of these fields may be investigated by sprinkling iron filings in the region around the conductors, as in the experiments outlined in Figure 32.1.

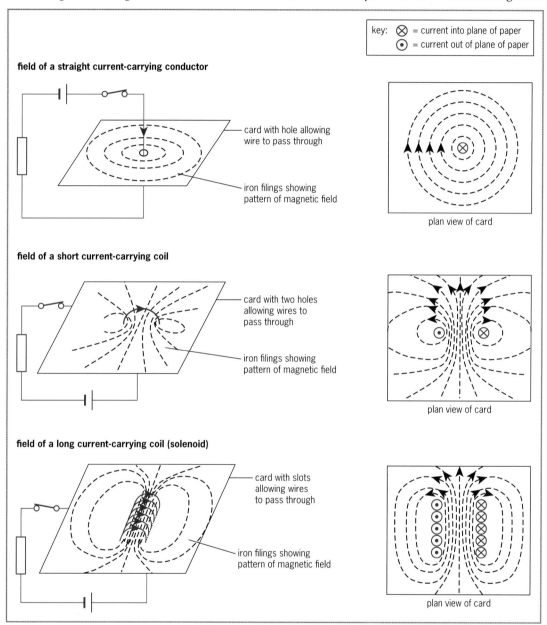

Figure 32.1 *Magnetic fields produced by electric currents*

Note the following:

- The magnetic field associated with the current in a solenoid is identical to that of a bar magnet.
- Magnetic field lines are directed out of the north pole and into the south pole of a current-carrying coil.
- The direction of the field can be obtained by using the **right-hand grip rule** described next.

Right-hand grip rule

1. For a straight conductor: Imagine gripping the wire with the right hand such that the *thumb* is in the *direction of the current*; the fingers will then be in the direction of the magnetic field.

2. For a coil: Imagine gripping the coil with the *fingers* of the right hand in the *direction of the current*; the thumb will then indicate the direction of the magnetic field (the end of the coil which acts as a north pole).

Applying the right-hand grip rule to each of the experiments in Figure 32.1 results in the field directions shown in the plan views.

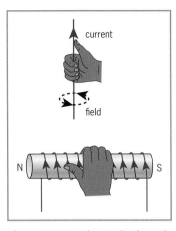

Figure 32.2 *The right-hand grip rule*

Magnetic fields of two parallel wires carrying current

The forces on the wires produced by the interacting magnetic fields are equal, in accordance with **Newton's 3rd law** (see Chapter 7).

- In Figure 32.3(a) the forces (*F*) of *attraction* are due to the *longitudinal tension* within the field lines.
- In Figure 32.3(b) the forces (*F*) of *repulsion* are due to the *lateral push between* the field lines.

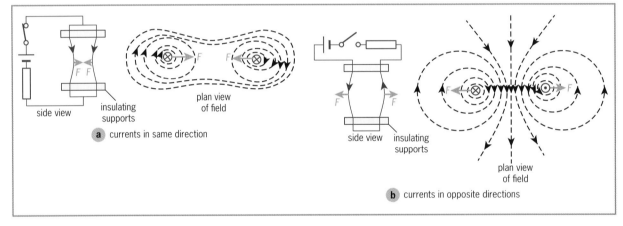

Figure 32.3 *Magnetic fields associated with parallel wires carrying currents*

Electromagnets

An electromagnet is an electrical coil wound on a soft-iron core (Figure 32.4). The core significantly increases the strength of the magnetic field when the current flows.

Electromagnetic relay

One application of an electromagnet is an electromagnetic **relay**. Figure 32.5 shows one type. When switch S_1 is closed the current in the coil creates a magnetic field which magnetises the two soft-iron 'reeds'. The adjacent ends of the reeds become opposite magnetic poles and attract each other, completing the circuit connected to terminals, T_1 and T_2. The reeds are protected from the environment by the inert gas in the glass enclosure.

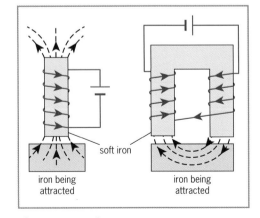

Figure 32.4 *Electromagnets*

Figure 32.6 shows another type of relay. When S_1 is closed, the current in the coil magnetises the electromagnet, causing it to attract the soft-iron armature. The armature then rocks on its pivot and closes the graphite contacts, completing the circuit connected to terminals T_1 and T_2.

These can be connected to a vehicle starter motor. When the ignition key, S_1, is turned on, the *low-current* circuit of the solenoid switches on the *high-current* circuit to the starter motor. Note that the wires in the high-current circuit must be thick.

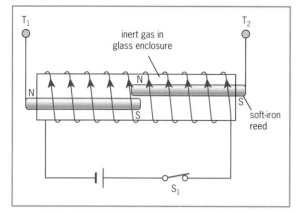

Figure 32.5 *Electromagnetic relay*

Figure 32.6 *Another type of electromagnetic relay*

Force on a current-carrying conductor in a magnetic field

Figure 32.7 shows a stiff wire hanging from a metal loop and immersed in a magnetic field. The lower end of the wire just touches the surface of mercury contained in a dish below. A force acts on the wire in accordance with **Fleming's left-hand rule** (described below), which pushes it out of the mercury and breaks the circuit. The current then diminishes to zero, the wire falls back into the mercury, and the process repeats.

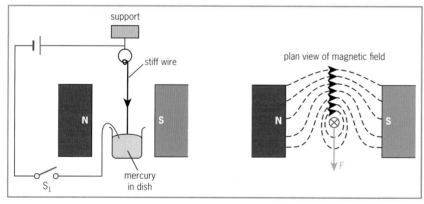

Figure 32.7 *Demonstrating the force on a current-carrying conductor in a magnetic field*

Fleming's left-hand rule

If the first finger, the second finger and the thumb of the left-hand are placed mutually at right angles to each other (Figure 32.8), with the **F**irst finger in the direction of the magnetic **F**ield and the se**C**ond in the direction of the **C**urrent, then the **Thu**M**b** will be in the direction of the **Th**rust or **M**otion.

The strength of the thrust (force)

The force is proportional to:

a) the magnitude of the current

b) the strength of the magnetic field.

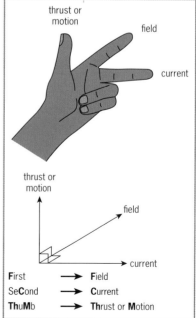

First	→	Field
SeCond	→	Current
ThuMb	→	Thrust or Motion

Figure 32.8 *Fleming's left-hand rule*

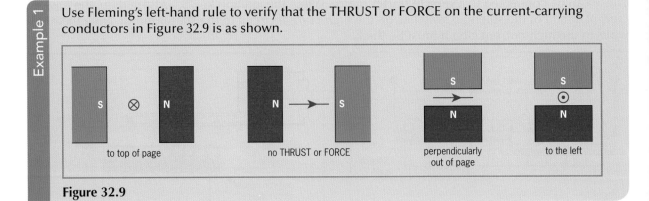

Figure 32.9

Deflection of charged particles entering a magnetic field

Moving charged particles that enter a magnetic field which is at right angles to their motion travel in a circular path (Figure 32.10), in accordance with Fleming's left-hand rule.

Note the following:

- The direction of current for the flow of *negative charges* is *opposite* to the direction of motion. Recall that the direction of an electrical current is the direction of flow of POSITIVE charge.

- No work is done since the force (thrust) is always *perpendicular* to the displacement.

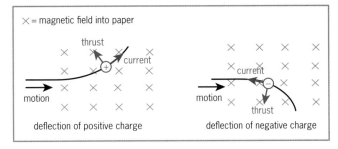

Figure 32.10 *Deflection of positive and negative charged particles by a magnetic field*

Simple dc motor

Current through a coil which is immersed in a magnetic field produces forces in accordance with Fleming's left-hand rule. Since the current flows in opposite directions in either side of the coil, the forces are in opposite directions, and the coil rotates about the axle.

The *left-hand side* of the coil in Figure 32.11(a) has a *downward force* on it, causing anticlockwise rotation. Half a revolution later (Figure 32.11(b)) it is on the *right-hand side* and requires an *upward force* to maintain the rotation. The split-ring is fixed to the axle and allows this to happen by switching connection between the coil and battery every half revolution as it rotates and rubs against the fixed graphite brushes (contacts).

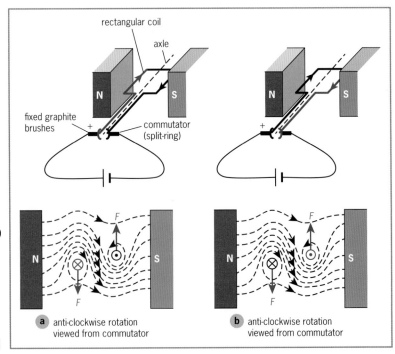

Figure 32.11 *Simple dc motor*

For a motor, the strength of the thrust (force) is proportional to:

a) the magnitude of the current

b) the strength of the magnetic field

c) the number of turns of the coil (each turn of coil produces its own force).

Electromagnetic induction

Two important laws

1. *Whenever there is relative motion of magnetic flux (field lines) linked with a conductor, an **emf** is induced, which is proportional to the rate of cutting of flux (**Faraday's law**). If the circuit is complete, this emf will produce a current.*
2. *The induced **current** is always such as to oppose the motion creating it (**Lenz's law**).*

Figure 32.12 shows a metal rod being pushed downwards through a magnetic field.

- As the conductor cuts through the magnetic field, an emf is induced which drives a current through the centre-zero galvanometer. The positive pole of the rod is the end which drives the current *into the external circuit*. This can be compared with a cell or battery – the rod is acting as a source of electricity.
- If the rod is now pulled upwards, the induced current is in the opposite direction.
- Moving the rod faster increases the magnitude of the current.

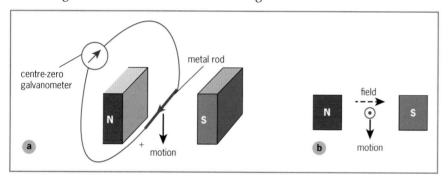

Figure 32.12 *Induced current in a metal rod*

Figure 32.13 shows a pole of a magnet being pushed into a coil.

- An induced current is detected by the galvanometer.
- Pulling the magnet out results in a current in the opposite direction.
- Keeping the magnet stationary in the coil produces no current.
- Increasing the speed of the magnet increases the magnitude of the current.
- Increasing the strength of the magnet increases the magnitude of the current.

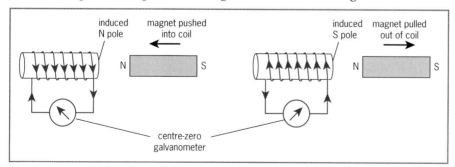

Figure 32.13 *Induced current in a coil*

As the rod in Figure 32.12 is moved through the magnetic field, and as the magnet in Figure 32.13 is moved into and out of the coil, the experimenter will experience a force *opposing the motion*. The opposition to the motion is in agreement with the principle of conservation of energy. The mechanical energy used to push against the opposing force converts to electrical energy induced in the conductor.

Direction of emf and current

The direction of the emf for the rod in Figure 32.12 can be obtained by the use of **Fleming's right-hand rule**, in which the fingers and thumb represent the same as they do in Fleming's left-hand rule (Figure 32.8). Apply the rule to Figure 32.12(b) to confirm that the induced current direction shown is correct.

The direction of the current in the coil in Figure 32.13 can be obtained by applying Lenz's law. If the N pole of a magnet is pushed *into* the coil it induces a N pole at that end of the coil, which opposes its motion. If the N pole of a magnet is pulled *out of* the coil it induces a S pole at that end of the coil, which opposes its motion. Then using the **right-hand grip rule** with the polarity of the coil gives the direction of the current.

Transferring electrical energy between coils

- Figure 32.14(a): On closing the switch, the current in coil A rapidly rises to some maximum value and then remains constant. In this time, the magnetic field associated with this current also grows to a maximum value and then remains constant. As it grows, the flux (field lines) enters coil B and *induces a current* in it. The magnetic poles induced in B are such as to *oppose the entry* of the magnetic field of A.

- Figure 32.14(b): When the current in A reaches its maximum value and remains constant, the magnetic field associated with it no longer grows, but *remains stationary. No current* is therefore induced in B at this time.

- Figure 32.14(c): If the switch in A's circuit is now opened, the current will rapidly fall to zero. The magnetic field associated with this current therefore also diminishes to zero. As it does so, the flux withdraws from B and once more *induces a current* there. The magnetic poles induced in B are now such as to *oppose the withdrawal* of the magnetic field of A.

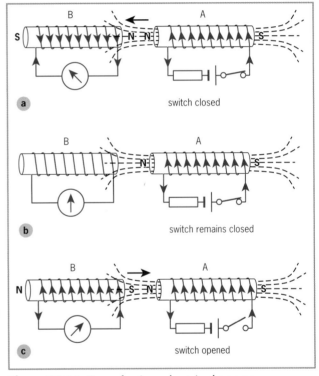

a — switch closed

b — switch remains closed

c — switch opened

Figure 32.14 *Transferring electrical energy between coils*

Use the right-hand grip rule to confirm that the directions of current in coil B of Figure 32.14(a) and (c) are correct.

Simple ac generator

A simple ac generator is shown in Figure 32.15. The coil is rotated with the sides P and Q cutting through the magnetic field. This induces an emf which drives current around the circuit in accordance with Fleming's right-hand rule. After every half revolution, the side of the coil which was moving downwards then moves upwards through the field, reversing the direction of the emf and producing an *alternating voltage*.

The alternating voltage is transferred to the external circuit by a pair of *slip rings* which rub on a pair of fixed graphite brushes as the coil rotates. This ensures that each side of the coil is always connected to the same output terminal for any coil position, allowing the ac generated in the coil to be transferred to the external circuit.

Note that the slip rings are rigidly connected to the shaft and coil and therefore rotate together. They are necessary so as to prevent tangling of the wires connected to the external circuit.

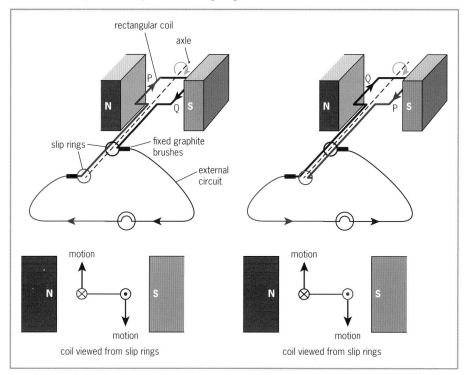

Figure 32.15 *The ac generator*

Assuming clockwise rotation, use Fleming's right-hand rule to verify that the currents in P and Q are as shown in Figure 32.15.

The variation in the emf produced during one revolution of the coil is illustrated in Figure 32.16. Use Fleming's right-hand rule with respect to the 'red' side of the coil for the positions shown to verify that the current alternates as illustrated by the graph.

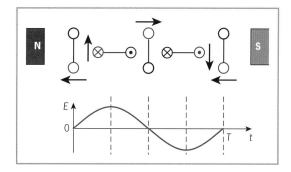

Figure 32.16 *Output of ac generator*

Transformer

*A **transformer** is a device that increases or decreases an alternating voltage.*

Figure 32.17 shows a simple transformer. The primary coil is connected to an ac supply of voltage V_p and the secondary coil delivers a voltage V_s to the device to be operated. The changing current in the primary coil produces a changing magnetic field which repeatedly grows into, and diminishes from, the secondary coil, thereby inducing an alternating voltage within it.

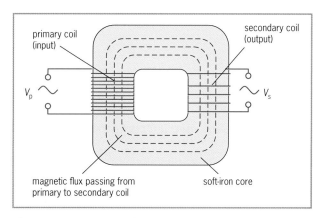

Figure 32.17 *A transformer*

- The *soft-iron core* allows the magnetic flux to easily pass from the primary to the secondary coil.
- *Direct current is not input to a transformer* because it cannot produce a changing magnetic field.
- Placing a *fuse in the primary coil* protects both coils from high currents, because current can only flow in the secondary if there is current in the primary.
- *Step-up transformers* increase an alternating voltage and *step-down transformers* decrease it.
- A transformer that increases the voltage decreases the current (see 'Calculations involving transformers' below).
- The coil with the *least number of turns* carries the *lower voltage* and therefore the *greater current*. It should be of *thicker wire* to increase its conduction and prevent overheating.

Long-distance ac distribution

Power stations generate electrical energy at alternating voltages, which has to be transmitted over long distances to the city where it is consumed.

The **power** lost as heat in the electrical cables is given by $P = I^2R$. In order to prevent large amounts of energy wastage, the transmission current (I) and the resistance of the cables (R) should be kept to a minimum. A step-up transformer at the power company increases the voltage and hence decreases the current. Where the electricity is to be consumed, a step-down transformer decreases the voltage to an appropriate value to be delivered to factories, homes and so on.

Advantages of using ac for transferring electrical energy

- Consumer appliances operate on several different voltages, which can easily be obtained from an ac mains supply by use of a transformer.
- Transformers step up and down ac *with minimum energy loss.*
- The ac can be transferred from the power station at small currents, resulting in *minimum energy being wasted as heat in the resistance of the transmitting cables.*
- By stepping down the transmission current from the power station, *thinner cables* can be used and therefore the *material cost is reduced.*

Calculations involving transformers

V_p and V_s = voltage across the primary and secondary coils

N_p and N_s = number of turns in the primary and secondary coils

I_p and I_s = current in the primary and secondary coils

P_p and P_s = power in primary and secondary coils

- For an **ideal transformer** (which is 100% efficient) the following holds:

$$P_p = P_s$$

$$\frac{V_p}{V_s} = \frac{N_p}{N_s} = \frac{I_s}{I_p}$$

Important note

The current ratio is inverted compared with the ratios for voltage and turns.

Example 2

The primary coil of an ideal transformer is connected to a 120 V mains supply and is used to operate a 60 W 12 V device (Figure 32.18). The primary coil is wound with 4000 turns of wire. Determine:

a the number of turns on the secondary coil

b the current in the secondary coil

c the current in the primary coil.

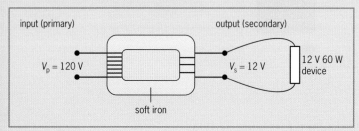

input (primary) output (secondary)

$V_p = 120$ V $V_s = 12$ V 12 V 60 W device

soft iron

Figure 32.18

a $\dfrac{N_s}{N_p} = \dfrac{V_s}{V_p}$

$\dfrac{N_s}{4000} = \dfrac{12}{120}$

$N_s = \dfrac{12}{120} \times 4000 = 400$

b $P_s = V_s I_s$

$60 = 12 I_s$

$I_s = \dfrac{60}{12} = 5.0$ A

c $\dfrac{I_p}{I_s} = \dfrac{V_s}{V_p}$

$\dfrac{I_p}{5.0} = \dfrac{12}{120}$

$I_p = \dfrac{12}{120} \times 5.0 = 0.50$ A

(Note that as the transformer reduces the voltage, it increases the current.)

Revision questions

1 Describe, with the aid of diagrams, experiments to investigate the magnetic field patterns around each of the following current-carrying conductors:

a straight wire **b** solenoid

Your diagrams should clearly indicate the direction of the current and the field.

2 Describe, with the aid of a diagram, one commercial application of an electromagnet.

3 Describe an experiment which indicates that there is a force on a current-carrying conductor placed in a magnetic field.

4 Figure 32.19 shows electrical currents flowing through magnetic fields. Determine the direction of the thrust on the conductors in each case.

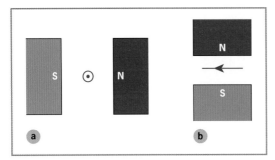

Figure 32.19

5 Sketch the magnetic field diagram for Figure 32.19(a).

6 With the aid of a diagram, explain the functioning of a simple dc motor.

7 Describe how an induced current can be produced in a metal rod.

8 Redraw Figure 32.20, showing the *current direction* in the solenoid and the *magnetic polarity* at its ends, for each of the following cases:

a The N pole of the magnet is pushed into the coil.

b The N pole of the magnet is left at rest in the coil.

c The N pole of the magnet is withdrawn from the coil.

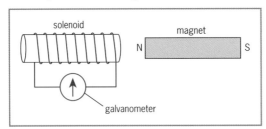

Figure 32.20

9 State THREE ways by which the current produced in question 8 may be increased.

10 Sketch a diagram of a simple ac generator.

11 With the aid of a diagram, explain how a transformer can transfer electrical energy from its primary coil to its secondary coil.

12 State TWO advantages of using ac for the long-distance transmission of electricity.

13 An ideal transformer has 4000 turns on its primary coil and 200 turns on its secondary coil. The primary coil is connected to a 120 V ac mains supply and the secondary to a 4.0 Ω device. Draw a circuit diagram of the arrangement, and determine:

a the voltage across the 4.0 Ω device

b the current through the secondary coil (and through the device)

c the current in the primary coil

d the power input and the power output.

Exam-style questions – Chapters 26 to 32

Structured questions

1 **a)** Complete Table 1 to compare the properties of the zinc-carbon cell and the lead-acid accumulator.

Table 1

	Zinc-carbon cell	Lead-acid accumulator
Electrolyte		
Rechargeability		
Terminal voltage		
Maximum current		>400 A
Internal resistance		0.01 Ω

(4 marks)

b) **i)** Distinguish between the directions of conventional current and electron flow. **(2 marks)**

   ii) State a type of conductor in which both positive and negative charges translate freely. **(1 mark)**

c) A charge of 480 μC flows through a resistor of resistance 500 Ω in a period of 12 ms. Determine:

   i) the current **(2 marks)**

   ii) the potential difference across the resistor **(2 marks)**

   iii) the number of electrons which flow (the charge on each electron is -1.6×10^{-19} C) **(2 marks)**

   iv) the electrical energy transformed. **(2 marks)**

Total 15 marks

2 **a)** Figure 1 shows two oppositely charged particles and Figure 2 shows a current flowing in a wire perpendicularly into the plane of the paper between two magnetic poles.

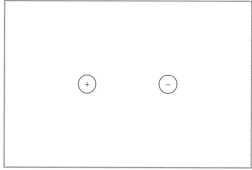

Figure 1

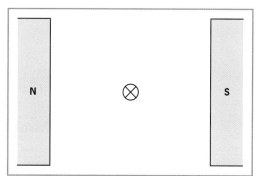

Figure 2

   i) Sketch the electric field lines between and around the particles of Figure 1 and the magnetic field lines associated with the current and magnetic poles of Figure 2. **(6 marks)**

   ii) By means of an arrow labelled F, show the direction of the force on the current-carrying conductor in Figure 2. **(1 mark)**

b) i) Determine the combined resistance between X and Y of Figure 3(a) and between P and Q of Figure 3(b). **(4 marks)**

A current of 1 A flows in the 4 Ω resistor of Figure 3(b). Determine:

ii) the potential difference across the parallel section of the circuit **(2 marks)**

iii) the total power used by the three resistors. **(2 marks)**

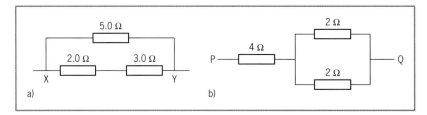

Figure 3

Total 15 marks

Extended response questions

3 **a)** Sketch graphs of current against voltage for each of the following components when the potential difference is varied across them. Both graphs should have positive and negative axes.

i) Filament lamp **(3 marks)**

ii) Semiconductor diode **(3 marks)**

A graph of current against potential difference for a particular component is a straight line and passes through the origin.

iii) What can you deduce about the resistance of the component? **(1 mark)**

b) The variable resistor (rheostat) shown in Figure 4 has a maximum resistance of 10 Ω.

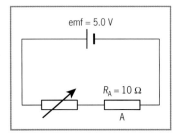

Figure 4

The rheostat is initially set to 0 Ω. Determine:

i) the current in the circuit. **(2 marks)**

The rheostat is adjusted to have its maximum resistance. Determine:

ii) the new current **(2 marks)**

iii) the potential difference across resistor A **(2 marks)**

iv) the power used by A. **(2 marks)**

Total 15 marks

4 **a) i)** Explain how a transformer can alter the value of an alternating voltage. **(3 marks)**

ii) State THREE advantages of using ac for transferring electrical energy. **(3 marks)**

b) i) Indicate, by means of arrows, the directions of the current induced in the metal rod and in the coil of Figure 5. **(3 marks)**

ii) Mark the induced north pole of the coil with the letter N. **(1 mark)**

iii) Indicate the polarity of the rod by marking + at the correct end. **(1 mark)**

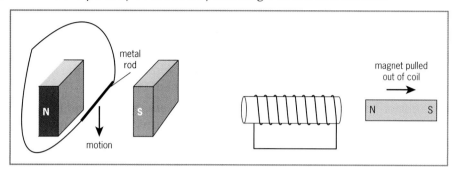

Figure 5

c) An ideal transformer has 6000 turns and 1000 turns on its primary and secondary coils respectively. It is used to operate a 100 W 20 V device. Determine:

i) the input voltage **(2 marks)**

ii) the current in the secondary coil. **(2 marks)**

Total 15 marks

33 The atom

Models of the atom

Evolution of the concept of the atom

≈400BC   The Greek philosopher, Democritus, suggested that matter consisted of small indivisible particles. He called these particles 'atomos', from the Greek word for indivisible.

1897   Joseph John Thomson viewed the atom as a *positively charged sphere* with smaller, *negatively charged, fixed particles (**electrons**) interspersed within it*, the resultant charge being zero. This is known as the **plum pudding** model of the atom.

1911   Ernest Rutherford proposed that most of the atom is *empty space* and that it contains a **nucleus** of very *concentrated positive charge*. He suggested that small negatively charged particles exist in a surrounding 'electron cloud', making the net charge zero.

1913   Niels Bohr suggested that the *negatively charged electrons orbit the nucleus in particular shells*. A unique energy value is required by an electron to exist within any shell.

1932   James Chadwick discovered **neutrons**, uncharged particles that exist together with **protons** within the nucleus of an atom. Neutrons were difficult to detect because, unlike protons and electrons, they have no charge, and are therefore unaffected by electric and magnetic fields.

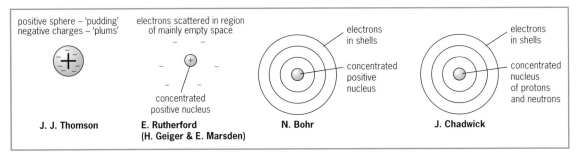

Figure 33.1 *Successive models of the atom*

The Geiger-Marsden (or 'Rutherford scattering') experiment

Ernest Rutherford worked with Hans Geiger, investigating the behaviour of alpha particles when fired through metals. In 1911, Geiger, together with a student, Ernest Marsden, carried out a research project in Rutherford's laboratory, measuring the angles of deflection of the alpha particles (Figure 33.2).

They shot alpha particles through a thin sheet of gold foil and observed the scintillations produced as the particles struck a zinc sulfide screen. The chamber was evacuated because alpha particles are stopped by just a few centimetres of air. The microscope could be rotated to observe the scintillations received at any angle.

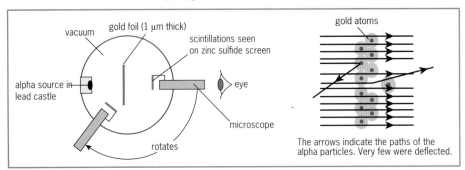

Figure 33.2 *The Gieger-Marsden (or 'Rutherford scattering') experiment*

Rutherford analysed the observations and made his conclusions.

Observations

1. Most of the particles passed straight through the foil without deflection.
2. Very few were deflected, but those that were, did so with extremely *high speeds*, even at large angles of deflection.

Conclusions

1. Most of the atom is *empty space*.
2. The nucleus is *extremely dense*, and consists of *positive charges* which repelled the positively charged alpha particles.

Structure of the atom

*The **Periodic Table** is a table of elements of increasing proton number, arranged so as to categorise their electronic configurations and chemical properties.*

Periods	I		II		III		IV		V		VI		VII		0	
1	H	1													He	2
2	Li	3	Be	4	B	5	C	6	N	7	O	8	F	9	Ne	10
3	Na	11	Mg	12	Al	13	Si	14	P	15	S	16	Cl	17	Ar	18
4	K	19	Ca	20												

Figure 33.3 *The first 20 elements of the Periodic Table: their symbols and their proton numbers*

- The **proton number** or **atomic number**, Z, of an element is the *number of protons* contained in the nucleus of an atom of the element. Neutral atoms have the same number of protons as electrons.
- The **neutron number**, N, of an element is the *number of neutrons* contained in the nucleus of an atom of the element.
- The **mass number** or **nucleon number**, A, of an element is the *SUM of the numbers of protons and neutrons* contained in the nucleus of an atom of the element.

$$A = Z + N$$

***Isotopes** of an element have the same atomic number but different mass numbers.*

Table 33.1 *Mass and charge of sub-atomic particles*

	Proton	Neutron	Electron
Relative mass	1	1	$\frac{1}{1840}$
Relative charge	+1	0	–1
Actual mass/kg	1.7×10^{-27}	1.7×10^{-27}	9.1×10^{-31}
Actual charge/C	1.6×10^{-19}	0	-1.6×10^{-19}

Representation of a nuclide

A **nuclide** is a nucleus with a particular number of protons and neutrons. It is represented by:

$${}^{A}_{Z}\mathrm{X}$$

where X is the symbol of the element. For example:

${}^{24}_{11}\mathrm{Na}$: this nuclide contains 11 protons and 13 neutrons

${}^{23}_{11}\mathrm{Na}$: this nuclide contains 11 protons and 12 neutrons

Representation of a subatomic particle

$$\overset{N+Z}{\underset{\text{relative charge}}{}}Y$$

where Y is the symbol for the particle. For example:

$^{1}_{1}p$: proton $^{1}_{0}n$: neutron $^{0}_{-1}e$: electron

Electron configuration

An **electron configuration** shows the number of electrons in each shell. See Figure 33.4.

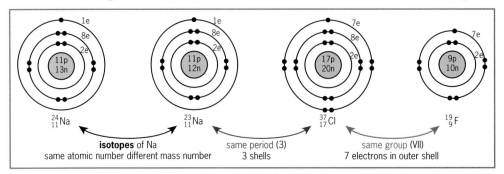

Figure 33.4 *Electron configurations*

For the first 20 elements of the Periodic Table, the shells can hold these maximum numbers of electrons:

1st shell: 2 electrons   2nd shell: 8 electrons   3rd shell: 8 electrons

Meaning of the periods and groups of the Periodic Table

Period: The period number indicates the *number of shells* of the atom.

Group: The group number indicates the *number of electrons in the outer shell* of the atom.

See Figure 33.4.

Revision questions

1 State the contribution made by each of the following in the evolving theories of the structure of the atom: Thomson, Rutherford, Bohr, Chadwick.

2 a) Describe, with the aid of a diagram, the important experiment of Geiger and Marsden.

b) State the observations made in the *Geiger-Marsden* experiment, and the conclusions drawn from those observations.

c) What made the neutron so difficult to discover?

3 a) Sketch the structure of the following atoms, showing, for each, the numbers and positions of its sub-atomic particles.

$^{26}_{12}Mg$ $^{40}_{20}Ca$ $^{19}_{9}F$

b) Using the same notation, state a possible isotope of $^{40}_{20}Ca$.

c) Represent the proton, neutron and electron using this notation.

4 Construct a table showing the mass and charge of the neutron and the electron, relative to the proton.

a) If the electron has a mass of 1 unit, what would be the mass of a proton?

b) What can be said of the numbers of protons and electrons in a neutral atom?

5 Define each of the following:

a atomic number   b mass number   c isotopes

34 Radioactivity

Radioactive emissions

Marie Curie's work in the field of radioactivity

Marie Curie was born in Poland in 1867. Following up on Henri Becquerel's work on the radiation emitted from uranium, she realised that the intensity of the rays was dependent only on the mass of the emitting sample. Since no environmental conditions could alter the intensity, she concluded that *radioactivity is an atomic phenomenon*.

In 1903 Marie and Pierre, her husband, shared the Nobel Prize in Physics with Henri Becquerel for their work on radioactivity, and in 1911 she was awarded another Nobel Prize, this time for the isolation of the elements polonium and radium. Her work opened the field of *radiotherapy and nuclear medicine*.

She died in 1934 from the cumulative effects of the radiation that she encountered during her investigations.

The nature of radioactivity

Radioactivity is the spontaneous disintegration ('decay') of unstable atomic nuclei.

The nucleus becomes more stable by emitting **alpha particles**, **beta particles** and/or **gamma waves**. Some of the properties of these types of emissions are outlined in Table 34.1.

Table 34.1 *Properties of radioactive emissions*

	Alpha particle (α)	Beta particle (β)	Gamma wave (γ)
Nature	2 protons and 2 neutrons tightly bound	1 electron	High-frequency electromagnetic wave
Symbol	$^4_2\alpha$	$^{\ 0}_{-1}\beta$	γ
Relative mass	4	$\dfrac{1}{1840}$	zero
Relative charge	+2	−1	zero
Speed (in air or vacuum)/m s^{-1}	2×10^7	Up to almost the speed of light	3×10^8
Ionisation of the air	strongly ionising on collision with neutral air molecules	weakly ionising on collision with neutral air molecules	very weakly ionising when the wave energy is absorbed by air molecules
Absorbed by	a thin sheet of paper or about 5 cm of air	a few m of air or about 3–5 mm of aluminium	several m of concrete (4 cm of lead absorbs 90%)
Detection of presence by	GM tube and accessories	GM tube and accessories	GM tube and accessories

Background radiation is the ionising radiation within our environment arising from radioactive elements in the Earth and its surrounding atmosphere, plus X-rays from medical equipment and high-speed charged particles from the cosmos.

Detection using the Geiger-Müller tube

Radioactive emissions may be detected by a **Geiger-Müller tube** (GM tube) and accessories. Radiation entering the tube produces a current which may be passed to one of the following:

- a **ratemeter**, which gives the rate at which emissions occur
- a loudspeaker, which produces a sound whenever the GM tube detects an emission
- a **scalar**, which counts the emissions.

*The **activity** of a sample of radioactive material is the rate at which the nuclei decay.*

*The unit of activity, the **becquerel (Bq)**, is the rate of one nuclear disintegration per second.*

Received count rate

The received count rate detected by a GM tube depends on the distance from the source to the detector. Experiments investigating the activity of a source should therefore maintain *a constant distance between it and the detector.*

The count rate observed will also include that due to background radiation. This *must be subtracted from the received count rate* to obtain the correct portion detected from the source being investigated.

Testing for the type of radiation

1. Absorption test (Figure 34.1)

- The background count rate is measured.
- The source is then placed in front of the GM tube and the count rate is again measured.
- A thin sheet of paper is placed between the source and detector and the count rate is measured. If the activity is reduced to the background count rate, then the source is an α-emitter.
- If the activity is unaffected, then the source is either a β-emitter or a γ-emitter. The paper is replaced by an aluminium sheet of thickness 5 mm. If the activity now returns to the background count rate, then the source is a β-emitter; otherwise, it is a γ-emitter.

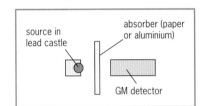

Figure 34.1 *Absorption test*

Alpha particles are readily stopped by air, and therefore for experiments where there is the possibility of α-emission, either the source must be placed very close to the detector or the apparatus should be set up in a vacuum.

2. Electric field deflection test (Figure 34.2)

- The count rate is taken with the electric field switched off.
- The electric field is then switched on.

   a) If the count rate is unaffected, the source is a γ-emitter.

   b) If the count rate falls and only returns to its initial value when the detector is shifted towards the positive plate, then the source is a β-emitter. The positive plate will attract the negative β-particles.

   c) If the count rate falls and only returns to its initial value when the detector is shifted towards the negative plate, then the source is an α-emitter. The negative plate will attract the positive α-particles.

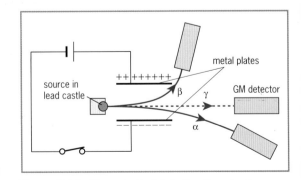

Figure 34.2 *Electric field deflection test*

3. Magnetic field deflection test (Figure 34.3)

- The count rate is taken in the absence of the magnetic field.
- The magnetic field is then directed perpendicular to the path of the rays as shown in Figure 34.3.

   a) If the count rate is unaffected, the source is a γ-emitter.

   b) If the count-rate falls, the detector should be shifted until it returns to its previous value. Current is a flow of charge and therefore α- and β-particles will experience forces in accordance with **Fleming's left-hand rule** (see Chapter 32). Remember that the direction of the current is the direction of *flow of positive charge*. Apply Fleming's left-hand rule to Figure 34.3.

   Although an α-particle has twice the charge of a β-particle, it is deflected less, because its mass is much greater than that of the β-particle (see Table 34.1).

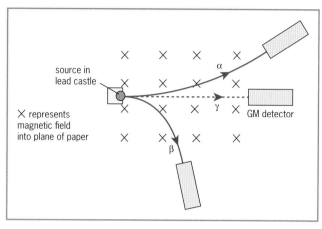

Figure 34.3 *Magnetic field deflection test*

4. The diffusion cloud chamber test

Radioactive sources produce cloud tracks in a device known as a **cloud chamber**. The tracks become visible as condensation occurs on ions created by the radiation, and are characteristic of the type of radiation as illustrated in Figure 34.4.

- α tracks: An α-particle has a mass of more than 7000 times that of a β-particle. The α-particles are strongly ionising on collision with other particles and produce *thick* tracks. The tracks are *straight* because α-particles are not easily deviated on collision with other particles.

- β tracks: β-particles are only weakly ionising, due to their relatively small mass, and produce *weak* tracks. The tracks are *randomly directed* because these particles deviate readily on collision with other particles.

- γ tracks: These tracks are *extremely weak* and *dispersed*. The ions in this case are produced when a γ-wave is absorbed by an atom, resulting in the ejection of an electron.

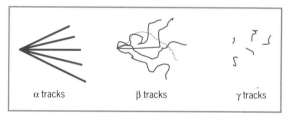

Figure 34.4 *Tracks produced in a cloud chamber*

Beta emission

Beta particles (electrons) are emitted from the nucleus of an atom. During beta emission, a neutron in the nucleus decays into a proton and an electron. The electron shoots out of the atom as a high-velocity β-particle, leaving the newly formed proton within the nucleus (Figure 34.5).

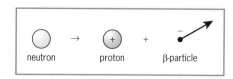

Figure 34.5 *Neutron decay and beta emission*

Equations of radioactive decay

Table 34.2 *Common symbols used in nuclear equations*

Alpha particle	Beta particle	Gamma wave	Proton	Neutron
$^{4}_{2}\alpha$ or $^{4}_{2}\text{He}$	$^{0}_{-1}\beta$ or $^{0}_{-1}\text{e}$	γ	$^{1}_{1}\text{p}$	$^{1}_{0}\text{n}$

- When an isotope emits an α-particle it becomes an element *two places back* in the Periodic Table.

$$^{226}_{88}\text{Ra} \longrightarrow {}^{4}_{2}\text{He} + {}^{222}_{86}\text{Rn}$$

- When an isotope emits a β-particle it becomes an element *one place forward* in the Periodic Table. The mass number is unchanged.

$$^{14}_{6}\text{C} \longrightarrow ^{\ 0}_{-1}\text{e} + ^{14}_{7}\text{N}$$

- When an isotope emits a γ-photon its *atomic number and mass number remain unchanged.*

$$^{234}_{91}\text{Pa} \longrightarrow ^{234}_{91}\text{Pa} + \gamma$$

Some nuclei may remain in an **excited state** (more energetic state) after emitting an α- or β-particle. A γ-photon is then emitted, returning the nucleus to its more stable, **ground state**.

$$^{238}_{92}\text{U} \longrightarrow ^{234}_{90}\text{Th} + ^{4}_{2}\alpha + \gamma$$

$$^{90}_{38}\text{Sr} \longrightarrow ^{90}_{39}\text{Y} + ^{\ 0}_{-1}\beta + \gamma$$

During radioactive decay, the decaying nuclide is called the **parent** and the new nuclide produced is the **daughter**.

The nature of the radioactive decay process

Radioactive decay is *random*. This can be compared to *throwing dice, tossing a coin or shooting at a target*. If a radioactive source is placed in front of a GM detector the following will occur, depending on the instrument connected to the GM tube:

- the ratemeter needle will flicker
- the 'clicks' from the loudspeaker will be heard at a random rate
- the scalar will indicate a random increment of the detected emissions.

Although the activity of a radionuclide is random, there is a definite period for half of a given sample to decay.

*The **half-life** of a radioisotope is the time taken for the mass (or activity) of a given sample of it to decay to half of its value.*

The half life of a radioactive material is *not affected by conditions external to the nucleus.* This includes:

a) physical conditions such as temperature and pressure

b) chemical conditions such as whether or not the isotope is in its pure state or chemically combined with some other element in a compound.

Graphs showing exponential decay

Figure 34.6 shows that radioactive decay is **exponential** with time. Note that the curve never meets the time axis but gets closer and closer to it. The activity (the rate of decay) is measured by the count rate, and is proportional to the number of atomic nuclei *remaining* at any particular time. It is therefore proportional to the mass at that time. The vertical axis of the graph can show mass, count rate (or activity), or number of nuclei remaining.

The half-life is found by choosing any point on the graph and finding the time for its mass, count rate, or number of nuclei remaining, to fall to half of its value at that point. An average from THREE decay periods gives a more accurate result.

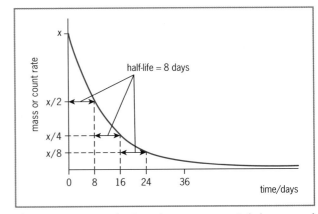

Figure 34.6 *Graph showing exponential decay and half-life*

Simulating radioactive decay

- About 300 dice are placed in a bucket. The number of dice, D, is recorded.
- The bucket is emptied (the dice 'thrown') and the dice with the value 6 facing upward are removed. The new value of D is recorded.
- The process is repeated using the remaining dice, recording the number of throws, N, and the new value of D, until fewer than 25 dice remain.
- A graph is plotted of D against N, as shown in Figure 34.7.

Note:

- The points on the graph are not exactly on the smooth curve drawn through them because the generation of the value 6 occurs at random.
- The exponential nature is indicated by the curve.
- As D decreases, the outcome of each throw becomes statistically less accurate.
- The 'half-life' of this decay can be found by reading from the graph THREE values of D and determining the corresponding time taken for D to fall to half of its value. These three half-lives can then be averaged.

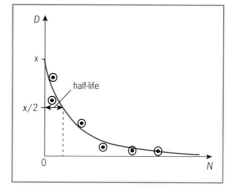

Figure 34.7 *Simulating radioactive decay: dice remaining versus number of throws*

Calculations involving half-life

The following Examples illustrate these two methods:

Arrow method

- Each arrow represents a half-life transition and points to half the value it originates at.
- The total time of decay is the sum of the half-lives.

Table method

- Particularly useful if a graph is to be plotted.
- The 'Time' column always starts at 0 and increases by one half-life for each new row.
- The 'Activity' or 'Mass remaining' column decreases to half its value for every new row.

Example 1

A radioisotope gives a count rate of 50.0 Bq. Determine the count rate after 40 years if its half-life is 20 years.

Arrow method:

$$50.0 \text{ Bq} \xrightarrow{\hspace{1cm}} 25.0 \text{ Bq} \xrightarrow{\hspace{1cm}} 12.5 \text{ Bq}$$
$$\phantom{50.0 \text{ Bq}} 20 \text{ y} \phantom{25.0 \text{ Bq}} 20 \text{ y}$$

After 40 years, the count rate is 12.5 Bq.

Table method:

Activity/Bq	Time/y
50.0	0
25.0	20
12.5	40

Example 2

A radioisotope has a mass of 200 g and a half-life of 25 ms. Determine the time taken for it to decay to a mass of 25 g.

Arrow method:

$$200\text{ g} \longrightarrow 100\text{ g} \longrightarrow 50\text{ g} \longrightarrow 25\text{ g}$$
$$\quad\quad 25\text{ ms} \quad\quad 25\text{ ms} \quad\quad 25\text{ ms}$$

Time taken to decay to 25 g = 3 × 25 ms = 75 ms

Table method:

Mass/g	Time/ms
200	0
100	25
50	50
25	75

Example 3

A radioisotope decays to $\frac{1}{8}$ of its mass in 12 weeks. Determine its half-life.

Arrow method:

With fractions, start with 1.

$$1 \longrightarrow \frac{1}{2} \longrightarrow \frac{1}{4} \longrightarrow \frac{1}{8}$$

So 12 weeks represents 3 half-lives.

One half-life = $\frac{12}{3}$ weeks = 4 weeks

Table method:

Fraction	Time/wks
1	0
$\frac{1}{2}$	4
$\frac{1}{4}$	8
$\frac{1}{8}$	12

Example 4

A radioisotope of mass 80 g has a half-life of 5700 years. Determine its mass 17 100 years ago.

Arrow method:

$$\frac{17\,100}{5700} = 3$$

So it has decayed for 3 half-lives.

Work backwards from 80 g for 3 half-lives:

$$640\text{ g} \longrightarrow 320\text{ g} \longrightarrow 160\text{ g} \longrightarrow 80\text{ g}$$

17 100 years ago, the mass was 640 g.

Table method:

Mass/g	Time/y
640	0
320	5 700
160	11 400
80	17 100

A radioisotope has a half-life of 30 days. How long will it take for its mass to fall by 87.5%?

Arrow method:

With percentages, start with 100%.

It falls BY 87.5% and therefore falls TO 12.5%.

$$100\% \longrightarrow 50\% \longrightarrow 25\% \longrightarrow 12.5\%$$
$$\quad\quad 30\text{ d} \quad\quad 30\text{ d} \quad\quad 30\text{ d}$$

It takes 3 half-lives, so 3×30 days = 90 days, to fall by 87.5%.

Table method:

%	Time/days
100	0
50	30
25	60
12.5	90

Radio-carbon dating

When an animal or a plant dies, its decaying C-14 (radioisotope carbon-14, or ^{14}C) is no longer replaced, so the ratio of C-14 to non-radioactive C-12 decreases with time. Every 5730 years the amount of C-14 in a dead specimen falls to half the mass it had at the beginning of that period.

If the amount of C-14 per gram of carbon in a living organism is known, together with the amount found per gram of carbon in an old specimen, the age of the specimen can be calculated.

In natural carbon there is only one atom of C-14 with every 8×10^{11} atoms of carbon. Due to this very small proportion of C-14 in a sample of carbon, even from a living organism, the count rate obtained from very old specimens is very low. This type of dating is therefore not useful for determining the age of samples which have been dead for over 60 000 years (about 10 half-lives).

A mass of 1.0 g of carbon from a living plant gives a count rate of 19.0 min^{-1}. An extremely old specimen is found and 6.0 g of carbon is extracted from it. The count rate produced by this sample is 28.5 min^{-1}. Given that the half-life of C-14 is 5730 years, determine the age of the old specimen.

We need to compare *equal masses* of the living organism and the old specimen.

For the old specimen:

6.0 g gives a count rate of 28.5 min^{-1}.

1.0 g gives a count rate of $\dfrac{28.5}{6.0} = 4.8$ min^{-1}

The activity of 1.0 g has reduced from 19.0 min^{-1} since the plant died.

Arrow method:

$$19.0\text{ min}^{-1} \longrightarrow 9.5\text{ min}^{-1} \longrightarrow 4.8\text{ min}^{-1}$$
$$\quad\quad 5730\text{ y} \quad\quad\quad 5730\text{ y}$$

So the age of the old specimen is $2 \times 5730 = 11\,460$ years.

Table method:

Count rate/min^{-1}	Time/y
19.0	0
9.5	5730
4.8	11 460

Uses of radioisotopes

Medical uses – cancer therapy

1. External beam radiotherapy

Gamma radiation from cobalt-60 can be used to destroy malignant growths (cancerous tumours). The treatment is only useful if the *cancer is localised* in a small region, because the radiation also destroys good cells.

This type of therapy has its problems.

a) Normal tissue is irradiated between the surface and the tumour.

b) The beam cannot be sharply focused so tissue surrounding the target can be affected.

c) Bone may shield the tumour from receiving radiation.

The use of Co-60 for external beam radiotherapy is no longer common. It has been replaced by high-energy X-rays, because the X-ray beam is much easier to control and a sharper focus can be obtained.

2. Surface and implant radiotherapy

Radioactive sources may be

a) stuck to the patient's skin to treat *skin disorders*

b) placed in a tumour in the form of needles, as in the treatment of *breast cancer*

c) placed into capsules and inserted into body cavities, as in the treatment of *cervical cancer*.

The sources used can have *short or long half-lives* because they can be removed from the patient at any time. Short-range radiations (α, β and low-energy γ) are used so that they are totally absorbed by the malignant region.

3. Radiopharmaceutical therapy

This form of treatment is used when a pharmaceutical (drug) can carry the radioactive source to the target site. An example is in the treatment of *thyroid cancer*. The thyroid uses iodine so if a patient is given a dose of iodine, it is targeted there. Iodine-131 emits β- as well as γ-radiation. Its β-radiation is particularly useful in destroying cancer cells. In order to protect others, patients should remain in the hospital until a safety level of radiation is reached.

It is important that for this form of therapy the sources have *short half-lives* so as not to expose the patients to excessive doses of radiation for long periods.

Medical uses – diagnostic

Radioisotopes used for diagnosis are preferably γ-emitters, because γ-radiation is least absorbed by the body.

1. Radioactive tracing

*A **radioactive tracer** is a chemical compound in which one or more elements have been replaced by radioisotopes, used to investigate chemical reactions by tracking the path it follows.*

In medical diagnosis a suitable tracer is given to the patient orally or as an injection, and a detector is used to follow its path through the body. Iodine-123 is used as a tracer to investigate the functioning of the thyroid.

2. Photography

The patient is given a γ-emitting radioisotope which can be targeted to a particular region within the body. A *scanner* or *gamma camera* is positioned outside the patient to detect the emitted radiation. Tumours present will show up as a shadow in the image, since they will absorb the radiation.

Iodine-123 can be used for *thyroid scans*. It only emits γ-radiation, unlike I-131 which also emits the stronger β-radiation.

Technetium-99m (Te-99m), also a γ-emitter, joins to phosphate compounds which collect in bones, so this is therefore important for *bone scans*.

Non-medical uses

Other photography

Gamma radiation is used in the photography of metal castings to investigate weak areas.

Other tracers

Water containing a γ-source can be pumped below the ground. Engineers then use detectors to trace its flow as it seeps through cracks to the surface. This gives them information of the strength of the foundations for potential building sites.

Radio-carbon dating

The age of an old organic specimen can be calculated by measuring the amount of carbon-14 it contains, as discussed earlier in the chapter.

Sterilisation

The objects to be sterilised are packed and sealed in plastic containers which are then irradiated by γ-radiation from cobalt-60 to kill bacteria. Some foodstuffs are also sterilised in this way.

Thickness measurements

Beta or gamma radiation may be passed through various materials, and by examining the amount of radiation that penetrates, the thicknesses of the samples can be determined. Strontium-90, a γ-emitter, is used for measuring the thickness of metal sheets (Figure 34.8).

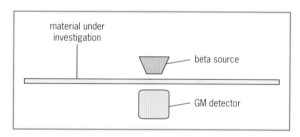

Figure 34.8 *Thickness measurement*

Choice of half-life in applications

Long half-life

Sources used for *thickness measurements* should have long half-lives so that their activity remains steady during the measurement. Sources used in *dating* must have very long half-lives so that they still emit, even after thousands of years. Radioisotopes used for *external beam, surface or implant radiotherapy* can have long or short half-lives because they may be removed from the patient's environment at any time.

Short half-life

Sources *given to patients orally or by injection* should have short half-lives so that they are not in the patient at dangerous levels for long periods. The half-life, however, cannot be *too* short, because time is needed for the radioisotope to be transported by the blood to the target site. The half-lives of some radioisotopes used in the medical field are:

technetium-99m (Te-99m) – γ-emitter – half-life 6 hours

iodine-131 (I-131) – β- and γ-emitter – half-life 8 days

iodine-123 (I-123) – γ-emitter – half-life 13.2 hours

Nuclear fission and fusion

*Nuclear **fission** is the splitting of a large atomic nucleus into two nearly equal parts, resulting in a large output of energy and a decrease in mass.*

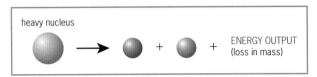

Figure 34.9 *Nuclear fission*

Nuclear power plants produce electricity by nuclear fission in controlled reactors. The 'atomic bomb' also utilises nuclear fission.

Two possible fission reactions of uranium-235 (U-235) are shown below. A stray, high-speed neutron penetrates the uranium nucleus and triggers the reaction.

$$^{235}_{92}U + ^{1}_{0}n \longrightarrow ^{141}_{56}Ba + ^{92}_{36}Kr + 3^{1}_{0}n + energy$$

$$^{235}_{92}U + ^{1}_{0}n \longrightarrow ^{144}_{56}Ba + ^{90}_{36}Kr + 2^{1}_{0}n + energy$$

*Nuclear **fusion** is the joining of two small atomic nuclei to produce a larger nucleus, resulting in a large output of energy and a decrease in mass.*

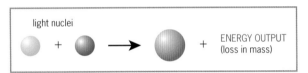

Figure 34.10 *Nuclear fusion*

Nuclear fusion is the process by which *radiant energy is produced by the Sun* – in the core of the Sun, energy is generated by two hydrogen nuclei as they join to form a single helium nucleus. The 'hydrogen bomb' also utilises nuclear fusion.

Two ways by which hydrogen nuclei fuse to helium:

$$^{2}_{1}H + ^{2}_{1}H \longrightarrow ^{3}_{2}He + ^{1}_{0}n + energy$$

$$^{2}_{1}H + ^{3}_{1}H \longrightarrow ^{4}_{2}He + ^{1}_{0}n + energy$$

These reactions require temperatures in excess of 10^8 K to allow the positive hydrogen nuclei to travel fast enough to overcome the very strong electrical repulsion that exists between them. The difficulty of maintaining these extremely high temperatures has been the main obstacle in the design of fusion reactors.

Einstein's equation of mass–energy equivalence

When nuclei undergo fission or fusion the resulting nuclei are, as in radioactive decay, *more stable*, and energy is released.

The energy output by a nucleus during radioactivity, nuclear fission and nuclear fusion is obtained by a reduction in its mass.

*The **mass defect** is directly related to the energy output:*

$$\Delta E = \Delta mc^2$$

This equation was famously proposed by Albert Einstein.

ΔE = energy output

Δm = mass defect

c = speed of light in a vacuum

Example 7

The Sun radiates energy at a rate of 3.6×10^{23} J s^{-1}. This energy originates from nuclear fusion reactions. Determine the loss in mass each second.

In 1 s, 3.6×10^{23} J is converted from mass to energy.

$$\Delta E = \Delta mc^2$$

$$\frac{\Delta E}{c^2} = \Delta m$$

$$\frac{3.6 \times 10^{23}}{(3.0 \times 10^8)^2} = \Delta m$$

$$4.0 \times 10^6 \text{ kg} = \Delta m$$

Example 8

The nuclide $^{210}_{84}$Po emits an α-particle to form $^{206}_{82}$Pb.

a Write an equation for the reaction.

b Determine the energy released by an atom of $^{210}_{84}$Po as it undergoes nuclear decay.

Atomic mass of Po-210 = 209.9829 u

Atomic mass of He-4 = 4.0026 u

Atomic mass of Pb-206 = 205.9745 u

1 atomic mass unit, u = 1.66×10^{-27} kg

Speed of light in a vacuum = 3.0×10^8 m s^{-1}

a $^{210}_{84}$Po $\longrightarrow$ $^4_2$He + $^{206}_{82}$Pb + energy

b Step 1:

Find the mass defect, Δm, in atomic mass units, u.

$^{210}_{84}$Po = $^4_2$He + $^{206}_{82}$Pb + energy

209.9829 u = 4.0026 u + 205.9745 u + Δm

5.8×10^{-3} u = Δm

Step 2:

Convert u to kg.

$5.8 \times 10^{-3} \times 1.66 \times 10^{-27} = \Delta m$

9.63×10^{-30} kg = Δm

Step 3:

Calculate ΔE.

$\Delta E = \Delta mc^2$

$\Delta E = 9.63 \times 10^{-30}(3.0 \times 10^8)^2 = 8.7 \times 10^{-13}$ J

Pros and cons of nuclear power stations

Advantages

1. In the absence of natural disasters, they do not contaminate the environment if carefully managed. They do not produce greenhouse gases such as methane or carbon dioxide, or other hazardous gases such as sulfur dioxide or carbon monoxide.

2. When compared to obtaining energy from fossil fuels, fewer lives are lost each year per unit of energy produced.

3. Many radioactive materials used in medicine are produced at nuclear power plants.

4. A small amount of nuclear fuel produces an enormous amount of electricity, and therefore delivery and storage of the fuel is relatively cheap.

5. A large supply of U-235 is available.

Disadvantages

1. Nuclear radiation can destroy or damage living organisms. It can alter the DNA of cells and can produce cancers and other abnormal growths.

2. Staff working with radioactive material are irradiated by radioisotopes which contaminate their surroundings, and may be contaminated themselves if they ingest the material.

3. Used radioactive fuel still contains radioactive material and is hazardous to the environment. It is usually stored under water in order to remove the excessive heat it produces. The water also acts as a radiation shield for the surroundings.

4. There is the possibility of a catastrophic effect if there is a critical malfunction at the plant. Huge explosions can spread the radioactive material over large areas and the radiation could impact heavily on the planet.

5. Nuclear power stations have to be shut down after several years because the plant and machinery become heavily contaminated. This is very costly and hazardous.

Hazards of ionising radiations

- Radiation 'burns' can be obtained by those receiving high doses.
- DNA may be damaged. This can cause changes which may lead to cancer or to genetic mutations.

Sources outside the body: If the source is several metres away, only γ-radiation is dangerous, because α- and β-particles cannot travel this distance in air.

Sources inside the body: If the source has been ingested or inhaled, α- and β-radiation are very dangerous, because the emissions will be heavily absorbed by the body cells. Gamma radiation is not as dangerous since much of it passes through the body and only a portion of the electromagnetic energy is transferred to the cells.

Figure 34.11 *The hazard symbol for ionising radiation*

The **tri-foil**, the international hazard symbol for ionising radiation, is shown in Figure 34.11. It has a yellow background.

Safety precautions against the hazards of ionising radiations

- The tri-foil hazard sign must be visible wherever ionising radiation is hazardous.
- All radioactive samples should be labelled by name, and as being radioactive and dangerous.
- The use of robotic arms, tongs or gloves should be employed when handling radioisotopes.
- One should never consume food or drink when in a location where there is radioactive material.
- Radioactive samples should be stored in lead containers.
- One should wear lead-lined clothing or stand behind lead-lined walls when working with radioisotopes.
- One should comply with current regulations on the disposal of radioactive waste.
- Nuclear weapon testing must be done underground.

Revision questions

1 Marie Curie realised that the intensity of radiation from uranium was proportional only to the mass of the emitting sample and that nothing could be done to change this.

    a What important conclusion did she make from this observation?

    b State the reason she was awarded EACH of her two Nobel prizes.

    c What important field did her work open for others to develop?

2 Define the following with respect to nuclear emissions:

    a radioactivity   **b** activity of a sample   **c** becquerel

3 The cloud chamber can be used to identify radioactive emissions.

    a Draw diagrams to illustrate the tracks associated with each type of emission.

    b Briefly describe and explain these tracks in terms of *strength* and *direction*.

4   **a** State the nature of each of the following:

        i   α-particle   **ii** β-particle   **iii** γ-wave

    b For each of the following, state the type of radiation (α, β or γ) that has the particular characteristic.

        i   Has the strongest ionising capability

        ii   Is stopped by a thin sheet of paper or a few cm of air

        iii   Has the strongest penetrating capability

        iv   Cannot be deflected by an electric or a magnetic field

        v   Is deflected most by an electric or a magnetic field

        vi   Can penetrate no more than a few mm of aluminium

        vii Is a particle of relative charge +2

        viii Is a particle of charge -1.6×10^{-19} C

        ix   Is comprised of particles of total charge $+3.2 \times 10^{-19}$ C

        x   Is comprised of particles of total mass more than 7000 times that of an electron

5   **a** What is meant by *background radiation*?

    b Identify THREE sources of background radiation.

6 Describe an experiment, using EACH of the methods listed below, to determine the type of radiation being emitted by a radioactive source.

    a absorption test   **b** electric field deflection test   **c** magnetic field deflection test

7 State the numbers that should replace the boxes in the following nuclear equations.

    a $^{214}_{\square}\text{Po} \longrightarrow \alpha + ^{\square}_{82}\text{Pb}$ **b** $^{\square}_{82}\text{Pb} \longrightarrow \beta + ^{210}_{\square}\text{Bi}$ **c** $^{99m}_{\square}\text{Tc} \longrightarrow \gamma + ^{\square}_{43}\text{Tc}$

8 A mass of 4.0 g of iodine-131 (I-131), of half-life 8 days, decays for a period of 24 days.

    a Define the term *half-life*.

    b What mass of I-131 remains after this time?

    c Sketch a graph of mass against time for the decay.

9 A sample of the metal sodium-24 (Na-24) at a temperature of 20 °C is left for a period of 30 hours. After this time its activity falls by 75%.

    a Determine the half-life of Na-24.

    b What would be the half-life if the temperature was 40 °C?

    c Would the half-life be affected if the sample was in the form of the compound NaCl?

10 It is said that radioactivity is a *random process*.

    a How can the use of a Geiger tube and accessories be used to verify this random nature?

    b How can an experimental plot of count rate against time illustrate the random nature?

11 A sample of 1.0 g of carbon from a live plant gives a count rate of 20 min⁻¹. The same mass of carbon is analysed from an old relic and gives a count rate of 5 min⁻¹.

    a Assuming the half-life of C-14 to be 5700 years, determine the age of the relic.

    b Why is C-14 dating not useful for ageing specimens over 60 000 years old?

12 **a** Briefly describe the use of the following in the medical field, stating a suitable radionuclide in each case:

        i tracers   **ii** external beam radiotherapy

    b State TWO problems with the use of external beam radiotherapy.

13 The following is about radioisotopes used in the medical field.

    a Explain why the half-life of a radioisotope given orally or by injection to a patient must be short, but not too short.

    b Name the type of radioactive emission that is least absorbed by the body.

In questions 14, 15 and 16 use: speed of light in a vacuum = 3.0×10^8 m s⁻¹.

14 1 g of matter is completely transformed into energy.

    a Write the equation needed to calculate the amount of energy produced.

    b Identify each quantity in the equation.

    c Name the scientist associated with this equation.

    d Calculate the energy derived from the mass.

15 A certain star is losing mass at a rate of 2.0×10^8 kg s⁻¹. Determine its power output.

16 Determine the energy released during the fusion of the hydrogen nuclei shown below.

$$^{2}_{1}\text{H} + ^{2}_{1}\text{H} \longrightarrow ^{3}_{2}\text{He} + ^{1}_{0}\text{n}$$

$(^{2}_{1}\text{H} = 3.345 \times 10^{-27}$ kg, $^{3}_{2}\text{H} = 5.008 \times 10^{-27}$ kg, $^{1}_{0}\text{n} = 1.675 \times 10^{-27}$ kg $)$

17 Briefly describe TWO advantages and TWO disadvantages of obtaining electricity from nuclear energy.

18 Alpha, beta and gamma radiation are ionising radiations.

    a Briefly describe the effects of ionising radiation on body cells.

    b Suggest a reason why a gamma source is usually less dangerous than an alpha or beta source when ingested or inhaled.

    c State THREE precautions that can be taken as protection against the hazards of ionising radiations.

19 **a** Define:

        i nuclear fusion   **ii** nuclear fission

    b Why do nuclei undergo fission?

    c Name the process by which the Sun liberates energy.

    d Name the process by which today's nuclear power stations generate electricity.

20 State the numbers that should replace the boxes in this nuclear equation.

$$^{235}_{\square}\text{U} + ^{1}_{0}\text{n} \longrightarrow ^{139}_{56}\text{Ba} + ^{\square}_{36}\text{Kr} + 3^{1}_{0}\text{n} + \text{energy}$$

Exam-style questions – Chapters 33 to 34

Structured questions

1 **a)** Complete Table 1 with reference to the nucleus of a carbon atom, $^{14}_{6}C$.

Table 1

Mass number	
Atomic number	
An isotope (represented in a similar manner)	
Number of electron shells in its atom	
Number of electrons in its neutral atom	

(5 marks)

b) Complete Table 2 to show the mass and charge of the neutron and the electron relative to that of the proton.

Table 2

	proton	neutron	electron
Relative mass	1		
Relative charge	+1		

(2 marks)

c) Carbon-14 is used to determine the age of old organic material. It has a half-life of 5700 years. In natural carbon there is ONE atom of C-14 with every 8×10^{11} atoms of carbon.

   i) What percentage of a sample of the isotope remains after a period of 17100 years? **(2 marks)**

   ii) Predict whether or not the isotope would be useful in determining the age of a specimen older than 60 000 years. **(2 marks)**

   iii) A sample of carbon-14 is heated in a furnace so that its constituent atoms obtain increased kinetic energy. By applying your knowledge of nuclear processes, predict how the half-life of the isotope is affected. **(2 marks)**

   iv) C-14 decays by emission of a beta particle to form N-14. Write a nuclear equation for the decay. **(2 marks)**

Total 15 marks

2 **a)** Complete Table 3 with reference to the properties of radioactive emissions.

Table 3

Property	Type of emission
Tracks produced in a cloud chamber are thick and straight	
Travels at the speed of light in a vacuum	
Strongly ionises the air it passes through	
Penetrates up to a few mm of aluminium	
Is deflected most by magnetic fields	
On emission, produces an element one place ahead in the Periodic Table	
Is electromagnetic in nature	

(7 marks)

b) Calculate the values of p, q, r, s and t in the following nuclear disintegrations, and rewrite the equations.

$$^{210}_{82}Pb \longrightarrow {}^{0}_{-1}e + {}^{p}_{q}Bi$$

$$^{p}_{q}Bi \longrightarrow {}^{0}_{-1}e + {}^{r}_{s}Po$$

$$^{r}_{s}Po \longrightarrow {}^{4}_{2}He + {}^{206}_{t}Pb$$

(4 marks)

c) A ratemeter detects a background count rate of 5 Bq. When a radioactive source is placed close to its detecting window, it detects a count rate of 85 Bq. If the half-life of the source is 20 minutes, what will be the count rate received after a period of 1 hour?

(4 marks)

Total 15 marks

Extended response questions

3

a) The 'gold-foil' experiment carried out by Geiger and Marsden revealed a better understanding of the structure of an atomic nucleus.

   i)   Briefly describe the procedure.

   ii) State TWO important observations of the experiment.

   iii) State TWO conclusions drawn from the observations.

(6 marks)

b) Iodine-131 (I-131) has an atomic number of 53 and is a beta-emitter with a half-life of 8 days. It decays to the element xenon, Xe.

   i)   Write a nuclear equation for its decay.

(3 marks)

   ii) 160 g of iodine-131 is left in a sealed container in the laboratory. Calculate the mass of the sample remaining after a period of 40 days.

(3 marks)

   iii) Sketch a graph of mass against count rate for the first 24 days.

(3 marks)

Total 15 marks

4

a) State THREE advantages and THREE disadvantages of generating electricity in nuclear power stations.

(6 marks)

b) i) The equation of the fusion reaction of deuterium, an isotope of hydrogen, is shown below. Table 4 indicates the atomic masses of the particles involved in the reaction.

$$^{2}_{1}H + {}^{2}_{1}H \longrightarrow {}^{3}_{2}He + {}^{1}_{0}n + energy$$

Table 4

Nuclide	Atomic mass/u
$^{2}_{1}H$	2.015
$^{3}_{2}He$	3.017
$^{1}_{0}n$	1.009

Calculate the energy released by the fusion reaction of two deuterium nuclei.
($1\ u = 1.66 \times 10^{-27}$ kg, $c = 3.0 \times 10^{8}$ m s^{-1})

(5 marks)

   ii) Determine the number of neutrons released in the nuclear reaction shown below.

(1 mark)

$$^{235}_{92}U + {}^{1}_{0}n \longrightarrow {}^{148}_{57}La + {}^{85}_{35}Br + neutrons$$

c) A certain star loses mass at a rate of 5.0×10^{9} kg s^{-1}. Calculate its power output.
(Speed of light in a vacuum $= 3.0 \times 10^{8}$ m s^{-1})

(3 marks)

Total 15 marks

Index